FOOT
ANALYSIS

FOOT
ANALYSIS

THE FOOT PATH
TO SELF-DISCOVERY

AVI GRINBERG

SAMUEL WEISER, INC.

York Beach, Maine

First published in 1993 by
Samuel Weiser, Inc.
Box 612
York Beach, ME 03910

Library of Congress Cataloging-in-Publication Data
Grinberg, Avi.
    Foot analysis / by Avi Grinberg.
        p.   cm.
    Includes index.
    1. Foot--Examination.   2. Alternative medicine.
    3. Reflexotherapy.   I. Title.
    RZ999.G45   1993   92-44831
    615.8'22--dc20   CIP
ISBN 0-87728-780-5
EB

Typeset in 11 point Palatino

Printed in the United States of America

99 98 97 96 95 94 93
10 9 8 7 6 5 4 3 2 1

The paper used in this publication meets the minimum requirements of the
American National Standard for Permanence of Paper for Printed Library
Materials Z39.48-1984.

TABLE OF CONTENTS

List of Illustrations vii

List of Tables xi

Foreword xiii

Chapter 1. The Method of Foot Analysis 1

Chapter 2. Foot Categories 21

Chapter 3. Technical Aspects of the Analyzing Process ... 49

Chapter 4. Physical Analysis 95

Chapter 5. Excessive Elements 109

Chapter 6. Element Relationships 119

Chapter 7. Dividing the Feet 145

Chapter 8. The Spine and the Foot 149

Chapter 9. Energy Patterns 159

Chapter 10. Expressing Time 171

Chapter 11. The Toes 179

Chapter 12. Emotional Potential 203

Chapter 13. The Technique of Foot Analysis 219

Chapter 14. Love and Creativity 247

Chapter 15. Resolving Unfinished Business 263

Chapter 16. The Benefits of Foot Analysis 271

Index 275

About the Author 287

LIST OF ILLUSTRATIONS

Figure 1. The four basic elements in the foot 8

Figure 2. How to find the basic potential of the
earth element 12

Figure 3. How to find the basic potential of the
fire element 13

Figure 4. Toes elevated and curled 18

Figure 5. The four elements represented in the
feet and body 22

Figure 6. Physical organs in the earth element area 24

Figure 7. Physical organs in the water element area 26

Figure 8. Physical organs in the fire element area 28

Figure 9. Physical organs in the air element area 30

Figure 10. Division between active and passive
elements 36

Figure 11. Division of the foot into the four elements 37

Figure 12. Dividing the foot and body into eight bands 39

Figure 13. Testing the ankle's range of motion 54

Figure 14. Manipulating the big toe 55

Figure 15. Manipulation of the other toes 56

Figure 16. Checking the tendons 57

Figure 17. The walking thumb technique 58

Figure 18. The moving fingers technique 59

Figure 19. Air indicators 65

Figure 20. Air indicators 66

Figure 21. Air indicators 67

Figure 22. Air indicators 68

Figure 23. Fire indicators 72

Figure 24. Fire indicators 73

Figure 25. Fire indicators 74

Figure 26. Fire indicators 75

Figure 27. Water indicators 77

Figure 28. Water indicators 78

Figure 29. Water indicators 79

Figure 30. Water indicators 80

Figure 31. Water indicators 81

Figure 32. Water indicators 82

Figure 33. Water indicators 83

Figure 34. Earth indicators 86

Figure 35. Earth indicators 87

Figure 36. Earth indicators 88

Figure 37. General indicators 91

Figure 38. General indicators 92

Figure 39. Examining Jane Doe's feet 98

Figure 40. The different shapes of the element-dominated
            foot 116

Figure 41. Earth in water 127

Figure 42. Fire in water 129

Figure 43. A line separating the fire and water element ... 132

Figure 44. Four examples of earth energy invasion
            in the fire element area 136

Figure 45. Spinal column as represented in the feet 150

Figure 46. Nine months of pregnancy shown
            in the foot 151

Figure 47. Signs of imbalances 151

Figure 48. Signs of difficult birth or abortion 156

Figure 49. Two typical lines found on the foot—
            transverse and lengthwise 160

Figure 50. The flow of sexual energy 162

Figure 51. The flow of the breath 164

Figure 52. The flow of digestion 165

Figure 53. The flow of energy in the spinal column 167

Figure 54. Lengthwise and horizontal lines on the region of the foot corresponding to the spinal column 168

Figure 55. The flow of energy to the arms 170

Figure 56. Time as expressed in the feet 172

Figure 57. Toes and their corresponding element 182

Figure 58. Toe 5 curled under toe 4 186

Figure 59. Toe 2 on toe 1 186

Figure 60. Toe 1 on toe 2 187

Figure 61. Toe 1 and 2 are very long 188

Figure 62. The division of the toes into seeing and hearing 189

Figure 63. The lateral division of the air element 191

Figure 64. Toe five without a nail 191

Figure 65. A long toe 2 192

Figure 66. A bunion on the air toe 193

Figure 67. Lengthwise division of the toes into active and passive elements 194

Figure 68. Toe 2 dropping into the passive region 197

Figure 69. Earth in air 198

Figure 70. Elevated toes 1 and 5 199

Figure 71. Cone-shaped toes 201

Figure 72. The areas where certain emotional energies are located in the water element 204

Figure 73. Love—the area between the water and fire elements 248

Figure 74. Separation line 250

Figure 75. The flow of creativity 258

LIST OF TABLES

Table 1. Common Air Indicators 64

Table 2. Common Fire Indicators 71

Table 3. Common Water Indicators 76

Table 4. Common Earth Indicators 85

Table 5. General Indicators 90

Table 6. Symptoms and Signs in
Jane Doe's Feet 100

Foreword

Foot analysis is a central—but not the only—constituent of the comprehensive Grinberg Method, developed and taught over the past decade by Avi Grinberg and now studied and put into practice by his dedicated and spirited team.

I am well-acquainted with Avi Grinberg and his team and, although skeptical about the method in the beginning, I became intellectually intrigued by what I saw and heard. Eventually I spent a good deal of time and energy examining the theoretical basis of their work to acquire at least an intuitive insight into the hows and whys.

Being an intellectual historian and comparatist, as well as a contextual relativist, I did not expect to find a full-fledged Western-type medical theory that provides a non-Western integrative view of the total human being, able to cope with many existential situations where modern medicine—or even modern psychiatry—has very little to say. What I did expect to find was a clear formulation of what is missing in our modern (or even post-modern) understanding of humankind, and a creative approach that might answer some of those needs. And indeed, that is exactly what I found superimposed on a conceptual system that appears to supply its practitioners with all the necessary intellectual scaffolding.

The practitioners of foot analysis do not interfere with the purely medical aspects of a person's health. They do not attempt to heal or charm away existing diseases, malignant growths, or immune deficiencies, although it often happens that such ailments are discovered in people unaware that they have a disease, and they are urged to consult a physician.

What they claim to do—and I have seen this happen time and again—is work together with the person, attempting to help mobilize inner energies (physical and mental in conflation) in order to fight any imbalance in the system. They systematically approach, with much empathy, that neglected area between body and soul where modern medical practice stops short. And indeed, how often we hear medical experts tell us that ultimately recovery depends on the determination, trust, and optimism of the patient. Unfortunately, medicine has little to say about the means of cultivating such an attitude, and here is where the Grinberg Method performs so well.

The accuracy of the insight into the state of the subject is astounding. The mental, physical, and psychological history of the person is spelled out with such accuracy and detail that it makes the interpretation of his or her state of health and probable future developments highly credible.

I have repeatedly seen old and young change their life style and mobilize their innermost being to achieve a balanced self. Time and again, through the intervention—if it can be called thus—and support from the practitioners of foot analysis, men and women reach the point where their inner balance is restored and they are at peace with themselves.

I know enough about Eastern philosophies to recognize some Eastern influence in the Grinberg method, yet the method is down-to-earth and not mystical in any sense. It is true that most Eastern medicine is also not mystical, but usually it lends a much deeper meaning to the conceptual infrastructure of the forces at work than does the Grinberg Method. Unlike most practitioners who seek to subsume what they diagnose in broad generalizations, foot analysis is oriented toward the individual.

My trust in the ability of this method to help and support others has grown over the years. All in all, it is a highly effective, well-designed system and will very likely become a successful tool to advance people's well-being. Intellectually it constitutes a fascinating approach to the ever-changing image of human beings.

—Yehuda Elkana

Professor Elkana is Director of the Van Leer Jerusalem Institute, teaches at the Cohn Institute of History & Philosophy of Science & Ideas at Tel Aviv University, and is a permanent fellow at the Institute for Advanced Study in Berlin.

FOOT
ANALYSIS

1

THE METHOD
OF FOOT ANAYLSIS

Over the course of history, many techniques have been developed that enable one to get a picture of the whole person by looking at one part or at something the person has created, or at the way in which the person responds to situations. Each of these techniques has a philosophy and a set of rules for drawing a portrait of the person from one particular angle. These techniques deal with peripheral organs.

Foot analysis is based on the principle that the feet show us how a person "walks" through life. Foot analysis is meant to combine physical, emotional, and spiritual dimensions into one. The perspective is holistic, and the principles of the method rest on a philosophy that merges East and West. We deal with the region that, physically, is the most remote from our senses, an area that modern human beings usually keep covered, protected, and out of sight. It is also an area, however, in which few defense mechanisms have developed, because socially it is relatively neglected and unimportant, less adorned and cared for.

An important stage in our growth as human beings is the transition from helplessly lying and crawling to moving about on our feet; this is also the stage when our individual personality begins to be clearly expressed. The entire person rests on the soles of the feet.

Any change, whether perceptive, cognitive, emotional, or physical, implies a change in how a person stands in the world. Abstract changes, too, such as a change in status or self-image, affect how people hold themselves, move, and express themselves; hence, situations that are enduring or strong enough will leave clear and unmistakable marks on the soles of the feet. Foot analysis is a technique that tries to understand the significance of those signs and combine them into an integral picture of the individual on all levels.

When we came out of the water, climbed down from the trees, or landed from outer space, the first thing we did was take a step, leaving our footprints in the sand. The footprints may have been erased from the sand, but their memory is retained on the foot, if they were truly significant in that person's life.

HUMAN ENERGY

Every human cell is surrounded by (and full of) the energy that sustains it, and the cell itself is its tangible expression on the atomic level. This energy is located around (and within) the entire body. Today it is possible to photograph it with Kirlian photography and to identify its tiny centers. This energy is like a bubble around the human body and is known by many names: aura, the cosmic egg of life, biofield, etc. This energy is focused and discernable at approximately 650 loci, called acupuncture points or nadis, and in a central system called the chakra system, which is similar to the body's system of endocrine centers. Each region and organ of the body has its own specific frequency of energy.

The harmonic state of this energy is called health on all levels—mental, spiritual, emotional, and physical. The basic disharmonious state of this energy is an excess or deficiency in a particular region or organ, as compared with the optimum harmonious level. Another possibility is that the quality (frequency) of the energy in a certain region switches to that appropriate to a different region, i.e., the energy controlling the region is not the appropriate one for it.

Vital energy is composed of the same elements that constitute the universe. Philosophy has known and defined these elements since antiquity—ancient Chinese philosophy, as well as Hinduism, Islam, Judaism, etc. In this book energy is divided into four elements, each of which is a frequency of that energy; together they make up the whole being. These elements are earth, water, fire, and air. We view a fifth element, the quintessential ether, as a mysterious factor linked to destiny and to the unique personality of each individual—an element that joins us all together in one single cosmos, as well as dividing us into separate individuals.

Each region of the body has a frequency that it requires in order to be harmonious and to function fully. Any deviation from the equilibrium point will affect the functioning of the organ or region. If the deviation is chronic and long-lasting, it will develop into an illness, and it will be imprinted in a particular fashion on the feet.

In the ancient division of energy centers, the body is divided into eight transverse strips, each with its own specific function. The functions are physiological, spiritual, mental, and emotional, and together they create the individual's psychophysical personality. At the root of the energetic-philosophical understanding of a person, is the claim that this energy (the person) was born into this life in order to develop and approach the source of that energy as closely as possible. Each of the major religions describes this process in a different style and according to its own system of rules.

In principle, in foot analysis, we view people as energy in the process of developing, and every obstacle they encounter is at the same time an opportunity to grow and evolve. From this perspective, we can represent a person's life as a flowing river: at some points it flows more strongly and at others more feebly; at some it turns into a marsh and at others it becomes a lake or a sea. In the feet we can see the phenomenon of disharmonious states trying to flow back to harmony.

Changes in energy that involve a deviation from harmony and exist as a chronic state over a long period of time, or that are acute and sufficiently traumatic to create a permanent alteration in the individual, will be expressed in the feet as signs that reveal fundamental states of surplus or deficiency, which together construct patterns of energetic behavior. The nature of the sign, its location, and the relationship between it and other signs on the feet are the major components of foot analysis. What do we see while we are analyzing the sole of the foot? We see a physical, emotional, mental, and creative level; the past, the present, and future tendencies.

WHO SEEKS FOOT ANALYSIS?

Why do people seek foot analysis? There are a number of reasons. Some people simply come out of curiosity, and they enjoy hearing about themselves. Often people who stand at a crossroads in their lives will have foot analysis to help them decide which aspect of themselves to choose, and which part of themselves to heed. We can not choose for people through foot analysis, but we can show them which powers are strong and relevant so they may take them into account when choosing. We will show them what they will be giving up by focusing on one aspect at the expense of another. We may illuminate certain aspects of personality that the subject has previously preferred to ignore.

Sometimes people come to a foot analyst and want to know why they don't feel good. On the surface, everything appears to be fine, but the person just doesn't feel quite right. We could find that they are alienated from certain aspects of themselves, which inevitably causes suffering and pain. Pain and suffering come to show us that we must do something, that we must change something for the sake of our "wholeness." We will not solve people's problems for them; it is impossible to solve someone else's problems.

When faced with an internal choice, people find themselves trapped in a cycle from which they cannot escape. They seek guidance in moving beyond the point where they are stuck. We refer them to forms of treatment that will reach them and that are appropriate for them. In keeping with the type of person who sits before us, we can advise the proper treatment to which he or she is best suited. Through foot analysis, we decide not what is objectively correct but what is subjectively appropriate.

At times, a person comes for analysis in a moment of crisis. Crisis permits people to be "reborn"; they can emerge from this state like small children, viewing the world as a new entity. This is an opportunity to show people who they are and what they have done until the moment of crisis, so they will not commit the same mistake again. Chronic patterns can begin at a very early stage in a person's life (conception, pregnancy, and beyond). It is possible that underlying the patterns and choices we carry out today are very early factors of which we are not consciously aware, but which influence us throughout the years.

Our goal is to illustrate these cycles for our subjects, to hold up a clear, untarnished mirror reflecting as little of ourselves as possible. We tend to see ourselves in others, to see in them the things we are not ready to see in ourselves. In order to avoid this, foot analysis requires repeated examination of many aspects that validate or nullify each other to ensure that we have truly seen something in the subject, not just an element of our own selves.

Symptoms of Imbalance

Foot analysis incorporates the following aspects:

1) *Touch*—This is a technique that involves thorough and rather deep palpating; the condition of the tissue we touch is a factor in the analysis itself.

2) *Dermatological Differences*—Differences not only in the texture and folds of the skin, but also in its color; peeling, blemishes, and similar characteristics—are all indicative of a person's condition.

3) *Temperature*—There are regions of varying temperatures on the foot that differ from person to person. A hot or a cold region indicates tendencies toward a surplus or a deficiency in the energy level of the corresponding region of the body.

4) *Structure*—The structure and interrelations of the bones show us the basic potential of that person.

This stage of understanding the energy level of the body may serve us in two ways: identifying pathological conditions and understanding—through the specific energy wave of the region or organ—the nonphysical energetic significance connected to it. For example, a clear state of imbalance in the region of the liver indicates not only the risk of a physical problem in the liver, but the likelihood of the presence of repressed anger. Each organ and region of the body bears an energetic significance related to other, nonphysical aspects of the person's existence. We divide these areas into four elements and study their interrelationship. From the energy pattern we discern on the foot, we can draw conclusions about the physical state of the body as well as other states of the person (behavioral, emotional, and all other components of the personality).

GAUGING POTENTIAL

Foot analysis may permit us to view others' potential and the ways in which they can realize it; from over- or underutilization of potential points, to a disharmony that may manifest itself in various physical symptoms.

We walk through life on our feet. The matters that are important to us, in which we cover a lot of ground and step out of harmony in some fashion, will be indicated on the foot because we have "passed through" them over and over again. The deep scars sustained by our feet from one painful step also remain there, some fading with time, others embedded throughout our lives. In principle, from the moment of conception until the moment of death—whether a function of an ingrained habit, a behavioral pattern, an emotional pattern, or any other pattern—we construct our personality, and a major portion of it is shaped by encounters with our surroundings that result in pain, fear, hardship, failure, and frustration.

We must view any deviation from the harmony of the individual pair of feet as an open-ended gestalt—a cycle that must be pursued to its conclusion in order to part with it, and a pattern that interferes with the free flow of that life energy. The beauty of foot analysis is that when conducted seriously, in depth, and with proper experience, it permits us to view our subjects' entire life process—all events with which they have not come to terms, even if they no longer remember or attach any great significance to them. Our feet show events that we may have forgotten but that still influence our life energy, creating and shaping the recurring paths of our lives. It is possible to reveal patterns of which the subject is unaware and the analysis itself can serve as a catalyst that brings these patterns out into the open and allows the subject to see them.

From the moment of conception, every situation appears on the foot. During pregnancy we engage in a symbiotic relationship with our mothers, and we enter the world with a vast collection of energy patterns of genetic origin, which comprise our basic potential. From this point on, the foot will indicate how much of that potential we have realized; how we have walked through life: if we are tired and heavy; if we have "floated" through life; if we have truly moved through our life or merely run in place; and what we are likely to create for ourselves in the future—for the path we have already walked often dictates the future toward which we are headed.

BASIC POTENTIAL
VERSUS ACTUAL CONDITION

Many of us experience a great disparity between our ability and its fulfillment. We feel we ought to be living a life other than the one we live. We wish to be other than what we are, not only in behavior and social status but also in self-expression and vitality.

Science recognizes that we utilize only a small proportion of our brain's capability. Most of us use a negligible share of our physical prowess, and few of us engage our creative abilities at all. Research on the discrepancy between basic potential and its degree of fulfillment sheds light on one of the unfathomed sources of human suffering. When we study people, we see that few achieve a level of life-fulfillment and actualization that meets their expectations.

The first cell of the embryo is composed of the parents' energies and contains all the information needed to construct a complete individual. It contains the individual's basic potential, which, in fact, struggles to actualize its inherencies from the moment of conception. It is much like a seed that contains an entire tree; the tree is the seed's potential, the actualization for which the seed strives. Just as snow affects seeds and causes some of them to freeze and die, some seeds grow into small, weak trees, and others become huge trees, even though all the seeds are the same size and meant to develop into the same trees. Similarly, everything that happens to the cell from the

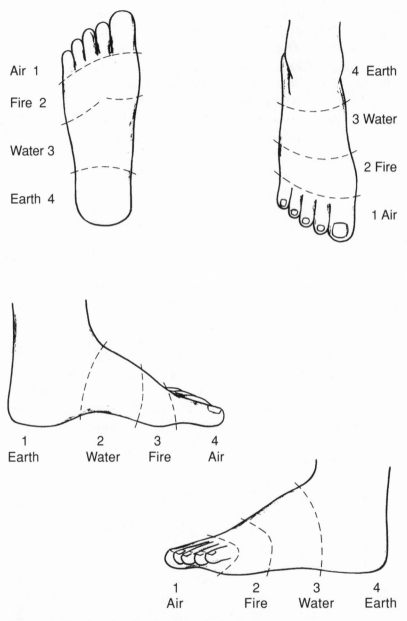

Figure 1. The four basic elements in the foot.

moment of its creation affects the essence and fulfillment of its potential.

This basic potential strives to actualize itself throughout a person's life and to correct or heal injuries that would delay or thwart this actualization. Defects that cannot be corrected or balanced, such as physical disabilities, will allow this actualization to occur only in part. Thus our potential redefines its limits and draws a new design for its actualization.

Basic potential includes the fundamental division of human energies that manifest themselves within the individual, and defines the initial potencies invested in these energies, which they will try to actualize in the individual's life. The intensity and importance of specific aspects of a person's life are determined at this most basic human level. Some of these abilities realize themselves through our very lives, circumstances, and other forces that act upon us. Others are flawed; they dissipate and disappear. Culture, education, environment, family, and other factors can cause people to swerve from the path of realizing their basic potential. Human beings are fated to pursue their personal actualization—and their very lives—in continuous struggle between the demand for realization and other forces that take us onto other paths.

We may divide people's inherent strengths into four basic energies that we call "elements": earth, water, fire, and air (see figure 1 on page 8). At any moment, we can study the state of these fundamental energies in a person and compare this state with the individual's basic potential. Thus we gauge people's degrees of inner harmony, of frustration, of struggle—and, of course, the suffering created by the disparity between these and total fulfillment.

Examining the internal breakdown of the four elements in an individual, we should distinguish between three basic states:

1) *Balance*—The element is completely realized; it plays exactly the role in the person's life intended for it by the basic potential.

2) *Surplus*—The element occupies a greater place in the person's life than that intended for it, meaning it also occupies space that belongs to other elements.

3) *Deficiency*—The element is not actualized, lacks strength, and fails to occupy the space intended for it by the basic potential. Thus it "invites" invasions by other elements, throwing all the energies out of balance.

Foot analysis was created to study and generate a portrait of an individual, composed of actualized potentials and "open circles" that thwart actualization. Calling people's attention to these unactualized powers opens new possibilities for actualization. Situations that people have perceived as problems that troubled them and required "correction" may now present themselves as renewed opportunities for growth and development for the actualization of potential.

Actualized potential creates harmony and fulfillment, vitality and joy in life. This is the state we call health. Unactualized potential creates suffering, pain, frustration, and chronic conditions. In fact, all of these are unsuccessful attempts by our energies to actualize themselves. They never stop trying to lead us to the life that we are supposed to live according to the potencies within us. Any symptoms of suffering represent an attempt to indicate a lack of actualization, a lack of correspondence between the reality we experience and the needs imprinted in our beingness.

Since everything we experience reaches us through the body, the body manifests its unresolved ("open") states on all human levels, including those that do not seem to be physical. For example, intensive bouts of fear may induce serious physical conditions such as diabetes; protracted fear with which the individual cannot cope may create a certain type of posture. These are chronic patterns that may include physical symptoms and sensations. We therefore study physical symptoms as manifestations of disparities between individuals' basic potential and existing conditions in all areas of life.

Any pain or symptom is actually an opportunity to "wake up" and rejoin the path toward the fulfillment of basic potential. Since this potential never gives up, we may understand why "chronic" conditions proliferate as they do. Any attempt to treat them is palliative only; it can offer relief but no solution. Often, too, attempts to suppress a condition create new symptoms. People tend to repeat their mistakes and re-injure the same parts of the body or areas of life. These are manifestations of failure in the actualization process. We invest much energy in the attempt to actualize our basic potential. When we fail, this energy finds itself in a vicious cycle, escapes our control, and denies us the right of its use. Thus, we forfeit the latent vitality and personal strength of our basic potential.

ANALYZING THE ELEMENTS

The foot reflects our basic potential through its structure, the condition and structure of its bones, and its congenital markings. Its condition at a given moment is reflected in the state of the tissue and in changeable markings and distortions. We may observe each element separately and thus ascertain whether it has actualized its basic potential.

Earth—The earth element is located on the heel and, three-dimensionally, spreads around the ankle to about four inches above it. To perceive the boundaries the basic potential creates in the heel, we "fold" the foot inward so the toes bend toward the heel (see figure 2 on page 12). The boundary between earth and water then appears clearly, permitting us to see whether the element in its current state is smaller or larger than its basic potential. If it is in balance, we expect to see full, healthy tissue filling the basic potential area throughout the heel region. This tissue should be reddish-brown—darker than the rest of the foot—and the skin should be slightly coarser than in the fire region.

Water—The water element appears in the vicinity of the arch, between the heel and the ball of the foot below the toes. We gauge the basic size of water after assessing the basic size of earth and fire, which delimit this element. When water is in balance (i.e., when it occupies an area as large as its basic potential), its tissue is the lightest in color on the foot. The skin is fine, soft, cool, and slightly moist. A striding line about one fourth the width of the foot is visible on the outer side.

Fire—The fire element appears around the ball of the foot below the toes. To examine whether this element fills or overflows the area destined for it by the individual's basic

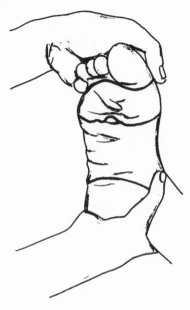

Figure 2. How to find the basic potential of the earth element.

potential, we stretch the toes backward, making the ball of the foot protrude (see figure 3); this shows the basic size of the element. When we release the toes from their stretched position, we observe the discrepancy between potential and actual size. When fire is in balance, we expect to find full, healthy, reddish tissue that fills, but does not exceed, the potential area of the ball of the foot. The skin should be coarser than that of the water region, but not as coarse as that of the earth region.

Air—The air element region extends from the base of the toes to their tips. To assess the full potential size of the air element, we stretch the toes and straighten them to their full length. The difference between the straightened toes and their natural state shows the difference between basic and existing potential. When air is in balance, we observe toes of basic-potential size. They are straight, flexible, splayed slightly but not too widely. The tissue should be full but not swollen; the toenails should be healthy. The skin is lighter than that of the fire region but darker than that of the water region.

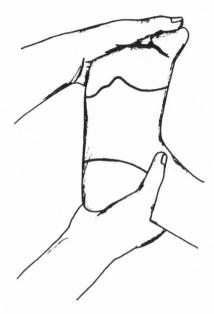

Figure 3. How to find the basic potential of the fire element.

ENERGY PATTERNS

An energy pattern is a condition built upon a permanent, chronic state of imbalance. This means that people who have several states of imbalance they have built up during their lives, with the aim of achieving some sort of balance in their existence, will construct them in such a way as to make them a permanent part of their everyday picture. In their outlook, feelings, and behavior, they will perceive them as a state of balance and as who they are. These states of imbalance are liable to be of longstanding, dating from periods a person cannot remember, such as pregnancy or early childhood.

Since we live with these "blocks" all our lives, we accept them as part of our personality and cannot perceive the imbalance, the loss of personal power, the decline in vitality and various aspects of existence. These patterns, viewed through our experiences, define ourselves, our limits, how we can and cannot live, what is correct and fair, and how we should be: I can, I want, I must. These patterns construct and comprise what we call the "ego," personality, and physical behavior.

For example, people who experience fear for an extended period during their youth acquire in their stance, posture, and muscular behavior a permanent pattern, a particular pulse rate, a particular way of breathing, a unique world view, a certain level of tension in their internal organs, a particular metabolism, etc.

By relating to the energy state and understanding the concepts of balance and imbalance, we comprehend that extended states of any type of imbalance—if they remain in the energetic body over a lengthy period—will take root there and continue to exist even after conditions appear to have changed. These patterns are likely to originate in certain preconditions. Such patterns may exist and surface on any level of the personality.

With reference to the distribution of our energy, we shall speak of eight levels into which a person's energy is divided. At each of these levels, we may find patterns of interlevel imbalance. For example, those who grew up with basic survival as the driving force in their lives will still, many years later, act instinctively in certain situations out of a need to survive and not out of careful consideration and thoughtful decision making, even when their survival is not at stake.

Most of these patterns are unknown to the subjects, or are known only through the symptoms they present, in the sense that they notice the imbalance only insofar as it prevents them from functioning and behaving in the way they think and perceive as "normal": pain, decline in functioning, or loss of control over performance, behavior that deviates greatly from social norms, or any emotional state that is hard to cope with. At times when these symptoms are not particularly pronounced or are hardly perceived, such people will feel "all right" and consider themselves healthy, but this does not mean they are free of patterns of imbalance.

Illness is a state of imbalance that has reached a climax or crisis; it is the symptomatic manifestation of the pattern. This definition views every illness and health problem as holistic, i.e., embracing the whole person. Let us take the example of pain in the hand. In order to understand and treat the condition, we should examine the client's patterns and states of imbalance, so as to comprehend the significance of the surface-level symptom. The repression of a symptom is liable to lead to the aggravation and neglect of a deeper state that may take the form of more severe symptoms in the future.

Chronic patterns are formed by permanent or recurring states of imbalance in human energy. When we view these patterns on the feet, we are actually seeing the permanent or recurring history of a person's life. Chronic patterns can be defined as those parts of a person's history that have not succeeded in balancing themselves. Within this history, we can discern several clear points of focus: Incomplete experience ("unfinished business"); Familial and genetic states; and Habits and routines.

INCOMPLETE EXPERIENCE

Under this heading we place all recurring life states that constitute any type of process affecting the subject's energy—specifically a process that never completed itself (gestalt). One of the most obvious conditions in people arises when panic reactions do not receive the attention that could restore the body's balance. We can observe this state in the difference between the reaction of an infant as opposed to that of an adult.

An infant reacts to panic by crying and demanding warmth, soothing, and some type of external response in addition to its personal response (it cries and later calms down). A particular energy in its body is generated and flows. The following physical phenomena occur: increased secretion of adrenaline into the blood; change in the breathing pattern; a particular state of the diaphragm; and a muscular state that is different throughout the body. By crying and expressing this energy, the infant releases it from its body; the hormones break down in the blood and are excreted. By demanding the time necessary for its body to return to a balanced state (slackened muscular tension and flaccid diaphragm), the infant creates a state in which the energy emanated is released, and balance restored.

Adult panic, by contrast, often fails to reach the point of physical and verbal expression; at times it does not even reach the person's level of awareness. Thus, instead of releasing this energy that has started to flow, the person represses it, ignores it, and does not experience it. Recurring panic reactions or an extended state of tension can lead to a phenomenon known as anxiety attacks, in which the body feels and acts out fear even with no cause. This state indicates how a specific pattern related to panic reaches the level of awareness, revealing the subject's imbalance.

In addition to panic reactions, there are many energy states in which people, due to their education or life situation, are incapable of living an experience fully and therefore cannot close the cycle and restore balance. Any past energy state that recurred or was so traumatic as to disrupt one's state of balance, e.g., the aftermath of an acute shock such as an accident, injury, rape, etc., or any other state of drastic change in energy that is not restored to balance later, remains within the person as a chronic pattern. Such states are likely to occur on the mental, emotional, physical, and all other levels.

The feet reveal a person's unfinished history. If this history had been completed/balanced, we would not see a state of imbalance on the foot. The states that are visible on the foot are those that express an imbalance. A 60-year-old man, for example, may show signs of laryngitis. He may claim that he has not suffered from this malady for the past fifty years, but the very existence of the sign on the foot points to the imbalance that is present in the region. It is likely to manifest itself in another symptom or form part of a general pattern that produces symptoms in other regions and other forms.

FAMILIAL AND GENETIC STATES

A familial state of imbalance recurs in a particular family, but is not passed on through the genes themselves (or may be passed on in this way, but the means to verify this do not yet exist). A genetic state *is* passed on by way of family genes. Both these states are likely to lead to a situation where a person, by virtue of being born into a particular family, will enter the world with a very deeply and unalterably imprinted state of imbalance. This is the basic state of the life energy of such people, and even it they achieve their own maximum degree of balance, they will still be in a state of imbalance compared to others.

Foot analysis permits us to view many manifestations of genetic or familial states. Severe genetic disturbances are expressed in a particular region of the foot (see chapter 2), and familial states appear on the foot even if the person does not exhibit the related symptoms. These states would be those related to the structure of the foot, such as the formation and arrangement of the bones, the shape of the arches, or indications of common patterns (see chapter 3) that occur not in the subjects themselves but in their blood relations. The more structural the state is, and the earlier its origins, the harder it is to restore balance.

Genetic or familial states appear in people in the deepest form, and they experience them as their own particular "I" on all levels of their psyches. Indeed, such states always represent imbalances of magnitude and form among the elements; this holds true less frequently in the case of other states of imbalance. It should be added that chronic illnesses in a family affect the children by virtue of their experiencing a state of imbalance—albeit in someone else but in a permanent and recurring fashion—that forms a part of the energy surrounding them, particularly at a young age.

Let us take as an example a man who grew up in a family where one member was an asthmatic. If he himself is not an asthmatic, one of his children probably will be. This person, by growing up in a family setting that caused his energy to enter a state of imbalance, will give expression to this imbalance with his children and thus reinforce the possibility of a similar imbalance in one of his offspring.

Similarly, a mother who is very fearful that her child will fall and is constantly yelling to be careful, puts her child under such pressure that it may lead to a fall. This paradigm, known as "self-fulfilling prophecy," is actually a manifestation of an imbalance in a human situation that affects all the individual energies involved. Most such states of imbalance are not perceived because they form an integral part of the individual's personality and are considered by the individual, and by others, as his or her normal state.

HABITS AND ROUTINES

A habit is a behavioral pattern that a person repeats, thus creating a chronic imbalance. Harmful habits are not necessarily those practices recognized by Western culture as pernicious (such as smoking, substance abuse, various addictions, consumption of high-cholesterol foods, breathing polluted air, etc.), but any habit that people may incorporate into their behavior that would take them out of a state of balance.

Examining the feet, we may discover many behavioral habits that are extremely personal. (The term *behavior* here encompasses physical, mental, emotional, or other aspects as indicated by the state of imbalance reflected in the foot.) These habits may manifest themselves in every level of a person's functioning.

Habits of Movement

Any situation that requires a person to perform the same movement or to remain in the same position for several hours a day over a lengthy period of time will create a chronic pattern of movement, posture, and permanent muscular state. Consequently, certain muscles will become stronger and others weaker, and many sets of muscles will lose their tone due to over- or underuse. Chronic patterns of movement will find tangible expression in the state of the muscles and tendons, and in the way the foot is placed on the floor or at rest. For example, a pattern of work performed while seated at a table, as is the case with a lot of people in the modern world, will be manifested in the toes being elevated and curled, and in the pronounced tension in the tendons of the upper foot. We will also see many accretions of tension in the lower back and in the back of the neck (see figure 4).

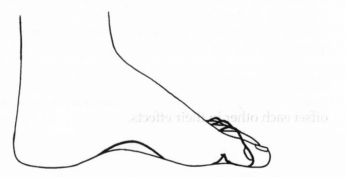

Figure 4. Toes elevated and curled signifies tension in the neck and shoulders.

Habits of the Senses

Most people focus on their head much of the time. The greater part of their attention is directed toward control of the senses in the head; they dissociate themselves from feelings and emotions. Most people, too, overuse their eyes and exhibit states of imbalance in the entire head. An example would be sitting in front of a computer or television for many hours each day.

Emotional Habits

Any state of emotional imbalance from which people are somehow unable to dissociate, such as a nonphysical addiction, is considered a harmful emotional habit. One example of this would be compulsive eating arising from a lack of satisfaction in any area. Such habits will appear on the feet in two ways: one, in the form in which the damage caused by the habit is expressed, and the other in such a way as to point clearly at the emotional origins of the problem.

• • •

Harmful habits come in too many varieties and combinations to list here. In principle, any recurring behavioral state that creates an imbalance, if it is repeated a great many times, will appear on the foot and command our attention, since the impact of such habits creates physical states that may manifest themselves as symptoms and as damage to the person's functioning. As we examine the feet, we observe and look for such habits by comparing the state of the subjects' feet with their work and other habits they describe to us—any habit in which they engage and which they do not balance. For example, the feet of a person who sits for ten hours a day and does not walk at all will not resemble those of one who sits for ten hours but walks for two hours each day. Thus we shall see that there are habits that may offset each other in their effects.

2

FOOT
CATEGORIES

This chapter categorizes and defines the observed demarcation of energy zones on the foot. An initial division into elements is presented here. The basic division is into four types of energy quality that coalesce to create life. It should be understood that none of these energies is capable of existing independently; only in combination do they form the fifth element, which is the totality of our life energy. In fact, we view the consolidation of these elements for life as the act that creates us as people; the balance between these elements characterizes the person as an individual.

THE FOUR ELEMENTS

In every person, a particular element may be present to a greater or lesser degree; it is the various combinations that create one's psychophysical personality. Over the course of human history, these elements have been defined, explained, and described in many philosophies that concern themselves with the essence of man, including religions, techniques of healing, astrology, etc. (Those interested in studying and understanding the elements themselves should consult the literature in this area.) We describe each of the four elements in terms of its physical/energy characteristics, in a manner that will provide an overall understanding of the concept.

The elements are earth, water, fire, and air. The division is vertical—from the earth, which we touch with our feet, to the air and sky which are at the head (see figure 5 on page 22). Earth and water are passive energies; fire and air are active. (Passive and active in this context mean that the energies are parallel and complementary.)

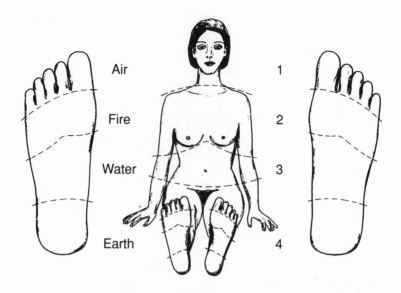

Figure 5. The four elements represented in the feet and body.

Earth: The Heavy Element—The lowest element from the per-spective of the erect human being is also the place through which we look at the person, i.e. the feet. In terms of the body, the part of concern to us—wherein the earth element is pre-dominant—commences with the feet and extends to the waist. Physically, it reflects the pelvis, legs, and thighs. The skeleton is a general manifestation of the earth element (see figure 6 on page 24). Its outstanding characteristic is the ability to absorb and receive, indicating great physicality, stability, rootiness, domesticity, permanence, sensuality, sexuality, fertility, sur-vival, perpetuation of the species, primal energy, and violence or submission for the sake of survival. Earth is self-sustaining, nondynamic, slow. It is an element in which gravity is most strongly expressed; it is where things fall. It is connected with the elimination of waste from the body, through which the unneeded material passes and is cleansed. Acquisitiveness, possessiveness, a need to amass things, cleanliness, and beau-tification are further attributes, along with maternal instincts, heightened sensual awareness, slow and lengthy processes of change, and dense energy in dark-colored waves, i.e., dark brown, maroon.

In principle, the earth contains the instinct to create new life and houses the true power of the human being. In life we attain but a meager degree of awareness and control of its power. The vast importance of this element in foot analysis is related to survival and the internal energetic power that a person has for coping with life. It is a passive element, indicating stability in the person's life; the ability to stand on the earth (I am responsible for my existence). Earth = "I need."

Water: The Sea of Emotions—Water resides above the element of earth. Physically, it reflects the abdomen and all the "soft" organs—those that contain bodily fluids, i.e., kidneys, intestines, a portion of the bladder. Within this region the intestines are in constant motion. Water represents all bodily fluids: blood, urine, intestinal contents, lymph, bile, hormones excreted in fluids, and cerebrospinal fluid (see figure 7 on page 26).

This energy is originally yellow. Water is the element that indicates uncontrolled flow in a person—the active parasympathetic system, smooth muscles in the intestines. Water is needed to cleanse the person. Water forms solutions. It can reverse itself, flow in opposite and changeable directions, be dangerous, frightening. Fear and other emotions emanating from it are the element of water. Water is emotional, romantic, deep, secretive, impulsive; it seeps into dryness, stands without movement, causes stagnation. Water can have a strong odor, produce bubbles, boil above and below the surface. It is a person's emotional world.

It also stands for renewal, giving and taking, the need for movement and dynamism in its flow. Water is the medium of digestion. It reduces other substances. It is an element where things are filtered and disposed of. Water can freeze, boil, and evaporate. Water doesn't show its true self on the outside; to understand it, one has to be within it. It reflects a person's emotional movement. Water is a feminine element, mysterious—not maternal and secure like the earth, but the shadowy, seductive side that attracts through its mystery. It is an element of emotional intuition, the ability to absorb what the other feels wordlessly.

The emanations of air and fire are digested through this element. Its movement is downward, trying to descend lower still. It can contradict itself (to be angry at someone and pity him or her at the same time). Things happen in it without being seen. It is as dangerous as the sea (stormy or calm); it can change into a swamp where one becomes bogged down; it can become something that is constantly turbulent—emotional turmoil. Water = "I feel."

1 SMALL INTESTINE	12 PELVIS
2 ILEOCECAL VALVE	13 GENITALIA
3 APPENDIX	14 OVARY
4 RECTUM	15 TESTICLE
5 ANUS	16 FALLOPIAN TUBE
6 BLADDER	17 UTERUS
7 HIP JOINT	18 PROSTATE
8 SCIATIC NERVE	19 SACRUM
9 LEG	20 COCCYX
10 THIGH	21 LUMBAR SPINE
11 KNEE	

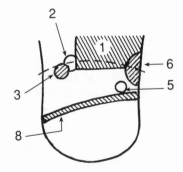
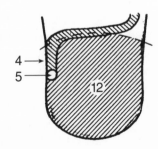

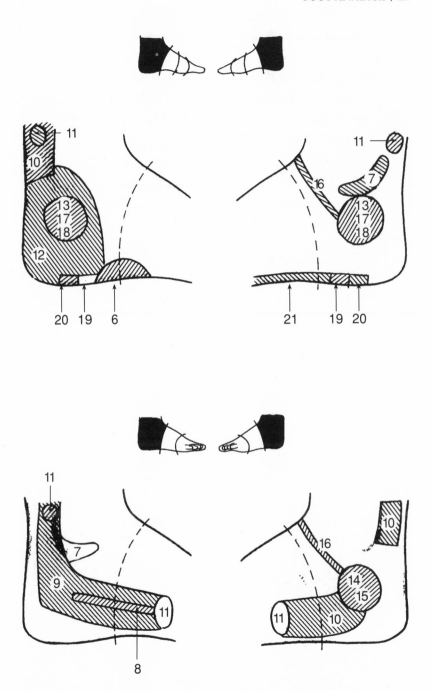

Figure 6. The physical organs that are in the earth element area.

1 HEART	13 ELBOW
2 SHOULDER JOINT	14 DUODENUM
3 LUNG	15 SPLEEN
4 ESOPHAGUS	16 SMALL INTESTINE
5 DIAPHRAGM	17 ASCENDING COLON
6 STOMACH	18 TRANSVERSE COLON
7 PANCREAS	19 DESCENDING COLON
8 GALL BLADDER	20 RECTUM
9 KIDNEY	21 ILEOCECAL VALVE
10 URETER	22 APPENDIX
11 LIVER	23 THORACIC SPINE
12 ARM	24 LUMBAR SPINE

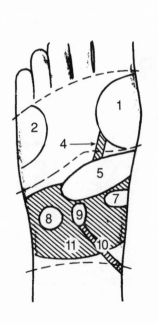

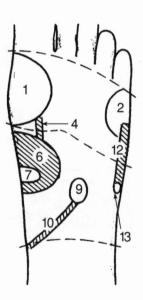

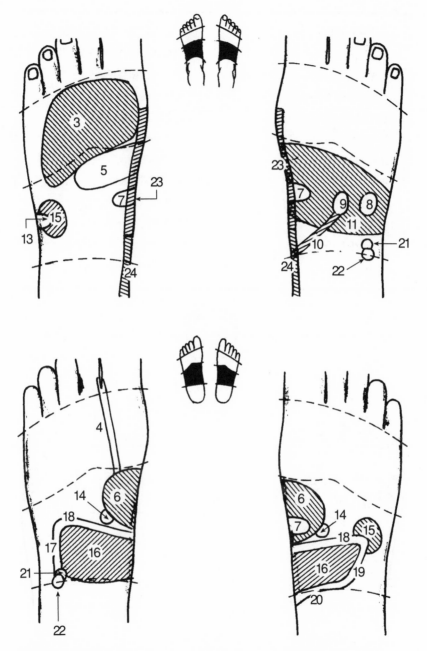

Figure 7. The physical organs that are in the water element area.

1 THYROID GLAND	11 THYMUS GLAND
2 EYE	12 SHOULDER JOINT
3 EAR	13 TRACHEA
4 INNER EAR	14 ESOPHAGUS
5 MOUTH	15 LUNG
6 JAW	16 HEART
7 TEETH	17 STOMACH
8 SINUSES	18 THORACIC SPINE
9 CERVICAL SPINE	19 ARM
10 THROAT	20 RIBS

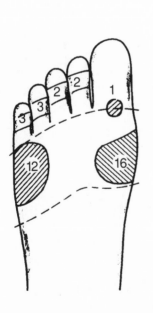 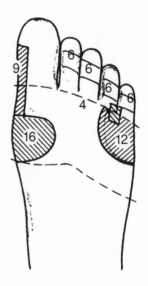

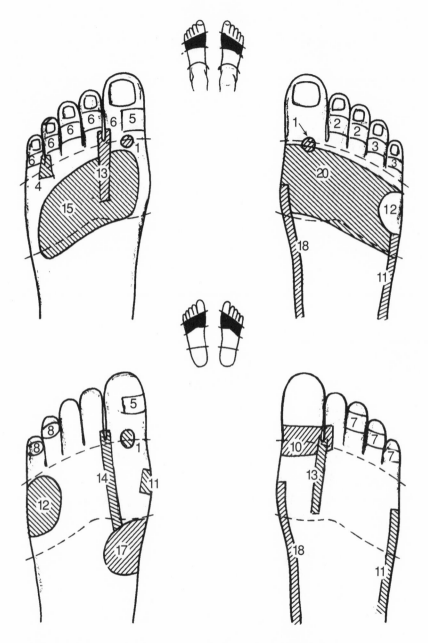

Figure 8. The physical organs that are in the fire element area.

1 PINEAL GLAND	10 CERVICAL SPINE
2 PITUITARY GLAND	11 SINUSES
3 EYE	12 JAW
4 EAR	13 TEETH
5 INNER EAR	14 TRACHEA
6 MOUTH	15 ESOPHAGUS
7 NOSE	16 HEART
8 THYROID GLAND	17 LUNG
9 THROAT	18 SHOULDER JOINT

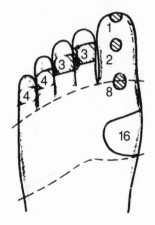 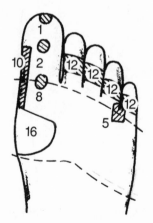

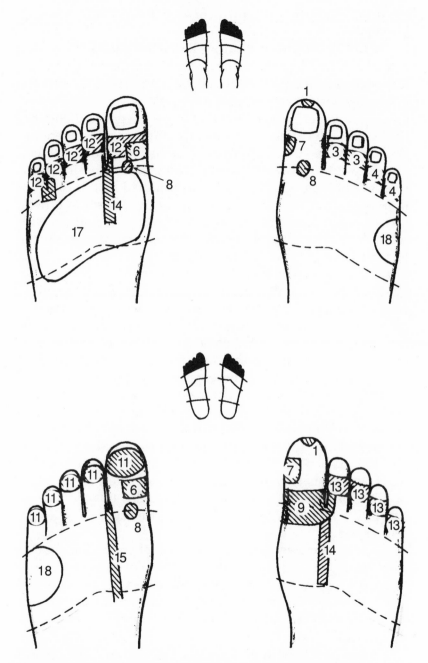

Figure 9. The physical organs that are in the air element area.

Earth and water complement each other. When they mix, growth becomes possible.

Fire: The Burning Shining Element—Fire is the region extending from the edge of the sternum to the shoulder blades. It encompasses the chest cavity, lungs, heart, ribs, chest muscles, and upper back. It represents the muscular system (see figure 8 on page 28). Fire is the region that burns oxygen and enriches the blood with oxygen, thus heating and providing energy to the body. A masculine, positive, dynamic, demanding element, it seeks ways to grow and to burn with greater intensity. It represents ambition, courage, lack of consideration. It is difficult, dominant. It burns/illuminates, seeks dynamism in others, takes from others in order to burn, may provide others with warmth or burn them in its fire. This element represents the ego, the internal power of the personality.

It is a region of doing. The hands are an expression of fire—busy, doing, dynamic, sharp; movements without warning; compulsiveness in connections; a tendency to be at the center of things; a tendency toward struggle with others; vocal outbursts. It is visible from afar as the color green. It seeks to expand its territory, its influence, its standing, its self-importance. Things are consumed in fire. It represents swift, impulsive decisions, the ability to be burned in a moment, as with a heart attack. With its pride, it cannot exist on its own and requires others to see it. It tries to make an impression; blurs and obscures the true reflection; appears from afar in darkness; leaves traces behind. It is hope, a place of inner balance. Fire has the ability to shine and shed light, the ability to give solely for the sake of giving, the ability to love unconditionally. It is individualism, independence; a feeling of "I," the primary seat of the ego, self-respect.

It is a hot element, striving to rise higher; an element that wants to expand, grow, achieve; an element of our ego—I want, I do. An element that contains strength and the capability of self-expression; the personal power of the individual—his or her self-presentation, charisma. From this area, people do things. Fire = "I do."

Air: The Element of Thought Perception—This region extends from the shoulder blades to the top of the skull, encompassing the upper portion of the head and shoulders. It represents the central nervous system, the brain, and the skin (see figure 9 on page 30). Air includes characteristics such as understanding, thinking, comprehension, organization, conscious memory, communicative ability, senses. It is related to the organs with which our lives are organized.

Air is a masculine, positive element, light blue in color, an element of space that serves two primary functions—conceptual space and communicative space. It contains the senses. Through it we receive information that we arrange in our conceptual space. All communication passes through it. Understanding, comprehension, organizational ability, intelligence, logic, intuition, instability in motion—all these are among its characteristics.

Air can be enclosed in definite borders. Expressive communication takes place within it; it permits messages to be relayed to the outside. Its energy is airy, light, elusive; it can be bored, cold, immobilized, engulfed in storm, disturbed, dangerous. Air has special, paranormal communicative abilities; it is creative, revitalizing, imaginative. It reaches every place; it does not exist in a vacuum. It represents the exercise of criticism, hearing, sight, taste, smell, conscious memory, speech, the ability to make use of existing information.

Air conforms to and encompasses all the other elements, can sweep things in its wake, can be clear or misty, can mislead, confuse, or delude. It is the ability to hover, to fly. It represents absent-mindedness, forgetfulness, a tendency to ignore, flightiness, impatience, and a demand for change. Through it we express ourselves, create, and are critical of what we and others create. This element is patterns, principles, conscious theories, explanations, speeches, words, writing. Air must be contained within another framework. It tends to disperse; it is not alone but is lonely. Air is swift.

Most Westerners have a large accumulation of tension in this region because all energies pass through this element; we are in it most of the time. Reflected in air are all mental actions we have taken in our lives (overexertion, underexertion). This element is exceedingly important to people today because it is the one we utilize the most. We use the lower portion of our bodies less and less, and our heads more and more. The element of air is like a computer, able to communicate with other computers. It is full of prepackaged, "bundled" software, such as prejudice.

Communication is carried out through air. From people's toes we may observe how they live with this element—what is in "their air." This element may point to the presence of intuition, special mental ability, various past states engaging one's physical head and its perceptual function. Any state in the element of air that represents a chronic departure from the norm emerges as a fixation in that person's perceptions. Air = "I think."

The element of fire heats the air and causes it to rise. Fire and air are masculine elements, and their tendency is to ascend. (I want something; the next stage is to think how to accomplish it—fire heats the air.) Air without heat will not move; fire without air will not ignite. They complement each other. Because they tend to rise, to expand, to achieve more, they are called active masculine elements. Air = light, fire = hot, water = wet, earth = heavy. Thus we have two descending, passive elements—feminine energies (earth and water)—and two ascending, active elements—masculine energies (fire and air).

We speak of the dichotomy of heaven and earth; out of their interaction man is created. Above the toes is the extreme of comprehension, below the heel is the extreme of sensations; we live between the two. Between the poles there must be tension as well as balance. If a state of imbalance occurs between the poles, whereby the feminine energy ascends and the masculine descends, the person's equilibrium is broken.

ZONES OF THE FOOT

Balanced distribution in a person's stride is two-thirds of the weight on the heel and one-third on and around the pads of the foot. In the latter zone there is a further distribution of weight: two-thirds of the weight in this region falls on the pad underneath the big toe, and one-third on the pads underneath the little toe. In other words, the pads underneath the big toe bear two-ninths of the body weight; the pads underneath the little toe bear one-ninth.

Walking on other areas is a departure from the state of balance. An example would be signs of walking on tiptoe. Dry, tough skin on the pads of the toes is evidence of pressure in the physical region corresponding to the toe that shows the tough skin. Pressure in the region indicates a nonflowing, unbalanced state. In practice, because most people are not in a state of balance, we hardly encounter the ideal distributions referred to above.

Division into Passive and Active Energies

The foot is divided into passive and active energies. The passive force seeks to descend (this is the part within us that wants to settle in one place and remain there forever); the active force strives to ascend, to renew, to change. See figure 10 on page 36.

Division into Four Elements

This is a division into elements:

- Air—Light, seeks to disperse.
- Fire—Hot, seeks to ascend.
- Water—Wet, cold; flows to the lowest point.
- Earth—Heavy and static; strongly influenced by gravity. See figure 11 on page 37.

Division into Active and Passive Parts of Each Element

This is a division into bands. Each element is bisected into lower and upper portions, representing passivity and activity, respectively. See figure 12 on page 39. We will discuss these bands and the various parts of the foot they represent.

Band 1: Lower Earth (passive element)—the region between the genitalia and the anus, which affects and encompasses the following organs: male and female sex organs, sciatic nerve, sigmoid colon, coccyx, sacrum, rectum, hips, thighs, cervix, lower pelvis, lower urinary tract, the lymphatic system in the groin, and the anus.

These energies relate to the primeval instincts of survival. This level exists within each of us, although we rarely encounter

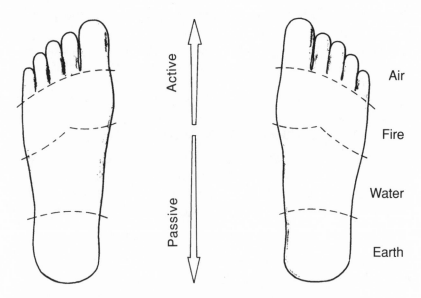

Figure 10. Division between active and passive elements.

it in the modern world. People utilize this energy only in war or sports, when they use it to break records and cross borders. We also invoke it to escape from a situation that threatens our existence; violence for the sake of defending one's existence occurs with neither thought nor emotion.

This is earth at its most extreme: tough, strong, containing dense energy—energy that causes people to do things without considering the consequences. It is a powerful energy capable of saving us if we know how to call upon it. It is our lowest energy, tending and striving to descend, to sink. Whenever it changes direction and ascends, we expect the destination to suffer from an extreme, uncontrollable intensity. An example of this would be the violence of a psychotic person.

Physiologically, hemorrhoids appear as a characteristic of pressure. The region is completely dried out; we observe a cracked and dry area at the tip of the heel, indicating that the energy in this area is in a state of great surplus and is not in balance with the other energies. This state occurs in people who spend a lot of time sitting, people who perceive themselves as fighting for their lives, people under financial pressure, and women during delivery.

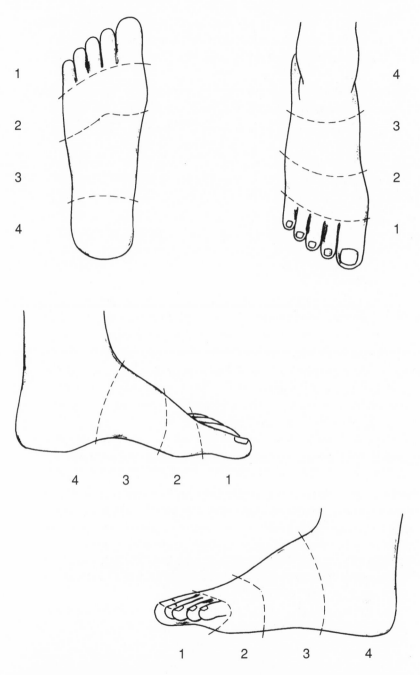

Figure 11. Division into the four elements seen from four sides of the foot. 1—Air; 2—Fire; 3—Water; 4—Earth.

This region contains a very important subzone: the rectal area, extending from the anal region to the testicles or perineum. This is a major energy center affecting the entire lower region (as we defined it) and the legs. A hernia in the groin indicates an imbalance in the lower earth region; the same is true of a cesarean section, which appears as a line between bands 1 and 2.

Band 2: Upper Earth (passive element)—the region extending from the end of the pubic hair to the line formed by the tip of the pelvic bones (band 2). It includes the following: male and female reproductive organs including the uterus, the ovaries, the fallopian tubes, the prostate, the bladder and a portion of the urinary tract; a portion of the descending colon, a portion of the ascending colon, a portion of the small intestines, the lumbar vertebrae, the appendix, the ileocecal valve, the muscles of the abdominal wall, and the muscles of the lower back.

This region is one of sexuality, fertility, perpetuation of the species; comfort, pampering, acquisitiveness, aesthetics, the need for things to be attractive, orderly, and clean. (This is where feces and urine reside before leaving the body.) It is a sexual and sensual region. If it is developed, warm, and attractive, it points to a person who enjoys physical contact and whose touch is warm. The paler, thinner, more narrow, and colder it is, the less sensual the person.

The earth element in this region, as elsewhere, tends to descend, but less strongly than in band 1. Here, in the second band, it ascends more easily. When one engages in a sexual fantasy, his or her earth ascends to air. In someone with constant sexual fantasies, earth ascends to air and stays there.

Upper earth contains an energy concerned with the end of pregnancy and with delivery. The moment of delivery is the boundary between the two bands. The father and mother contribute energy that passes outward from this region—from the feminine portion of both their energies.

It is from this interface between the two bands that energy is emitted when we reproduce and when we die. Earth—our bones—is the last part of our bodies that remains. Bands 1 and 2 are concerned with the lowest physical level of the person, primarily the skeleton and bones. The largest and heaviest

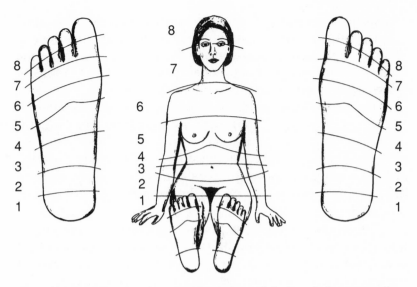

Figure 12. Dividing the foot and body into eight bands by separating each element into an active and passive state.

bones of the body, the pelvis and the femur, appear within the earth element. An example of the effects of earth would be women in menopause, which is characterized by a leakage of calcium from the bones (loss of earth qualities). Pregnant women also lose calcium.

Band 3: Lower Water (passive element)—the region extending from the line formed by the tip of the pelvis to a point approximately three fingers above the navel (band 3). It contains: part of the liver, part of the transverse colon, a portion of the urinary tract, parts of the descending and ascending colons, the lower T-vertebrae, the small intestine, muscles from the abdominal wall, back muscles, and the bladder. This is the band where we digest, accumulate water, and process all fluids. The fluids intermingle in the small intestine. (In the large intestine, they are absorbed.) Band 3 contains primarily the small intestine, causing us to speak of the mixing, grinding, and addition of substances more than their absorption.

It is an area we cannot see into from above. It exudes the mysterious, the nebulous. It is a region of emotional intuition; we feel things without knowing how. It houses aspects of our

emotions of which we are unaware (the emotional unconscious), emotional drives of whose origins we are unsure. It is
the dark region of our emotions. In this band are registered the
most elementary of our emotional patterns—life situations to
which our conscious psyche is blind.

This is the softest region in the body. It is protected by
the smallest amount of bone and muscle; it is very vulnera-
ble. Unconscious emotional manipulations are directed toward
it. It is the region where we digest the emotions of which we
are not aware, where we process and organize experiences.
This is not a conscious act of will, but something that happens
nonetheless.

This region contains the power of emotional perseverance
and resilience in the face of difficulties. (A surplus in the region
is a sign of someone who carries the unwillingness to concede
too far.) It is from here that the first emotional patterns in childhood emerge. Freudian analysis is meant to reach this region, as
is hypnosis. But it is hard to reach on an "aware" level. It houses
the emotional tie between mother and child. (The instinctive
connection is in earth.)

Band 4: Upper Water (passive element)—a region extending from three fingers above the navel to the solar plexus. It
contains a portion of the stomach, the pancreas, the solar plexus,
the lower diaphragm, the duodenum, the upper portion of the
liver, the spleen, the central thoracic vertebrae, the lymph
glands of the upper abdomen, part of the transverse colon, the
kidney, a portion of the vagus nerve, and the lower chest cavity
(the lower portion of the lungs).

The water is clearer and more transparent here. This band is
where conscious fear resides. The kidney—responsible for the
absorption, breakdown, and elimination of fluids—characterizes fear and is the organ that most typifies this band. Severe
traumas, such as car accidents, war, assault, rape, and so on,
leave their marks in this band. Most of us have many such
marks here. The shock of fear can cause the pancreas (which
is found in this band) to cease to function, thus bringing on
diabetes. The classic characteristic of this band is anxiety.

In the upper portion of the band, we find the diaphragm.
By means of its movement it interfaces between fire and water,
between masculine and feminine energy. Lack of movement in

the diaphragm indicates a lack of stomach movement. The spleen, the liver, the stomach, and the diaphragm are organs that lie between fire and water. When the boundary is unclear—when water pushes one way, or fire the other—we can see how active or passive the person is.

The accumulation of fluids in the body (upper or lower) is a function of this band and not of the lower water. This region is connected with phenomena in which water invades other areas. For example, an allergy affecting the eyes and nose indicates a surplus of water in the fourth band that has spread and ascended. All outwardly expressed emotions, such as laughter, weeping, and anger, emanate from this band. It is here that long-term, chronic illnesses are generated, persisting over the course of many years.

It is not customary to notice or mention things that reside in the element of water. Most people have trouble coping with the contents of their digestive systems, and most of us indeed suffer from stomach problems. The most extreme possibilities of the element of water are:

A) We are swept away by our emotions, disengaging our thought processes and our will. Water exerts total control; water permeates the entire foot.

B) We become completely "dry," feeling nothing. Here water disappears from the foot (or is compressed into a small area).

The element of water is problematic for us. It is changeable, emotional; people pass through and shift among many different states (unlike thought, which can remain unchanged). Any unresolved emotional state appears in water. Many people who cope well on all other levels can become entangled by their emotions.

• • •

Thus far we have discussed the passive sector—earth and water—elements that do not create but react to what is happening around them. Earth is a static element that represents the heavy things in our lives; water is a dynamic and variable element that flows naturally downward.

In modern civilization, people tend to dissociate themselves from their passive traits, for these contain forces that are
hard to control: instinctiveness, sexuality, unrestrained drives,
fear. We have tried to create systems that would control these
energies, lest they drag us in their wake. Many cultural rules
and frameworks are meant to govern these energies. We take a
dim view of fear, violence, and indiscriminate sex. All our cultural rules about sexuality are aimed at quarantining this energy
to keep it from running wild, bursting forth, and dominating us.
Prostitutes, for example, live around this band; generally this
behavior is connected with their existence and with violence.
(The reference here is to prostitutes who ply this trade due to an
overpowering urge or for lack of choice—for the sake of their
existence.)

The more we try to control the passive energy by applying
active energies, the more we become dependent upon them.
When we look at these regions in foot analysis, we encounter all
our stigmas and personal inhibitions with regard to the contents. These are heavy contents that tend to sink, both because
heaviness is a characteristic of passive energy and because of
our cultural conceptions.

Band 5: Lower Fire (active element)—the region encompassing the diaphragm, the upper abdomen, part of the liver,
the lower section of the esophagus, sternum, the solar plexus
(located on the line between water and fire), the ribs, the lower
portions of the lungs, the heart and the bronchial tubes, the
chest cavity, the muscles and the major blood vessels of the
chest, the lower part of the upper T-vertebrae, the thymus
gland, the muscles of the upper back and shoulders, the sternum, and a part of the trachea.

Fire is an element of ego. Part of the ego concerns itself with
control and action; the other part disregards these. The lower
fire band is not concerned with control. It contains the reasons
for what a person does, the power underlying the action. It
houses traits and drives that have nothing to do with the "I
shoulds" of life.

This band is the basis of the element of fire. Fire is at its
hottest here (sizzling coals). But it's not so active. It is more
concentrated, with fewer upward eruptions. It is a heat that is
difficult to control. This band is the home of love, the ability to
share this warmth with others, and affection coupled with inner
power and warmth (a basic warmth, from which one can give).

This region throbs with the power of inner self-confidence. When we act from the heart—not because of the outcome but for its own sake, for our own personal satisfaction—we act from this band (as shown in expressions such as: "I take it to heart" or "Dictates of the heart"). From this band we communicate with others, not conversationally or emotionally, but in terms of the particular characteristics of our active personality, our charisma, the power we radiate. Chemistry between people who work together stems from here. (Rather than asking how we may do something for another, we ask how we can do it together.) Action from this band precedes action emanating from band 6. Before we act, we choose. Choice and the ability to choose come from this band.

Cowardice and courage originate here. Courage without thought appears as a surplus; cowardice manifests itself as a deficiency. When the fire burns itself out, the water rises and extinguishes the coals. (It takes courage to love.)

The region may contain hate as a motivation for action. The foot analysis may observe the residues of separations that touched the heart, the effects of the subject's having parted with the object of a heartfelt connection. It is in this zone where a person feels like an "I"—without affectations. It may become a hole, a prison, or a place of refuge. This is the place where most people tend to be hurt and through which they die: approximately 50 percent of the population die of heart attacks, which occur in this region. Sudden, swift death is a characteristic of this band, as opposed to the long-term illnesses that typify band 4.

Band 6: Upper Fire (active element)—this region encompasses the hands, the shoulder blades, the vertebrae from the last neck vertebra to sixth or seventh vertebra, the upper reaches of the esophagus, the lungs, the bronchial tubes, the ribs enclosing the chest cavity and the heart, the major muscles of the chest and shoulders, the throat, the neck muscles, the trapezius, the shoulder joints, the thyroid gland, part of the trachea, the tonsils, the lymphatic system, the major blood vessels connecting the head and body, part of the vagus nerve.

This is the band of action, the creative drive. The hands emerge from the junction of fire and air. They form a bridge between the two elements, which collaborate in the creative act. Fire is most active here. This is the region of control, of attempts to expand and spread, of the urge to attain more influence. We express ourselves through this band. It is a sensitive region in many people; it proves problematic for those who do not do what they themselves want. Asthma, a classic physical condition arising in this region, represents a state of heavy demands upon oneself, of "What must I do?" when these are dictated not by personal needs but by the surroundings. Often the band may become a suffocation zone.

A person whose upper fire region is balanced and large, has good hands. Certain people are good at everything they do. They have hands that succeed in doing things. This region contains the thymus gland, a significant factor in our growth and development. Its influence is particularly intensive during the period when the patterns of our ego become ingrained (by the age of 16, for most of us). Many people with developmental problems have a sunken chest.

Fire tends to rise, reflecting the needs of the ascending ego. Fire is related to the way a person behaves and expresses things. There is a tendency to spread out from this region, to encroach upon others' boundaries. A forceful and domineering person is in a state of surplus here. There is a strong connection between the elements of fire and air along the shoulder line, since the shoulders move between fire and air. On the boundary between fire and air we find the thyroid gland, the passageway between the two elements, between one's strength and the way in which one moves outward and flows toward the air. People often have something in their element of fire that cannot come out. It remains stuck in their throats; throat obstruction represents a block in self-expression.

Band 7: Lower Air (active element)—the region encompassing the chin, the throat, the mouth, the upper and lower jaw, the tongue, the gums, the nose, the lower sinuses, the teeth, a portion of the eyes, parts of the inner and outer ears, the optic and auditory nerves, the brain stem, the lower portions of the brain, a significant portion of the skull and its component parts, the hair, the facial and trigeminal nerves, the cheeks and eyelids, the facial muscles, the lachrymal glands, the eyebrows, the temples, and the pituitary gland. Also situated in this band are the upper portion of the shoulder line (primarily in people who tend to raise their shoulders), and the larynx.

Air is the medium of communication. The lower air band concerns itself with communication and outward expression, i.e., speech; the upper band deals with inward-flowing communication. The two bands are not always directly connected.

People do not always speak their minds; the bands exist independently of one another. From this band, we ingest (swallowing food) and emit (speaking). The ways in which we swallow in and speak out are strongly interrelated. At times there is an outburst of fire alone, without thought, and sometimes we articulate only those thoughts that we have considered. The balanced outward flow should be the result of a combination of air and fire.

People have problems with this band: trouble with the teeth, gums, jaws, throat. Most of us go through problems with the throat and tonsils in childhood; this occurs during the period in which we begin to hold things in rather than letting them out. By failing to express what we want and what we don't want, we create a surplus in the region. Children easily express things emanating from the element of water: anger, fear, etc. Parents have patience for such things up to a certain point, beyond which they do not permit the child's water to control the situation. This leads to problems in the lower air region. Screaming and spitting, for example, are forbidden. We are sad; tears well up and we don't let them flow. The result is a sense of strangulation in the throat. A regular, chronic situation such as this creates a problem in the throat; whatever we have not said remains there in the form of a surplus.

It is from this region, too, that the nerves branch out to the hands. Control of the hands originates in air. Spontaneous creativity, unrelated to thought, comes from fire. Nonspontaneous creativity, related to thought and to the senses, comes from air. Actions originating in the lower air zone are very quick. The shortest stage of the digestive process takes place in the mouth. Speech is quick. The only thing quicker is thought, which occurs in the upper air zone.

Band 8: Upper Air (active element)—this region encompasses the upper skull, the brain, the cerebral cortex, the scalp, local blood vessels, the pineal gland, and upper sinuses. Here is where we sort, catalogue, and arrange our thoughts. It is the site of the breakdown into cause and effect; data absorption; visual and verbal memory; concentration; the ability to draw conclusions; aspects of nonspontaneous expression such as writing, which involves thought and reliance on prior information.

Taking place here are organization, orderly arrangement, use of mnemonics, etc. When we express ourselves spontaneously, we write without knowing what we are writing, paying no attention to grammar, rules, and all the rest. The reference here is to "official" writing, not poems. Unstructured writing arises from the lower air, fire, and water regions. Intuition is located in this band of upper air. Western thought has degenerated to a process of logic; for everything there is an explanation. The region can reduce everything to equations and stereotypes. Because of the characteristics of air, however, things are invented here without the person being aware of their origins. Within this region is the possibility to explain everything. Some of us utilize this band only partially, analyzing and explaining past events. These people's thinking is characterized by the processing of historical information; they neither think creatively nor overstep boundaries.

Within this element a paradox exists between logical thinking and a definite lack of boundaries. We may see movement of the toes beyond the line of the big toe. Part of the air element has transcended the air; thus logical thought does not coexist with these abilities. This element contains the concept of religiosity, in that it is thin, delicate, and the most abstract of all the elements. It comes closest of all to ethereal energy. Here we find inquisitive people, those who wish to know why we exist, those who do not settle for logical explanations.

Since air is the clearest material, it is through this band that the connection with infinity is formed. Things can fall here from infinity; thus explaining how we can know without knowing how we know. We are freed from our bodies here. From this site, people experience "religious awakenings" and daydreams. Certain spiritual abilities emanate from this band. It embraces our longing to touch infinity and detach ourselves from basic needs, from emotion, from the ego, and so on. Even if all the needs of the other bands have been met, there will remain a hunger for something else. Then people go in search of God—each in his or her own way. When true meditation takes place, it occurs in the upper air; air provides us with every possible opportunity to fantasize. Most of us, however, do not make use of this freedom, instead developing ingrained and well-planned thought patterns.

• • •

We are put together in the form of a rainbow of colors—a spectrum ranging from lower earth to upper air. No human activity emanates from one band alone. There must be a tension between the poles. This tension is us. The two poles must work together. People who are caught up in their own existence will not be spiritual. Some of us find ourselves stuck at one pole and then, propelled by the intensity at that pole, leap to the other.

There is a flow of ascending energy between the bands. Something has threatened my existence; immediately, I think what to do. An example would be a man sitting on a bus who sees a pretty girl. Just as something starts to happen in the lower elements, his air puts a halt to things. "Not on a bus," it says. "You're married." First the visual information descended from air to earth. He saw her and desire ascended to his head. Finally, his air descended and controlled his earth.

In all, the result is a cyclical, recurrent movement of ascent-descent-ascent. This cycle is completed only when we die. We are born with several clear-cut traits: characteristics of intelligence, genetic problems and attributes, and a fifth element that helps us circulate the energy through the ascent-descent-ascent cycle. If we overload or halt this cycle, we die. We are born with enough of this basic energy to sustain the cycle; the level of our energy is set at the time of our birth. The choice of whether to burn it, waste it, or fulfill it is left to us.

3

TECHNICAL ASPECTS
OF THE ANALYZING PROCESS

Before we examine all the various aspects of the analyzing process, we must consider the following conditions that interfere with or make foot analysis impossible.

1) Dry, tough skin over the entire foot. (The person should have a pedicure and then wear shoes for two weeks, after which chronic patterns will emerge.)

2) Mycosis or other severe infections of the foot. This is an illness of the foot itself, but if it has spread, all the indicators disappear. In a severe case, nothing can be done.

3) Circulatory problems in the feet. Severe problems alter both color and texture. Any condition we observe on the foot will look more severe than it is, since a problem exists in the foot itself. It is difficult to obtain an accurate reading, because the feet appear older and more problematic than they really are. In any such case, we regard everything we see as less acute.

4) Burns and partial amputations. When parts of one foot have been amputated, we draw conclusions about the missing area from the other foot. Our only inference is that, due to the amputation, the region of the body corresponding to the site of the amputation was damaged.

5) Paralysis of all or part of the foot. Because the paralyzed region indicates a dead state, we cannot draw any conclusions and must seek appropriate findings from the other foot.

6) Treatments involving medications that contain hormonal substances or cortisone. These treatments modify the state of the entire body. Cortisone reduces swelling. The feet change shape, confusing our observation. Examples include artificial insemination, chemotherapy, and radiation therapy (which particularly affects those parts of the foot corresponding to the areas irradiated).

7) General paralysis, paraplegia, or quadriplegia. The feet of people who cannot walk are smooth, swollen, and edematous. We may discern much in the first half-year, but almost nothing afterward.

8) Amputation of one foot. After an amputation, a person transfers considerable pressure to the second foot. We can learn a great deal from that foot, but we must take into account that it is filling the role of two feet and scale down what we learn from the indicators. (We should use less pressure; it is advisable to palpate a hand in place of the missing foot, and to carry out the mapping in accordance with the hand.)

9) When the toenails are unattractive, we ask if the person uses nail polish frequently. Nail polish and acetone stain the nails.

10) A foot that was in a cast for six months may affect the way a person walks. Sometimes people do not recall such a condition, even if it was recent. A limp caused by such a situation will be temporary, and the states indicated in the area where the person treads when limping are less pronounced than they appear to be.

When we observe the feet we compare them not with an ideal, harmonious, prototypical foot but with the state of balance that that particular foot is capable of attaining. At each age, the foot possesses different characteristics; we do not expect an octogenarian's feet to exhibit the same picture as those of a 16-year-old. Thus we are comparing the foot to itself. The observation must be thorough, covering the entire foot from four inches above the ankle to the tips of the toes, including the areas between the toes, behind the heel, around the ankle bone, and on both sides of the foot. Because the indicators we seek might be small, we need good overhead lighting (preferably not fluorescent light, which distorts the colors of the foot). Some of the indicators we see may be marks from a shoe or sock, an injury to the foot, and other conditions related to the foot alone, with no bearing on the person as a whole.

The process of examining the feet comprises several stages. First we ask the person to stand barefoot so that we can observe the following:

1) To find the dominant foot we ask the person to step forward in order to see which foot takes the first step. We also ask the person to stand on one foot in order to see which foot he or she trusts more. Sometimes we have to repeat the different tests to get a definite indication of the dominant foot; the one the person trusts to stand on and to step forward with.

2) To determine regions used in walking—which parts touch the ground, and which are in the air—we can try to move parts of the feet, such as toes, pads, and heels to check the distribution of weight while standing. We expect the person to put most of the weight on the heels, some on the pads, and very little on the toes and outer sides of the feet. Here we look for deviations from the above description.

Next we ask the person to sit down on a chair or a table with straight legs and the feet facing us so that we can observe the following:

1) We compare the size of the feet with the size of the body, checking whether there are noticeable disproportions.

2) We compare the size of the feet and the length of the legs to each other.

3) We compare the arches of the two feet. This will indicate differences in the muscles of the two sides of the back.

4) We divide the feet into the four elements and compare the size of each element to the basic potential size (see chapter 1).

5) We complete a detailed visual examination of the feet, which creates a three-dimensional map of the person. We compare the condition of each spot on the foot to the balanced state of the element in which it is located. We note each imbalance that we find and mark it on a contour of the feet. The indicators that we use are excesses of elements in their territories or in territories of other elements.

Earth—Dry and rough skin which might also be flaky, black-and-blue blood vessels or spots, calcifications of tendons, bands of muscles or joints, contortion or wild growth of bone, crystalline lumps, dark warts or corns, warm areas, thick toenails.

Water—Swollen areas, wet, cold and edematous, moist peelings. The tissue is thin and soft, perspiration, ticklish spots, hypotonic muscles, light color, soft and wet toenails.

Fire—Red, hot, inflamed areas, small sores, dry skin (but not very rough or flaky), the muscles and tendons are hypertonic.

Air—Empty areas, cold, dry and light in color, the muscles are hypotonic and very delicate, the skin has no flesh beneath it.

EXAMINATION OF THE FEET BY TOUCH

We palpate the entire foot from the area four inches above the ankle to the toes and between them. We do this to gather information from what we feel physically in the feet and from the client's responses. In the examination by touch, we use several techniques related to various aspects of the foot:

1) Temperature—This stage commences with a delicate touch aimed at noting and comparing the temperature of the feet. We look for differences in temperature in various regions on each foot, again comparing both feet. The same touch discerns differences in texture of the skin within each foot individually and between the two feet.

2) Flexibility—We use different techniques to check the flexibility of different parts of the feet. Manipulating the ankle must be done carefully; incorrect movement may cause discomfort and even harm. We grasp the right ankle firmly with the left hand (and vice versa) at the joint. The second hand holds the foot from the inner side under the big toe. An equal amount of pressure must be applied and maintained by both hands. The movement is a 360 degree rotation, with the hand grasping the ankle constituting the axis. The ankle and its limitations should be felt throughout the movement. We rotate the feet in both directions. Then we move the foot upward and downward. We note any

limitation in movement of the ankle. By rotating the ankle, we examine the mobility of the pelvis and the hips. Difficulty in movement indicates stiffness and accumulated tension in the corresponding parts of the body (see figure 13 on page 54).

The technique for manipulating the big toe is essentially identical to that used to manipulate the ankle, except that the flexing is performed on the joint of the big toe. For the right foot, the left hand grasps the top of the toe (the grip extends to the base of the toe); the right hand holds the foot from its inner side and the index finger reaches under the base of the joint of the toe. Pulling gently with the left hand, we slowly rotate the big toe several times in both directions, and move it up and down. Pay attention to the fact that the circular rotation of the big toe is limited by the structure of the foot. By moving the big toe, one feels if the joints are stiff, creaking, painful to the touch, or restricted in mobility. Limited mobility in the big toe indicates that the nape of the neck and the throat are in a state of tension, since this area corresponds to the middle joint of the big toe. The more problematic the joints of the big toe, the more severe the condition (see figure 14 on page 55).

Manipulation of the other toes is similar to the manipulation of the big toe. The difference is that the other toes can be moved to all sides and their joints are not restricted in their mobility. By manipulating the toes, we gauge tension and other conditions in the head and shoulders. Significantly, excessive freedom of movement is indicative of hypertonia, particularly in the shoulder area. The more one tends toward surpluses and accumulations of tension, the stiffer, closer together, and more lacking in mobility his or her toes will be, with a greater tendency to "pop" at the joints. The greater the deficiency, the greater the lack of sensation and almost unrestricted mobility of the toes (see figure 15 on page 56).

Manipulating the bones in the fire area is done by placing both hands with the thumbs underneath the foot, and resting the pads of the fingers between the foot's tendons. Holding a bone in each hand, we move the bones upward, downward, and toward each other and note whether they can be separated. By manipulating these bones we examine the mobility of the upper back and chest.

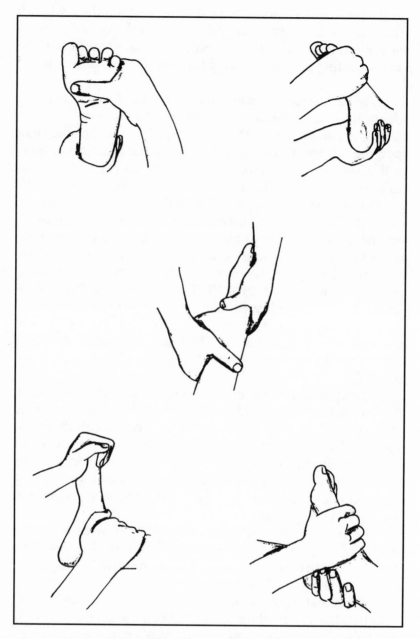

Figure 13. The ankle is rotated in all possible directions in order to test the ankle's range of motion.

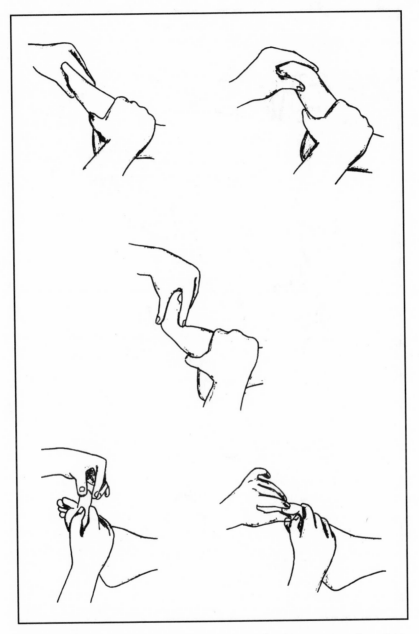

Figure 14. The big toe is moved in various directions to test for cricking and difficulty in movement.

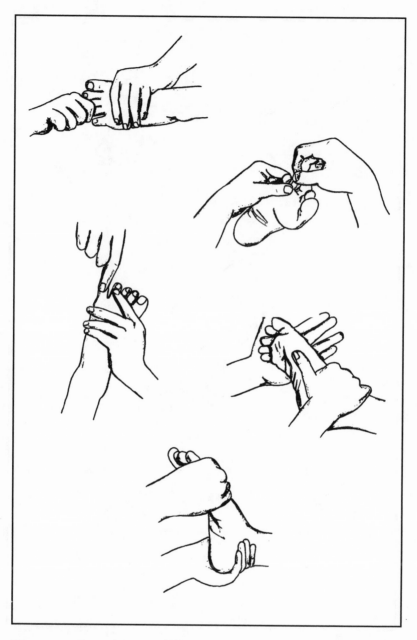

Figure 15. Each of the toes is moved in all possible directions to test for any lack of movement, rigidity, loss of flexibility or over-flexibility.

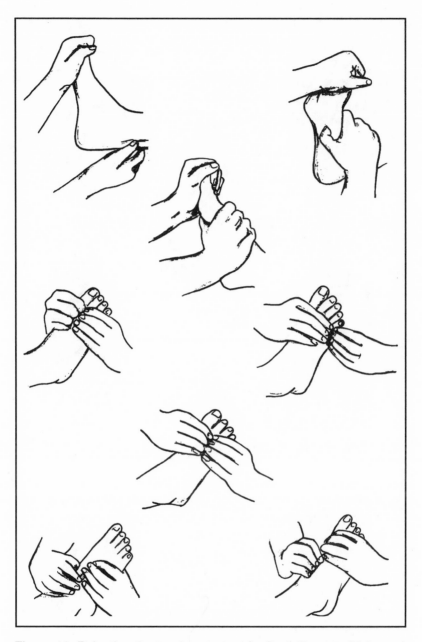

Figure 16. Palpating the tendons to test for flexibility, sensitivity and movement.

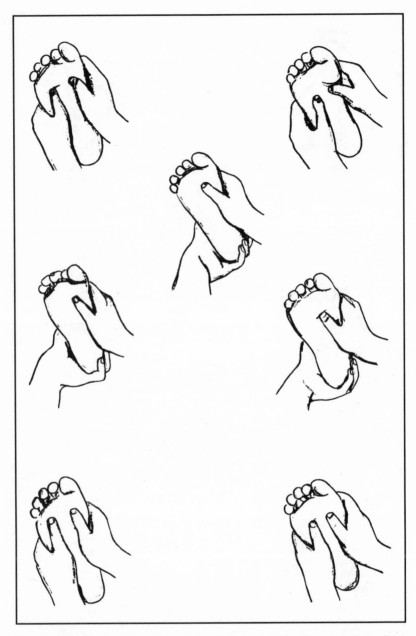

Figure 17. The walking thumb technique (using the thumb to find anomalies in the tissue) is used to palpate the bottom of the foot.

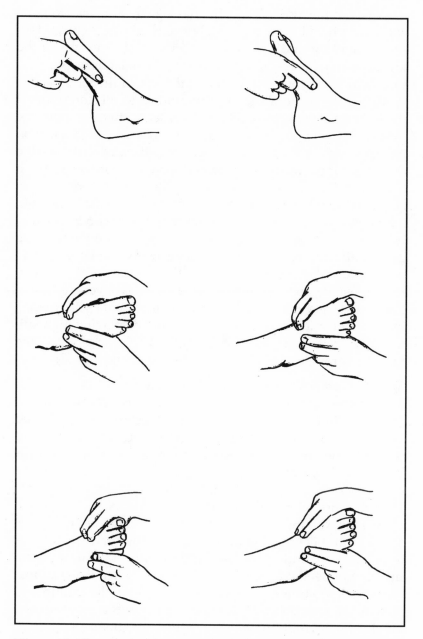

Figure 18. The moving fingers technique (using the fingers to find anomalies in the tissue) is used to palpate the top part of the foot.

We can flex the tendons by massaging each one along its entire length while it is completely stretched. The Achilles' tendon's condition indicates the condition of the muscles of the low back and the thighs. To stretch it to the maximum, push the foot away from you. The tendon in the sole of the foot, the one that goes along the water element, indicates the condition of the muscles of the belly and back. In order to stretch it, push the toes away from you. The tendons of the toes, which go down on the upper side of the foot from each toe to the ankle, indicate the condition of the muscles of the entire back. In order to stretch them, bend the toes toward you. By flexing the tendons, we acquaint ourselves with their condition—a state that reflects to a high degree the muscular system of the entire body. A calm, relaxed person is one with a flexible foot whose tendons are pliant and supple. The higher the level of accumulated tension in the muscular system, the more the tendons will be short, hard, sensitive, and insufficiently mobile. The converse is true in a state of deficiency; a foot that is too weak to hold itself together, instead spreading apart in mid-stride and displaying high vulnerability, reflects a state of degeneration and hypotonia in the muscles throughout the body (see figure 16 on page 57).

3) Palpation—We begin approximately four inches above the ankle bone, applying constant pressure and employing the "walking thumb" and "moving finger" techniques (explained below) in a slow and thorough pattern covering every inch of the foot. The pressure should be such that the person can bear it comfortably, except perhaps at certain points. At this stage of the examination, we make note of certain regions and points in accordance with indicators of elements in excess.

In the walking thumb technique we use the upper joint of the thumb, keeping the other joints stationary. Pressure is applied at the end of the pad underneath the nail, with the upper joint bent at an angle of 90 degrees. When the examination of one point is completed, we straighten the thumb and slide to the next point. Thus we attain a flowing movement of bend-press-relax-straighten-move from one point to the next. The pressure applied originates not in the thumb but in the other fingers, which remain in place on the other side of the foot. By contracting the hand and applying force from the supporting fingers on the other side, we exert a controlled pressure, avoiding, of course, excessive pressure and tension in the joints of the thumb. With this technique it is possible to work continuously over wide areas of the foot (see figure 17 on page 58).

The moving finger technique is identical to the walking thumb, except that the guidelines apply to the finger or fingers. The examiner should take care to hold the fingers at a comfortable angle for working on the foot and to position the upper joints of the finger at an angle of almost 90 degrees when applying pressure (see Figure 18 on page 59).

The moving thumb and moving finger techniques identify all points that are sensitive and particularly responsive to touch. Where the elements are in a state of balance, the pressure is pleasant. Where surpluses or deficiencies exist the pressure causes pain, other unpleasant sensations, or a lack of feeling. In addition, the examiner's fingers can discern differences in muscle tissue, crystalline lumps, swellings, and differences in sensation in specific areas. Thus we may map out areas of imbalance.

4) Odor—Note if the feet have a distinctive odor that is sharp or special in some way.

Common Indicators

Common indicators are signs that recur in a highly similar fashion in many people who suffer from chronic conditions. A large percentage of people who evince one of these indicators are found to suffer from a condition either medically diagnosed as identical or experienced similarly.

The indicator of asthma, for example, suggests a state of imbalance in the bronchial region. If this indicator appears on the foot, we know there is a strong probability that the individual has breathing problems. Even when the individual who shows the common indicator does not suffer from the condition indicated, more precise questioning shows the existence of an imbalance in the region, manifested in certain symptoms that the individual displays. An indicator of asthma in people who have not been diagnosed as asthmatic, or who do not define themselves as such, corresponds to difficulty in breathing during exertion, recurrent bronchitis in childhood, or damage to the respiratory organs caused by air pollution.

If the individual does not report a chronic condition that corresponds to the indicator, several possibilities exist:

1) The condition once existed and is presently inactive, but the tendency is still present.

2) The condition is latent or formative; it may surface in the future.

3) Someone in the family (usually not more than one generation apart) suffers from this condition, and the person lives with the effect that the condition has on the family. Perhaps, too, the condition tends to "run" in the family.

4) The indicator was caused by a foot injury and is therefore irrelevant.

It is important to remember that different people experience an imbalance differently, even when its manifestation on the foot is similar. Thus, the common indicators are only markers that help us identify conditions; we must still pinpoint each individual's variation of any condition suffered.

The most common indicators are visible changes in the structure or the shape of the foot. A chronic pattern that is stabilized and entrenched in the body will eventually create a change in the way that the person uses his or her feet. After a period of time this will cause either changes in the structure of the foot (such as curled toes) or it will create deep, visible lines or grooves in the tissue. The beginning of a chronic pattern of imbalance starts with the presence of an unbalanced energy in a specific element or organ. This is created either when the element's energy is far too strong in its own territory thereby "pushing out" all the other qualities that are necessary to balance the element (each element needs the other three elements so it can be balanced), or when the energy of the element becomes weak and the energies from the other elements become stronger and more dominant in its territory. For example, the presence of dry, rough skin on the shoulder area, what we call the invasion of earth energy into the fire element, shows a chronic condition where the earth energy is much too strong, thus affecting and changing the qualities in a specific area in the fire element. On the physical level, this may mean a calcified shoulder joint (too much earth) and loss of muscle tone and flexibility in the shoulder muscles (weak fire).

Some common indicators are not defined by the clear presence of an element invading into another element, but instead are seen as lines on the foot—a result of changes of structure and not as another energy's quality. Since a chronic pattern is actually the result of the body learning how to react and respond to the world, many times the habit pattern stays in the body even though the imbalance that caused the chronic pattern has passed. For example, if a child had bronchitis many times prior to age 12, we may see on the foot what we call an asthma sign—a branched line over the bronchial tubes area. The adult may not notice any breathing problems but we can see that this body is still behaving and acting as if breathing is still a great effort. The respiratory system is weak and susceptible to problems as this adult ages.

In order to diagnose the feet, you need to understand the four elements, and the chronic conditions that affect the qualities of each element, so that you can easily see the most common chronic problems that people have. In almost every pair of feet there are at least two or three common indicators. Seeing them immediately makes the beginning of the analysis easier and gives the analyzer confidence to go further. Most of the common indicators are described on a physical level—which is only a shallow understanding of what they mean—but at this stage it allows you better access to understanding the feet. To make learning the elements and their symptoms as easy as possible, we will explore each element (air, fire, water, earth) separately.

Common Air Indicators

Common indicators in the air element show the loss or the weakness of the qualities of this element. It is expressed not only by symptoms in the head area but also in loss of concentration and memory, weakening of the senses and fading of intellectual abilities. Described in Table 1 is a list of symptoms or conditions that appear either from other energies becoming stronger in the air region or from the learned habits of the air element. In both cases we see an unbalanced situation disturbing and clouding the element's abilities.

Table 1. Air Indicators.

Condition	Ailment
1. Ingrown toenail on big toe and/or other toes.	Recurrent headaches or migraines.
2. Swollen, red toe pads.	Sinusitis.
3. Little toe is bent, red, callused, or curled under the forth toe.	In women, a disturbance in the menstrual cycle (irregularity, pain, difficult menopause in older women). In men, prostate problems.
4. Toes that curl under or over one another, or deformities of the toes.	Problems affecting the head. (Toes 2 and 3 the eyes; toes 4 and 5 the ears.) See figure19a on page 65.
4a. Pronounced marks in the area corresponding to the eyes (transverse lines in the middle of toes 2 and 3).	Vision problems. See figure 19b on page 65.
4b. Pronounced marks in the area corresponding to the ears (the base of toes 4 and 5).	Hearing problems, vertigo, tinnitus (ringing in the ears). See figure 19c on page 65.

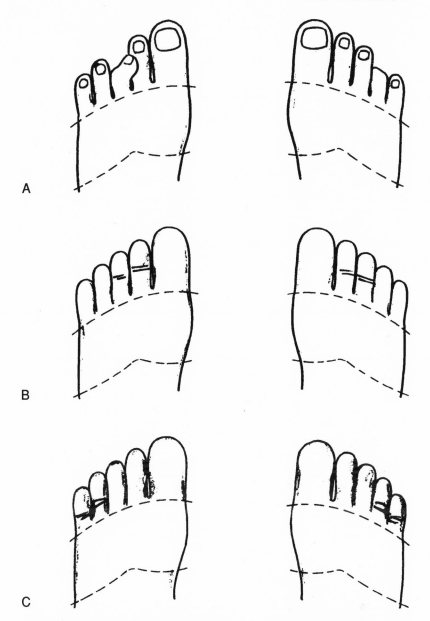

Figure 19. Air indicators: a) toes can curl in different directions and in many different ways; b) marks corresponding to the eyes; c) marks corresponding to the ears.

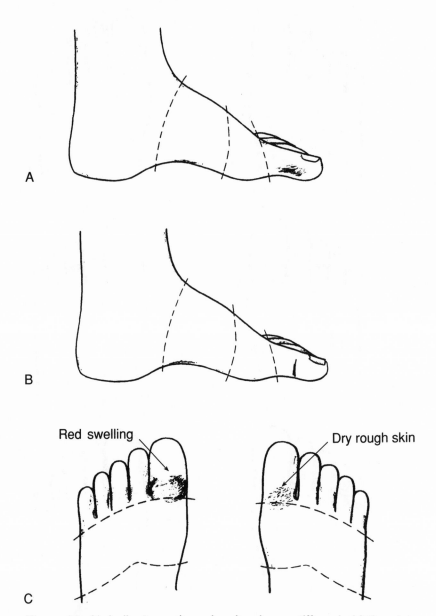

A

B

Red swelling

Dry rough skin

C

Figure 20. Air indicators: a) marks showing a stiff neck; b) the sign for an old whiplash; c) throat problems.

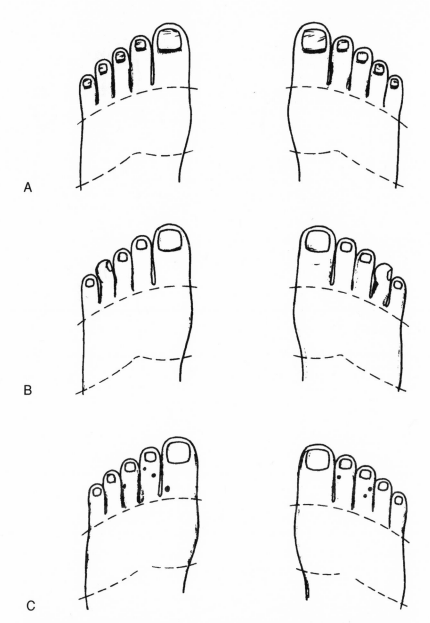

Figure 21. Air indicators: a) discoloration under the toenail indicates gum and teeth problems; b) curled toe 4 signifies possible dyslexia; c) beauty marks on the toes means an unusual capacity for dreams and visions.

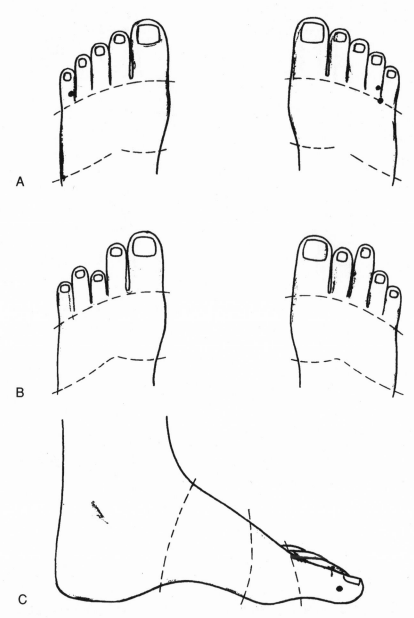

Figure 22. Air indicators: a) beauty mark in the area of the middle ear indicates vertigo; b) very long or very short toe 3 signifies basic imbalance; c) beauty mark in the area of the upper spine may indicate a genetic problem.

Table 1. Air Indicators (continued).

Condition	Ailment
5. Dry, tough skin on the outer side of big toe.	Problems in the upper vertebrae, with pressure radiating upward into the head or a pain or numbness in the arms. See figure 20a on page 66.
6. A deep line on the outer side of the big toe or a little lower.	Whiplash (a severe blow causing the head to fly backward). See figure 20b on page 66.
7. Redness, swelling, or signs of pressure on the area corresponding to the throat.	Sensitivity in the throat, nodules on the vocal cords, tendency toward laryngitis, past tonsillectomy, hoarseness, tendency to expectorate. See figure 20c on page 66.
8. Lines on the toes.	Scars on the head.
9. Marks under the toenails (differences in color) and mycosis of the nails.	Problems with teeth, gums, or hair. See figure 21a on page 67.
10. Toe 4 is turned such that its nail points toward toe 5 or toe 3.	Learning disabilities (dyslexia); faulty transition from auditory to visual learning and vice versa; any eye or ear problems unrelated to the physical functioning of hearing and sight. See figure 21b on page 67.

Table 1. Air Indicators (continued).

Condition	Ailment
11. Beauty marks or birth-marks on the toes.	Unusual capacity for dreaming. See figure 21c on page 67.
12. Beauty mark in the upper portion of the foot on the base of toes 4 and 5.	Problems with balance and the middle ear. See figure 22a on page 68.
13. Toes 4 and 5 are numb.	Pressure or other difficulty between the lower lumbar vertebrae (L4 and L5).
14. Numbness in the big toe.	Pressure or other difficulty between S1 and S2 vertebrae.
15. Toe 3 is very long or short (relative to the toes alongside it).	Irresolvable problem in the basic balance of the person (i.e., immune system or mental/emotional equilibrium). See figure 22b on page 68.
16. Beauty marks in the area corresponding to the topmost point of the spine.	Genetic problem or disease. See figure 22c on page 68.
17. Big toe "creaks."	Stiff neck.

Common Fire Indicators

Common indicators in the fire element inhibit the burning of fire. Breathing, muscle tone and the heart may all be affected physically. Creativity, self-expression, confidence and manual abilities may be lessened. The fire element is the doing element and thus work and behavior with others will be strongly affected by chronic patterns in it. See Table 2 for a list of symptoms or conditions that appear when the fire element is not balanced.

Table 2. Fire Indicators

Condition	Ailment
1. Dry, tough skin underneath toe 5, and restricted flexibility of the lower joint of the little toe.	Shoulder problem. See figure 23a on page 72.
2. Elevated, inflexible toes, and taut tendons in the fire region (at the top).	Tension in the neck and shoulders. See figures 23b + c on page 72.
3. Branching line, a deep fissure in the region corresponding to the trachea, or a long, dry strip of skin over that region.	Asthma. See figure 24a on page 73.
4. In children over 2 years, transverse lines in the skin in the region of fire.	Stridor. See figure 24b on page 73.
5. Calluses throughout the fire region; dry, tough, grayish, stiff skin.	Excessive smoking, angina pectoris (obstruction of the blood vessels feeding the heart); emphysema (impaired lung function). See figure 24c on page 73.

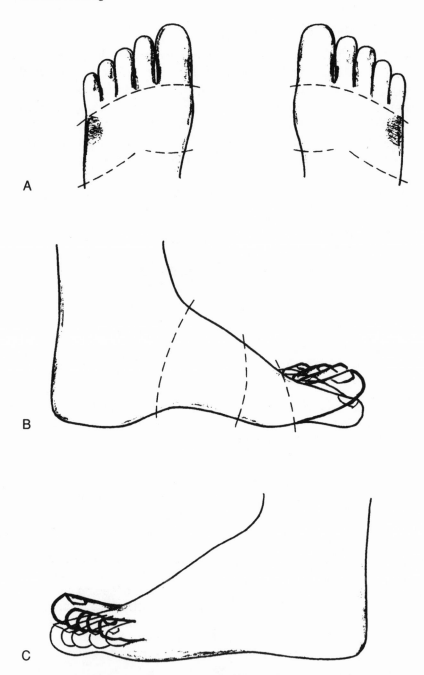

Figure 23. Fire indicators: a) dry skin here indicates shoulder problems; b and c) elevated toes due to short tendons in the fire area.

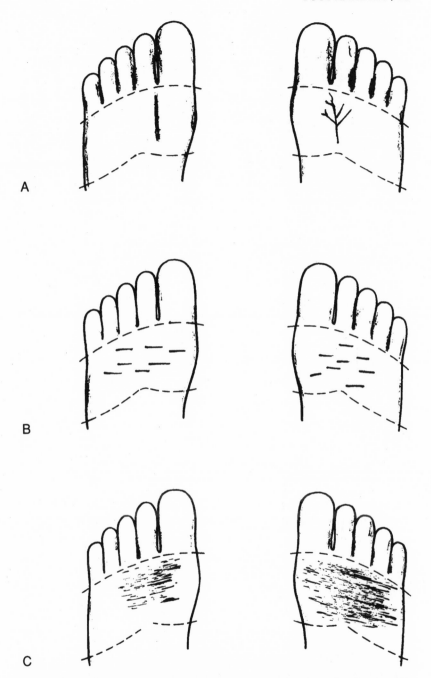

Figure 24. Fire indicators: a) straight line or branch-like lines indicate asthma; b) vertical line in the fire region signifies stridor; c) dry, rough, gray skin covering the fire element indicates emphysema.

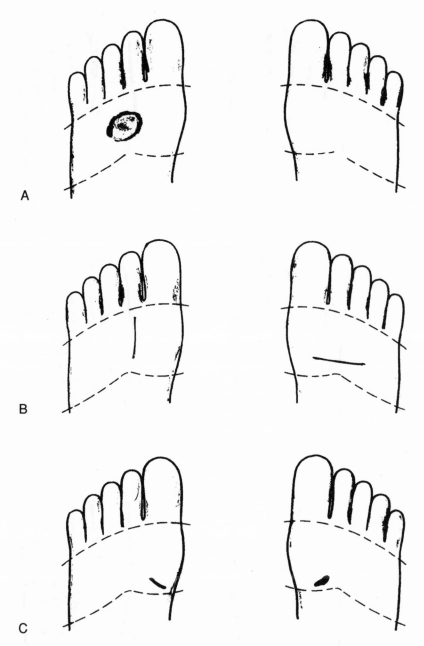

Figure 25. Fire indicators: a) rough dry skin in a small area surrounded by red skin indicates the person had a mastectomy; b) vertical or horizontal line in the fire element indicates the death of a
loved one; c) deep, small scar or line in the heart area is an indication of a previous heart attack.

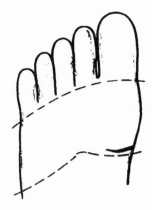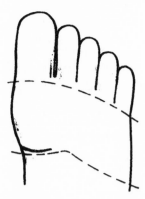

Figure 26. Fire indicators: curved line near the border of fire and water is a sign of an old separation from a relationship.

Table 2. Fire Indicators (continued)

Condition	Ailment
6. A dry area smaller than that of angina pectoris and surrounded by a red area.	Mastectomy. The indicator appears on the side where the operation was performed. See figure 25a on page 74.
7. A swollen, sensitive, red fire area.	Pneumonia or another pulmonary problem.
8. A straight line along or across the fire element.	Death of a loved one. See figure 25b on page 74.
9. A small, very deep indentation or fissure in the area corresponding to the heart, or a small, tough callus there.	Previous heart attack. This will appear on one or both of the feet. See figure 25c on page 74.
10. A light mark in an other-wise healthy heart area.	Prolapse of a heart valve.
11. A line between fire and water in the area corresponding to the heart.	A sign of separation. See figure 26.
12. A lengthwise line (similar to that produced by the death of a loved one).	Open-heart surgery.

Common Water Indicators

Common indicators in the water element (Table 3 below) show digestive imbalances in the flow of fluids in the body. Problems like constipation or bladder weakness are clearly disturbances in the water element. The water element represents the emotional world, so the same chronic patterns show how a person experiences his or her emotions on a deeper level. The way a person deals with fear, the number of chronic patterns, and all the old emotional history is buried under waves of water!

Table 3. Water Indicators.

Condition	Ailment
1. Deep, pronounced lines or fissures in the area corresponding to the stomach.	Ulcer, irritable stomach. Red lines and pain in area indicative of active ulcer. See figure 27a on page 77.
2. A star-shaped mark, another pattern of lines, a hole, or a beauty mark in the area corresponding to the diaphragm.	Herniated diaphragm. See figure 27b on page 77.
3. Transverse lines in the area corresponding to the diaphragm.	Shortness of breath; strong contraction of the diaphragm; nonallergic breathing problems. See figure 28a on page 78.
4. Darker color and a sharp pain in the area corresponding to the gall bladder.	Gallstones. See figure 28b on page 78.
5. A concentration of grooves in the area corresponding to the liver and spleen (on both feet).	Allergy. It can be an allergy that affects the skin. See figure 29a on page 79.

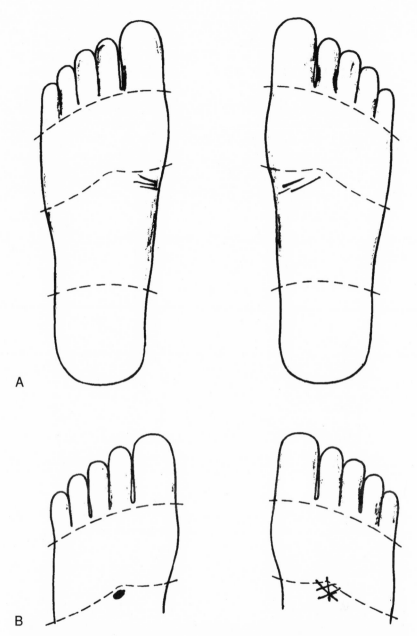

Figure 27. Water indicators: a) lines on the stomach area indicate an ulcer; b) marks on the diaphragm area indicate a herniated diaphragm.

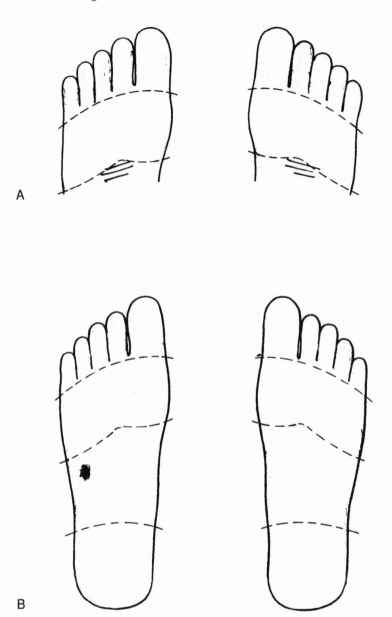

Figure 28. Water indicators: a) horizontal lines on the diaphragm area signify a contraction of the diaphragm; b) marks that indicate a gall bladder problem; seen only in the right foot.

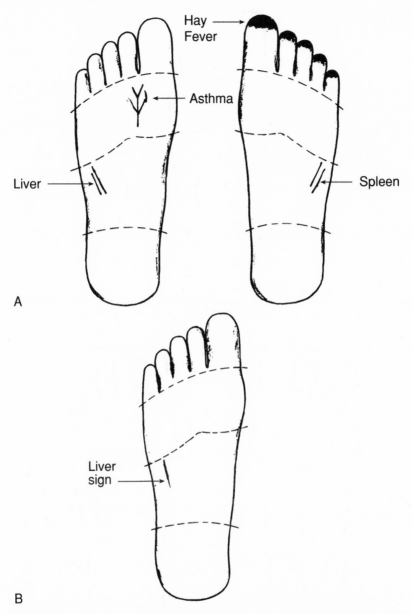

Figure 29. Water indicators: a) lines on the liver and spleen area indicate allergies. They can also appear with the indicator for asthma, meaning the person has allergic asthma, or they can appear coupled with strong indicators on the pads of the toes, in which case the person has allergies affecting the sinuses, eyes, and/or ears; b) line on the liver area means the person has had a liver problem.

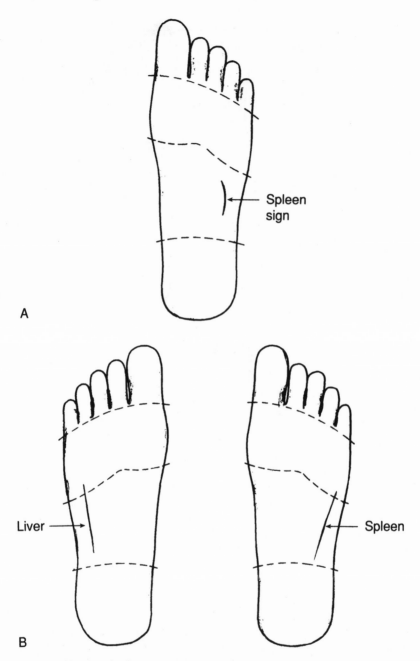

Figure 30. Water indicators: a) line on the spleen area indicates a tendency for low fever; b) lines on the liver and spleen areas signify a tendency for arthritis.

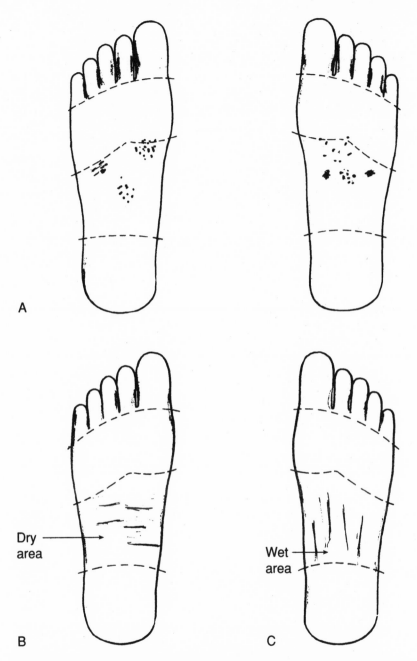

Figure 31. Water indicators: a) red spots in the water element are an indication of colitis; b) horizontal lines and dryness in the area of the water element are an indication of constipation; c) vertical lines and wetness in the area of the water element signify diarrhea.

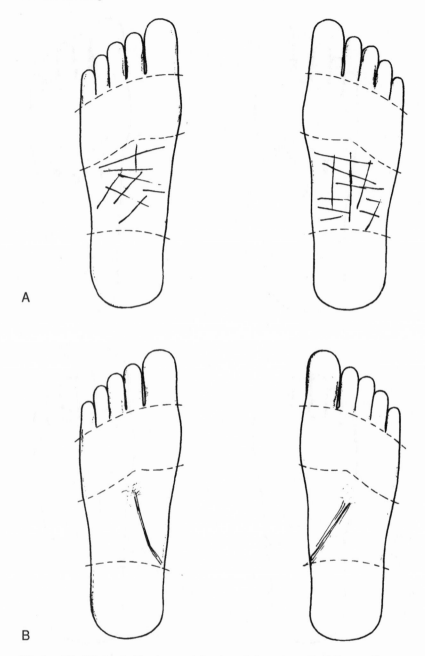

Figure 32. Water indicators: a) horizontal and vertical lines all over the water element area indicates an irritable intestine; b) deep lines from the kidney to the bladder area indicates chronic problems of the urinary tract.

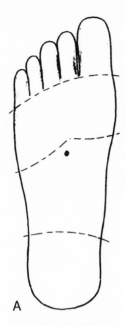

A   B

Figure 33. Water indicators: a) beauty mark indicates a genetic imbalance of the kidney; b) thin dry lines from the kidney to the bladder area mean not enough fluid is supplied to the body.

Table 3. Water Indicators (continued).

Condition	Ailment
5a. If grooves are coupled with strong indicators on the pads of the toes.	Hay fever; allergies affecting the sinuses, eyes, and/or ears. See figure 29a on page 79.
5b. If coupled with an indicator of asthma.	Allergic asthma, or an allergic reaction in the breathing system. See figure 29a on page 79.
6. One deep line over the liver.	Previous hepatitis, impaired liver function. See figure 29b on page 79.

Table 3. Water Indicators (continued).

Condition	Ailment
7. One deep line over the spleen.	A previous illness characterized by fever, and a present tendency to low fever. See figure 30a on page 80.
8. One deep line over the spleen and liver, beginning in the fire region and descending to the earth (under toes 4 and 5) on both sides.	Existing or incipient arthritis. See figure 30b on page 80.
9. Red spots or small blemishes in the soft region of water, or an unusual rash in the water region.	Colitis, small sores on the intestinal walls. See figure 31a on page 81.
10. Transverse lines and general dryness in the water region.	Chronic constipation. See figure 31b on page 81.
11. Vertical lines and wetness in the water region.	Chronic diarrhea. See figure 31c on page 81.
12. Criss-cross lines.	Tendency to alternate between diarrhea and constipation; irritable intestine. See figure 32a on page 82.
13. Dryness in the kidney region and lines from the kidney to the bladder.	Kidney stones; chronic problems of the urinary tract. See figure 32b on page 82.
14. Beauty marks on the area corresponding to the kidney.	Genetic or familial kidney condition. See figure 33a on page 83.
15. Lines from the kidney region to the bladder coupled with general dryness of the foot.	Person does not drink enough. See figure 33b on page 83.

Common Earth Indicators

Common indicators in the earth element (Table 4 below) show us imbalances in the bones, the hormonal system, the reproductive system, and, of course, in the legs. Looking at the disturbed quality of earth we can also see how stable the person is, and how he or she deals with family and with sexuality. The earth element shows us how a person deals with the world, how he or she handles survival needs as well as the other basic needs of daily life.

Table 4. Earth Indicators.

Condition	Ailment
1. Pronounced indicators of deficiency or surplus in the bladder region.	Chronic bladder problems. A surplus indicates inflammation. See figure 34a on page 86.
2. Strip between earth and water; transverse line below the ankle bone, or strip between earth bands 1 and 2 (the bands are explained in detail in chapter 2).	Cesarean section, hysterectomy, abortions. See figure 34b on page 86.
3. Line in the lower-back area between earth and water.	Lower-back problems. The deeper the line and the older it appears, the more chronic the problem. See figure 35a on page 87.
4. Very dry, tough heel with sensitive red spots in the center, or a red, sensitive, swollen mark in the middle of the earth region.	Acute sciatica. A lump in the region indicates a chronic inflammation in the sciatic nerve.
5. Deep lines and cracks accompanied by a ring of dry, tough skin surrounding the heel.	Hemorrhoids. See figure 35b on page 87.

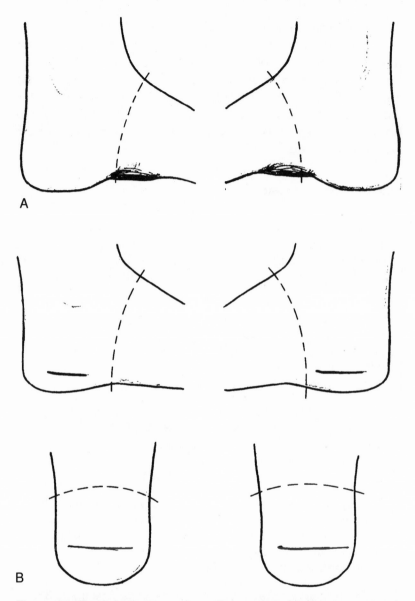

Figure 34. Earth indicators: a) swollen, red and hot area, or empty and cold area, may indicate chronic bladder problems; b) the line that appears after a cesarean or lower stomach operation.

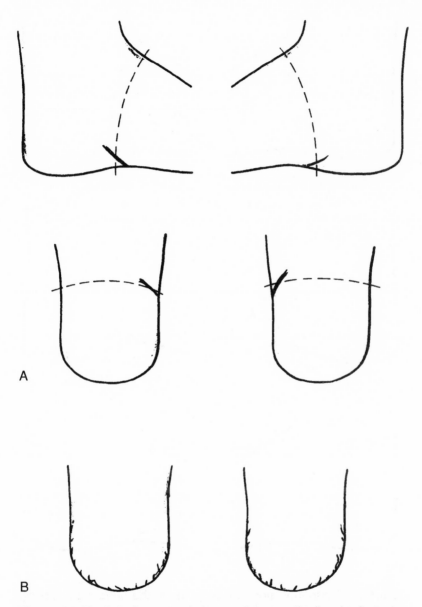

Figure 35. Earth indicators: a) deep groove on the border between the earth and water elements indicates a tendency for lower back pain; b) edges of the heel marked with cracks and dry skin indicates hemorrhoids.

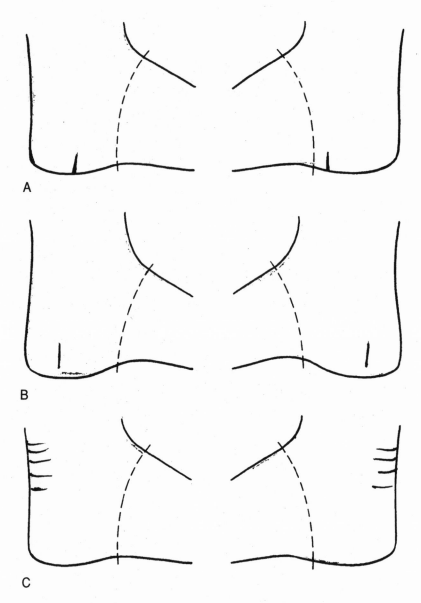

Figure 36. Earth indicators: a) deep line in the anus area may signify a fissure there; b) vertical line in the womb or prostate area
may indicate a birth trauma; c) lines on the Achilles' tendons show
cramped muscles in the lower back and indicate a tendency for
menstrual cramps in women.

Table 4. Earth Indicators (continued).

Condition	Ailment
6. Deep line in the area corresponding to the anus.	Anal fissure (burning, bleeding, painful anus; back pain; lower-abdominal pain). See figure 36a on page 88.
7. Longitudinal line below the ankle bone (higher than the anal region, toward the water element.)	A difficult labor and delivery (not the woman's own birth). See figure 36b on page 88.
8. Short, thickened, rigid Achilles' tendon with transverse lines.	Shortening, pressure on the lower back and posterior muscles; tendency for menstrual cramps in women. See figure 36c on page 88.
9. Swelling around the ankle joint.	Menstrual cramps.

General Indicators

The following table lists conditions that encompass the entire foot and are not element specific. These conditions are usually spread throughout the body or affect a system that is not located in one element's area, but runs through a few elements. These conditions cannot be seen unless we look at the foot as a whole. High blood pressure, for example, is caused by too much pressure in the blood vessels, and this condition is manifested all over the foot.

Table 5. General Indicators.

Condition	Ailment
1. Foot tends to dryness; surplus of the type characteristic of earth; sticky dryness; odor of acetone pervades the foot and/or a lump, protrusion, or very deep line in the area corresponding to the pancreas.	Diabetes.
2. Full, red, warm, swollen foot.	Hypertension (not due to a pathological/clinical renal disturbance). The feet appear as if the fire element has taken control; muscles are in a hypertonic state.
3. Foot is pale, cold, soft, light, thin, with a large element of water.	Hypotension.
4. Comparison of the arches with both feet adjacent to each other, when one arch is deeper than the other.	Scoliosis. See figure 37 on page 91.
5. Foot suffers from extreme shortage or surplus of energy.	Fatigue, grogginess.

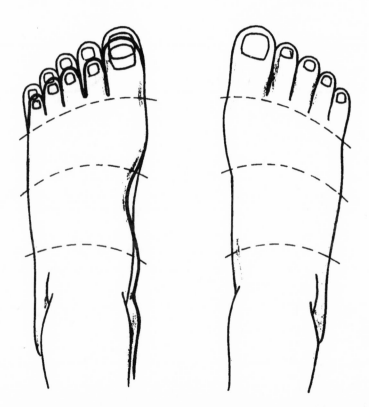

Figure 37. A big difference in the arches of the feet indicates a contraction and shortening of one side of the back as the spine curves to the side. Could signify scoliosis.

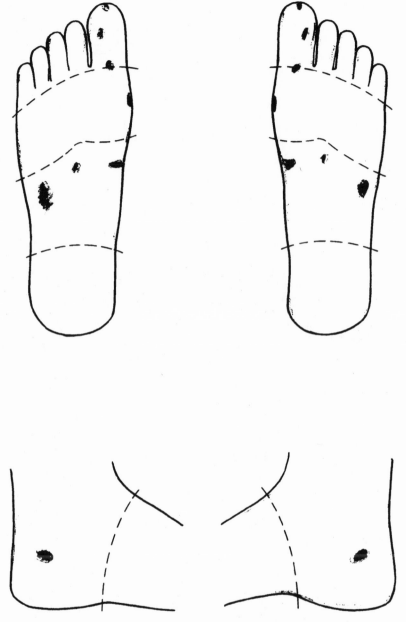

Figure 38. Nine points corresponding to the vitalizing and immune systems.

Table 5. General Indicators (continued).

Condition	Ailment
6. A state of extreme deficiency or emptiness encompassing the whole foot.	Tendency to malignant or degenerative diseases such as cancer. If a tumor exists, there will be pronounced indicators of surplus surrounding the area of the foot corresponding to that of the tumor, since the tumor creates pressure.
7. A straight well-defined short line appearing anywhere on the feet.	Surgery or deep scars that have scar tissue; the possibility of adhesions underneath the scar.
8. General coldness and wetness of the foot; feet that perspire and get cold while being touched.	The person has intense anxiety or is going through a fearful period.
9. Pain in the nine points that represent the endocrine system, the hormonal system, and the vitality; some show signs of imbalance.	The immune system is low; recovering from an illness; autoimmune disease. See figure 38 on page 92.

4

PHYSICAL ANALYSIS

After completing all of the procedures described in chapter 3, we continue our examination with an in-depth physical analysis of specific symptoms, their location, and probable cause.

THE INTERVIEW

To properly analyze our subject on the physical level, we must initially conduct an interview to determine the following:

1) Height, weight, age.

2) Health history, including severe illnesses, operations, injuries, fractures, traumas, etc; recurring, chronic, or traumatic states, past and present, resolved and unresolved.

3) Past and present medications, if used regularly.

4) Patterns and life style relating to sleep, dreams, diet (what, how, and when), alcohol, tobacco, drugs, meditation, and other regular activities (sports and hobbies).

5) Occupation.

6) Level of tension and stress.

7) Genetic illnesses and problems in the family, such as diabetes, hypertension, epilepsy, cancer, mental illness.

Generally a short interview of this type will reveal a number of facts germane to the subject's past and present condition, and provide the analyst with a basic profile and valuable background information. The following example illustrates what we might expect to learn from a typical interview.

General Information

Name: Jane Doe

Age: 25

Weight: 130 pounds

Height: 5' 8"

Children: none

Eating habits: vegetarian for the past ten years

Medications: none

Physical activity: regular exercise

Smoking: no

Drinking: no alcohol

Case History

Medical History: Stridor as an infant, passed after age 3. Laryngitis and ear infections until age 8, and two recurring infections each year since then. Appendectomy at age 6, no complications.

Commenced menstruation at age 12; never had regular cycle. Menstruation accompanied by pain on first day of cycle. Problem resolved only when she took birth control pills.

Sensitive stomach since childhood; heavy, oily foods cause discomfort, occasional heartburn, and nausea following overeating.

Viral hepatitis at age 16, no complications. Car accident at age 18, whiplash. Subsequent sensitivity in the nape of the neck; slight limitation in rotational movement of the head.

Pain and sensitivity in the left shoulder since age 20, treated by physiotherapy with no appreciable relief. Numbness in the hands, primarily the left. Does not take medication. Treated once by acupuncture for relief of shoulder condition. Experienced relief for six months.

Present symptomatic state: headaches, periodic sensitivity of the stomach, heartburn, limitation of head movement, severe pain in the left shoulder, numbness in the hands, irregular menstruation and cramps on the first day of the period. No medication or treatment.

Eating Habits and Exercise—Eats irregularly. A vegetarian for approximately twelve years. Does not try to balance her diet, does not take vitamins, does not smoke, does not consume alcohol; drinks 3 quarts of fluids daily. Regular exercise, twice weekly on an ongoing basis, concentrated on utilization of the skeletal muscles. Works sitting down approximately eight hours daily. Almost never walks; drives about one hour a day.

Sleeping Habits—Sleeps approximately six hours a night, wakes up tired, does not recall dreams, under tension most of the time for reasons stemming from work, loneliness, and lack of satisfaction in life.

Menstrual Cycle—Irregular menstrual cycle from its inception, except for three years when she used birth control pills. On first day of menstruation, abdominal cramps, bloating of abdomen, aggravation of back pain that radiates to left leg.

Patient's Explanation of Symptoms—Patient explains the condition of the nape of the neck, shoulder, and hands are a result of the accident at age 18. She attributes the condition of her stomach to nervousness and tension. As for her menstrual cycle, she states that her mother had a similar condition and required hormone therapy in order to become pregnant.

Past or Present Conditions—Following the interview, we create a table, with one side listing the client's current complaints and past medical problems, and the other side listing the symptoms that are reflected in the foot (see Table 6 on page 100). We attempt to find, for every condition described by the person, its corroboration as manifested in the entire foot, using our understanding of states of surplus and deficiency. We divide the body into left and right sectors and the foot into four parts, each corresponding to one of the four elements. See figure 39a and b on page 98.

In other words, when a person complains of pain in the left shoulder, we examine the left foot in the region corresponding to the left shoulder with respect to the element of fire, attempting to discern any state of surplus or deficiency. If no such state is apparent, we leave that space blank temporarily,

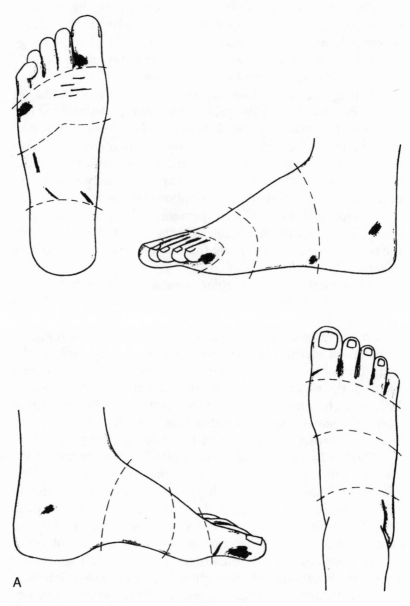

A

Figure 39. Examining Jane Doe's feet: a) mapping the imbalances on the right foot;

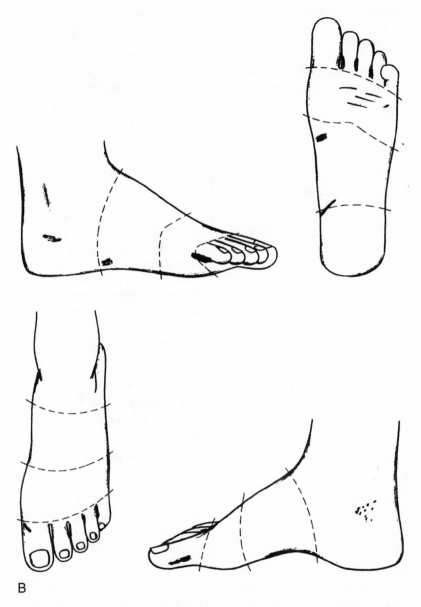

B

Figure 39 (cont.): b) mapping the imbalances on the left foot. See Table 6 on page 100 for a description of what these markings indicate about Jane Doe's health.

Table 6. Symptoms and Signs in Jane Doe's Feet.

Past or Present Condition	State of the Feet
1. Irregular menstrual cycle. Pain on the first day of period.	Region of uterus indicated. Sensitivity in region of ovaries. Sensitivity in region of pituitary gland. Air in surplus of fire; fifth toe small, red, bent.
2. Recurring infections, both fungal and other types.	Same as above.
3. Pain in lower-back, radiating to the right foot.	Deep crack in skin in the region of the lower back. Regions of sensitivity and pain when palpating lower-back area. In right foot, sensitivity and tension in Achilles' tendon; in left foot, sensitivity is less severe and indications are weaker (fire in earth).
4. Nervous and sensitive stomach.	Cracks and fire signs around stomach reflex; soft, white area on both feet (air in water).
5. Past hepatitis.	A line in the skin over region of liver.
6. Chronic pain in left shoulder.	Dry, tough skin; callus on the pad under the fifth toe; brown spot on left foot at point corresponding to shoulder joint (earth and air).
7. Numbness in the fingers, particularly on the left side.	Signs of definite surplus of earth in region corresponding to nape of neck on both feet— dry, tough skin. Along the area of both hands, partic- ularly the left, pronounced sensitivity discernible upon palpation.

Table 6. Symptoms and Signs in Jane Doe's Feet (continued).

Past or Present Condition	State of the Feet
8. Recurring laryngitis and ear infections in childhood.	Region of throat is red, swollen, sensitive. Toes 4 and 5 clearly smaller than toes 2 and 3.
9. Recurring headaches.	Signs on the nape of the neck and surpluses of fire in the entire region of the head.
10. Appendectomy at age 6.	Old scar, barely visible, at region of appendix.
11. Injury to nape of neck at age 18 (whiplash).	Deep, red line in region corresponding to nape of neck (lower cervical vertebrae) on upper foot; sensitivity to touch (fire in air). Difficulty in moving big toe without "creaking" of joints (earth in air).
12. Stridor in childhood.	Small transverse lines on fire region; old, white, insensitive (air in fire).

returning to it at the end of the diagnosis to see which indicators appearing on the foot might be causing the pain in the left shoulder. If the person's history included states for which no corroboration is found on the foot, the imbalance has passed and the state no longer exists. If the person nevertheless complains of the condition, evidence of it—however irregular— should be presumed to exist, and we must take pains to discover it.

When a person complains of pain or a problem, we first attempt to identify it on the foot, and then examine several other factors:

1) When a person complains of pain at a particular site, we examine the entire band (see division to eight bands in chapter 2) in which the organ is found, not only the exact location of the organ itself.

2) Sometimes a problem in one place points to a problem elsewhere, too. For example, a problem in the nape of the neck is a reasonable indication of a lower-back problem. Parallels: hips and shoulders, elbows and knees, feet and hands, mouth and anus, nape of the neck and lower back.

3) When one paired part of the body is injured, the other attempts to fill its role, to the detriment of both.

4) Any sign on the spinal column may indicate a problem in the nerve circuits branching out from that site. In the case of such a problem, we also examine the spinal column in order to determine if a local problem there has caused the condition that led to the client's complaint.

Any form of analysis that relies on the client's memory is not perfect for people tend to forget or they repress unpleasant states. Thus, in most cases, we discover patterns and numerous states of imbalance of which the person is completely unaware or whose existence he or she has forgotten at the time of the interview. At the conclusion of this type of analytic examination, we therefore face a certain number of regions and patterns that are apparently not characteristic of the person. We can ask such people to check with their parents or try to remember past experiences which we may describe to them in accordance with the regions where we find imbalance.

For example, an indicator of surplus of another element in the region corresponding to the throat, uncorroborated by the client, would dictate the need to ask him or her about past states of laryngitis, hoarseness, nodules on the vocal cords, tonsillitis, thyroid problems, and so on. In other words, we should inquire about the organs and the regions indicated, not necessarily in relation to the client's medical history but in terms of the symptoms that may be caused by a problem in the functioning of these organs. An example would be a change in weight due to a thyroid imbalance.

Examination Without an Interview

This type of examination starts with the feet; we examine the feet thoroughly, addressing ourselves to all known aspects. We divide this process into stages. At the end of each stage we draw conclusions, record them, and continue on.

Patient History

Name: _____

Age: _____ Any children? _____ How many? _____

Weight: _____ Height: _____

Smoking: _____ Drinking: _____

Occupation: _____ (What type of physical activity does the work entail?) _____

_____

_____

Habits of movement (list regular habits, if any): _____

_____

_____

Diet (type of food and drink, manner of consumption): ____

_____

_____

Medications: (type, dosage, duration of use): _____

_____

_____

Exercise (relevant only if regular): _____

_____

_____

Familial genetic problems (remembered or diagnosed): ____

_____

_____

General Characteristics

Does the person always begin walking with the same foot? If we ask him to stand on one leg does he stand on the same leg and does this match the dominant side as reflected in the use of the hands?

Is there a dominant element on the left side (an element that occupies the major portion of the foot), and what are its characteristics as manifested in the foot? Is there a dominant element on the right side? Is there a discrepancy between the form of the feet and the form of the body? Are there differences in form and structure between the two feet?

Compare the walking regions of each foot. Are there any differences in the structure of the arches? Compare the form of the upper and lower arches and the movement of the toes relative to the foot.

Visualization

This stage is limited to a visual examination of the feet, and is distinguished from palpation only for purposes of practice and understanding. First, look for any elements whose imbalance is most blatant. This item is intended to direct our attention to the most problematic energy regions, so that we may address them more seriously and describe them. Has one element "invaded" the territory of another, thereby reducing the latter's size?

Are there boundaries and partition points between elements? Pronounced separations indicate a discrepancy between adjacent elements. The better delineated the boundary, the greater the discrepancy. Difficulties in the flow and balance between these two elements will be present.

All points indicating surplus in that element's energy or showing indicators of another element's energy are recorded and marked for each element individually, thus facilitating clear understanding and an orderly, detailed, point-by-point recording of the state of the foot as a whole. Clearly visible sites of imbalance are listed by element areas, noting what other element appeared in this area causing the imbalance.

In this stage, we gain an understanding of the state of the elements and of the mapping of the foot into areas of imbalance and balance, as indicated through visual examination. We draw conclusions on the basis of this map, and from the state of the spinal column as well—by comparing arches and by noting the state of imbalance in the area. If distinct signs of any state appear during visualization, we observe their appearance in order to match them to the personal story of this and future clients. We also see if this sign is indeed part of a universal pattern.

Palpation

We map the foot by states of imbalance, following the corresponding sections of the chart and using the techniques of the moving finger and walking thumb. List all areas of imbalance—earth, water, fire, and air—by means of palpation and manipulation of the foot, seeking conclusions as to the states of the tendons, the joints, and the toes in motion. These conclusions permit the mapping of sensitive regions of the body that are not in a state of balance. Through palpating and moving the foot, we learn about the muscular system, the tendons, and the skeleton (their flexibility or tension), and gain a thorough understanding of the state of tissue, muscles, sensitivity to pain, and so on.

Conclusions

This section combines the two forms of examination. Most regions that show symptoms in visualization show imbalances by palpation, too. Our conclusions are derived from a combination of both approaches, giving us a detailed, in-depth picture of the person and a complete mapping of areas of deficiency and surplus. From these we draw further conclusions about the spinal column, posture, the muscles, and any differences between the left and right foot. It is also possible to discover systemic (nonlocal) imbalances, clear patterns in the person, and possible symptoms originating in the above.

By means of the information gathered thus far, we may draw conclusions about the client's activity, as well as physical and emotional behavior. It is now clear to us that specific systems are indicated in a particular way. The observed state indicates a change in functioning, generally as a direct corollary of the type of indicator—deficiency or surplus. By using the list generated by previous conclusions, we can compare personal recounting with our diagnosis. Verification of the specific state indicated on the foot as against the personal history related and recalled by the person, is done by reviewing each element in sequence and elucidating the state by the points of surplus and deficiency discovered thus far, coupled with systemic indicators such as posture.

There are several individual and conflicting factors to consider:

- A state reported by the client.

- Unexplained states observed on the foot.

- Past and present states that left no indication on the foot and were not described in the diagnosis thus far.

- The state of the four elements—earth, water, fire, and air.

States that do not appear on the foot but are included in the recounting, we attempt to explain through the foot. States observed on the foot that have not occurred or do not exist, we attempt to explain by discovering family tendencies, latent predispositions, or a particular manner of moving the feet.

By this stage we may have acquired information contained in the foot but not explainable in any way thus far. These states may point to future states and should be mentioned in our recommendations to the client.

We must take special notice of any imbalance in body systems. For example, constipation is probably a result of systemic damage, i.e., injury to the digestive system or a more specific state in the region of water. Our map of deficiencies and surpluses may show entire regions in the body that are no longer in balance. One element may be in high surplus, or the entire region of the feet may be seriously swollen and edematous. The body map of the foot is used to pinpoint more accurately those organs that are in a state of deficiency or surplus.

Life-Threatening States— the Way They Look on the Feet

1) *Malignancies*—A malignant state indicates a problem in the immune system. Since the immune system is found throughout the foot, we should expect to find the entire foot in a state of deficiency. The greatest state of deficiency usually occurs in the heel, since this is the site of our existential energy. Most people who suffer from a malignant illness have lost their vitality. If a lengthy, problematic emotional state preceded the cancer, we will notice that the element of water is in control throughout the foot. Cancer signifies concession. It is a state that generally originates in an old pattern. We therefore look for patterns of concession and weakness.

People are struck by cancer and, for that matter, by other ailments in those places that are already weak. We expect to see the foot of such a person in an extreme state of deficiency. A particular indicator will appear in the area of the tumor. The foot will emit a strong odor and the person will complain of weakness, fatigue, weight loss, lack of drive, and decline in appetite. A person in such a state must be referred for a medical checkup.

2) *Severe Heart Problems*—A heart attack is a function of extreme surplus in the region of the chest. We expect to see a chronic surplus there: a region of fire with a surplus of fire, or a state of earth in fire. The region of fire would be callused and gray; a state of angina pectoris, blockage of blood vessels surrounding the heart, would be present. Along with the chronic surplus, we should expect to find a state of acute surplus: a red stain, sharp pain upon touch, sensitivity, and warmth in the region. The person complains of pressure in the chest; nausea or heartburn; numbness in the hands; a prickly sensation in the chest; grogginess; weakness; dizziness; chills; excessive sweating. A person in such state must be sent to a hospital immediately.

3) *Hypertension*—We find indications of a surplus of fire. The foot is red, hot, with a tendency to excessive swollenness. If these symptoms are coupled with a surplus of fire in the toes, the client runs a risk of cerebral hemorrhage. This person's blood pressure must be lowered immediately.

5

EXCESSIVE ELEMENTS

While completing a thorough examination of the feet, it is important to consider the various zones in relation to one another. When earth, water, fire, or air exceeds its normal region, this may be a clear indication of problems in a corresponding area of the body. Let's look at some typical examples of excessive elements, the associated physical characteristics they suggest, and their energetic significance.

TOO MUCH EARTH

When a large earth region penetrates the water region, we would expect to find the following: dark color; tough, dry, cracked, warm skin; dry, tough, skin peelings; deep cracks and markings; darker marks in the area (freckles, moles, etc.); protruding or varicose veins around the ankles; the sides of the sole under the ankle are thick and inflexible; differences in the structure of the ankle bone; Heberden's nodes (an overgrowth of bones near the joint—any such hypertrophy in an element indicates a surplus of earth occurring within another element). The greater the surplus in earth, the more pronounced the dryness and brittleness. (In the visual examination of the foot, the region appears to be in extreme surplus.)

For women a state of excess earth can show difficult, painful menstruation, fibroids, and heavy bleeding. Earth has become so hard that water can hardly penetrate it; it has turned into stone. The muscles of the pelvis and posterior are extremely tense and rigid. The feet have vascular and circulation problems; the earth is very hard and does not let water pass through.

Constipation may occur. This points at one or more of the following: hemorrhoids, anal fissure; an enlarged prostate; urinary tract, cervical, and uterine infections; fatigue; a feeling of heaviness, primarily in the lower portion of the body; pains in the knees; traumatic injuries to the lower portion of the body (fractures, sprains, etc.); sciatica; vascular inflammation in the feet. It also indicates difficulty in late pregnancy and delivery, ectopic pregnancies, obstructions in the ovaries and/or fallopian tubes (possible sterility), and/or painful ovulation (menstrual symptoms around the time of ovulation).

In men, the conditions indicated are a tendency for premature ejaculation, or difficulty in ejaculating at all. People with strong sexuality who do not exercise it reach a state of earth in surplus because of their accumulated, unreleased energy. All features of earth are susceptible to overintensity. The region becomes dry; water either accumulates above it like a swamp, or dries up. Consequently, waste material that is supposed to flow out now accumulates in the earth.

Earth Characteristics

These people become set in their ways, static, stuck; they are less capable of changing, stubborn; likely to clash with others over matters of sex and money. Other characteristics include compulsive acquisitiveness; the need to reinforce self-confidence through material security; sensuality that becomes distorted into sexuality; aggression and violence. These people treat every situation as a matter of life or death. The aggressiveness and violence may remain internal and not become outwardly apparent.

There is a tendency toward physicality—typified by athletes—an obsession with physical activity, not merely for pleasure but for the sake of achievement; engaging in sports that require monotonous exertion (weight lifting and running); an attempt to reduce every situation to a practical level; esthetics, at times exaggerated (things must be "just so"); an attempt to preserve well-defined boundaries of identity ("This is me, and I am protecting this way of being"). The family or any other social structure will be very important and will be defended and protected as a part of the self.

Earth in surplus tends to expand into the water region, inducing people to choose security over emotional development. They attach less importance to their inner feelings; they repress emotional states in order to function. Such a person aims to function successfully, not to experience anything special. People who exhibit signs of intense violence have almost no water; earth occupies almost the entire water element and joins with fire.

Too Much Water

When excesses in this region manifest themselves, the area corresponding to the water element is large, wet, white, and cold. We may find wrinkled skin with peelings that are thin, soft, and wet; shallow, moist markings that are not deep and not dry; soft tissue with small lumps; excessive flexibility of the tendon extending from the big toe to the heel (the toes can be stretched very far back); special markings in the area corresponding to the kidneys and urinary tract. In the upper water band on the back of the foot, swelling may occur.

All the organs in this region contribute to the flow of fluids through the body. When the region is in surplus, fluids flow at high speed. Characteristics of this state include diarrhea; heavy urination; an abdomen distended by fluids; enlarged spleen and liver; flatulence; intestinal diseases, such as amoebic dysentery, colitis, and gastritis; lower-back problems; ovarian cysts; a benign tumor in the intestine, liver, or spleen; fatty masses throughout the body; skin diseases; allergies; circulatory problems throughout the body; a ruptured diaphragm; abdominal pain; spastic colon.

Anxieties may be experienced on the physical level as well, transcending their emotional context. This may be expressed as a rapid heartbeat; sensitivity to touch in the area of the abdomen (any contact induces pain); psychosomatic tendencies, i.e., the onset of asthma following a separation; a tendency to suffer from cold during winter and in general; frequent chill in the feet; a tendency toward colds; a strong odor emanating from the foot.

Water Characteristics

Water is more dynamic than earth. It generally flows downward. When water is in surplus, it attempts to escape from any part of the body, thus producing states of perspiration in the hands and feet, easily induced tears; fear, emotional turmoil, pain, and a tendency toward hysteria.

TOO MUCH FIRE

When a surplus exists, the foot is wide in the fire region. A large fire area penetrates the water and air regions, causing the toe pads to create a fold of skin under the lower joint of the toes, since the element seeks more volume for itself. The skin is dry, warm, red, and tough, but not stiff and thick (as in earth). Stiffness is evident when moving the big toe. The upper tendons (on the back of the foot) connecting the toes are shortened, tending to elevate and curl the toes (the influence of fire in surplus over air). If we apply force to the toes, we may straighten the tendons. (They are not fixed; this is not a surplus of earth.) All the muscular bands in the region are in a state of hypertonia.

The organs in the fire region may be seriously strained and overburdened. All the muscles in the body, primarily those in the chest and upper back, tend toward extreme tension. The client is most likely overextending himself or herself. The nature of fire sets the stage for short, terminal, pathological states such as heart attack (explosive states and overloaded functioning), scoliosis, hypertension, pressure in the chest, heartburn, stomach ulcer; sensitive and painful chest and upper back muscles; benign cysts and fibroids in the breasts; painful breasts during menstruation or ovulation; and difficulties in nursing. Fire in surplus signifies heavy use of the hands. Those who write all day show a surplus in the relevant region of the upper fire band, on the side where they write.

Fire Characteristics

Such people are intensely busy with themselves. They take events personally, as if everything is directed toward them.

They undergo vicarious experiences, such as suffering a heart attack while watching an exciting television show. They force their will on others, trying to control and dominate. They are egocentric, interested in controling others to their own advantage. They are highly judgmental, always trying to have the last word. They cannot stand being wrong; the ego is always right. In terms of creativity and action, they push too hard. If they are salaried workers, they annoy their bosses; if self-employed, they cannot relax because they are constantly trying to push onward. They do not work well on a team. As employers, they are not nice to work for. They are controlling and domineering, blind to others' needs. Such people do not realize that others hurt.

Too Much Air

Indications of an excess in the air region are: very flexible, long, thin toes, pale colors, a lot of skin over bony knuckles, big toe pads, cold dry skin, soft thin pale toenails, toes bent in different directions, toes 2, 3, and 4 are usually longer then the big toe, different marks that appear and disappear in one day. Usually people with an excess of air have a lot of muscle control over their toes.

The state of extreme excess in the air element might show conditions that are not clearly physical nor clearly mental, such as irregularities in the central nervous system, or electrical malfunctions like epilepsy, vertigo, dizziness, migraines, and other severe mentally related problems. More common are problems like headaches, tension at the back of the neck, sleeping problems, tiredness, and mild depression. As the skin is a part of the air element, extremes in the the air element might show skin problems.

Air Characteristics

These people tend to overuse the air quality. They are inclined to talk to themselves excessively and overuse their senses. Often the voice in their heads keeps them from sleeping. If these people are absorbed in one direction only, focusing their thoughts entirely on the reality their imagination creates for them, others will see them as disconnected and will call them "airheads."

These people may have problems concentrating, will probably daydream a lot, and will be very busy communicating their situation to everyone. You could think of this type as someone who, according to the popular American song, is always "blowing in the wind."

THE ELEMENT-DOMINATED FOOT

A foot that manifests the characteristics of one element above all others informs us that it is this element that governs the client's life. This is not a temporary influence, e.g., a person dominated by the element of air throughout a period of university study, but rather an influence felt throughout his or her life in all activities. We rarely encounter a foot that provides a classic manifestation of one element alone; this would be a very extreme case. We do, however, see feet in which one element is dominant.

Earth-Dominated Foot— Personal Needs Take Over

The foot is large, wide, hot, heavy, inflexible, dry, and cracked; it has a great deal of dry, tough skin or calluses; there are differences in the bone; sensitivity is limited only to a heavy touch—a light touch irritates. The heel is marked more than any other region. The foot is large, wide, and flat, and has a small, flat water region. Water rests on the earth; ankle mobility is restricted. The foot appears older than the person's chronological age. The toes are short or curled. We often find dry, tough skin at the tips of the toes—walking toes. Other manifestations: a short, thick, inflexible Achilles' tendon; prominent (varicose) veins; hard toenails—thick and cracked with a tough, thick skin texture; unusually short muscles and tendons; general inflexibility, no special strength (see figure 40 on page 118).

The foot is pleasant to the touch (because it is warm), clumsy (although it may appear attractive). Such people may not be able to relax, but their strong sensuality permits them to form relationships through touch—they enjoy touching.

Earth figures prominently in everything they do—relations with people, creativity, etc. The characteristics of earth accompany them at all times. Intellectually they are limited to the concrete, physical world, abstaining from intuition or abstract thought. They are attached to the family and any social structure they belong to.

Water-Dominated Foot— Emotions Take Over

Narrow foot, high arch, large water area pushing into fire and earth. The foot tends to be wet, cold, and highly pliable. The joints may overflex. The foot is light in color, almost hairless, very sensitive to touch, and can change color and feeling rapidly during the course of the examination. (Changeability is a characteristic of water.) The more secure the person feels, the warmer, drier, and more attractive his or her foot will be (see figure 40 on page 116).

If such a person has a severe problem, the water will produce strong odors in the feet. (It is water that generates foot odor.) In many cases, there are great differences between the feet due to the tendency of water to create states of conflict, i.e., an imbalance or discrepancy between the movement of both feet. A person governed by water is mercurial, passing through smooth, calm waters and suddenly experiencing hysterical seas. Mood swings and contradictions proliferate in this site of the foot. This is a person who can descend into emotional storms.

Fire-Dominated Foot— Self-Importance Takes Over

A large foot, particularly in the fire region; very warm. Fire has invaded and taken over some of the area of water and air; muscle tone is strong but flexible. There is a tendency toward calluses in the fire region (see figure 40 on page 116).

The foot is presented in a controlled manner (the person does not merely "throw" the foot forward). It is more sensitive to touch than an earth-dominated foot, but less so than a water-controlled foot. The skin is taut and pleasant to the touch, with a feeling of fullness in the flesh (rather than swelling caused

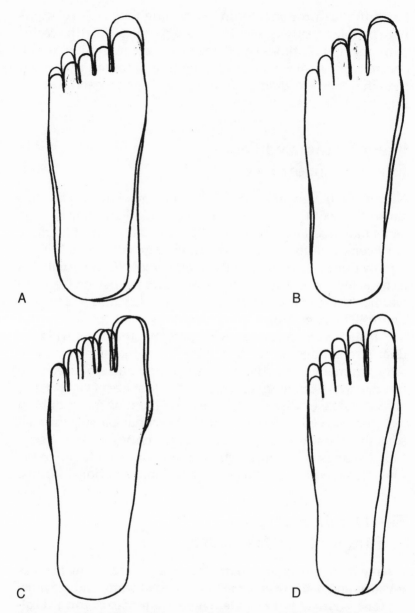

Figure 40. The different shapes of the element-dominated foot: a) a typical earth-dominated foot—broad, short, and heavy; b) a typical water-dominated foot—large water element area with cold and wet foot; c) a typical fire-dominated foot—wide area of the fire element with muscular, red, and hot foot; d) a typical air-dominated foot—long and thin with long toes and loose white skin.

by water). The toes are typically medium-sized. If fire has ascended to air, toes may bear red marks.

Air-Dominated Foot— Thought Takes Over

Slender, light, dry or wet, flexible, and splayed (the toes are spread out). The flexibility is different from that of water. The toes are long, pale, and hairless, with large spaces between them; the muscles throughout the foot are hypotonic. The veins are deep within the tissue, and the toes are generally long and very flexible. The skin is soft and delicate and can be lifted off the foot (see figure 40 on page 116).

Air is airy, lacking content and mass, causing a surplus of skin without "filler" underneath. Air exudes a feeling of emptiness—neither the fullness of fire, nor the swelling of water, nor the hardness of earth.

FEET IN BALANCE—A SIGN OF HEALTH

Feet in balance with themselves and the other elements exhibit health and harmony. This does not mean that the person is unlikely to suffer or become ill, rather it reflects the way he or she will cope with everything encountered in life. People who, in every life situation, experience all the facets of which they are constituted—who feel, are present, express themselves in work, think, absorb, and understand; permitting none of these aspects to assume dominance—exhibit balance in life. Whenever and wherever the elements are out of balance, they strive, by their very nature, to return to a balanced state. In the case of feet that are more-or-less harmonious, these processes will be of shorter duration, leaving fewer scars and markings on the person's individual energy. The tendency to waste energy on inappropriate matters is reduced. We discover through examination any element that is lacking or diminished, any element that has become stronger, conflicts among elements, and changes in the location or function of elements in the foot. Any of these situations points to an imbalance.

6

ELEMENT RELATIONSHIPS

Imagine a room with four people. The first is preoccupied with money, sex, and survival, and wants nothing to change. The second is emotional and is prone to constantly changing moods. The third is strong, always wants to be right, is domineering, and strives at all times to prod, to act, to change things. The fourth is an intellectual. When four individuals of such different natures are placed together, they may interact in several ways: 1) peace; 2) conflict—constant struggle; or 3) alienation—noncommunicating. In the light of this analogy, let us examine the four elements and the relationships that may exist among them.

1) *Peace*—For the four people in the room to interrelate peacefully, they must first be in a state of inner peace, at peace with themselves. If such a state exists, we would find each element in balance within its region, with no deviation or spill over. The boundaries between the elements would be defined but not sharply marked. Peaceful relations among the elements show that each accepts the others, allows them to be present, and neither controls them nor is controlled by them.

   A state of peace among all four elements is in fact a state of equilibrium. This is a dynamic state that always fluctuates slightly. Equilibrium is not static; there is a flow among the elements, and no chronic conditions arise. This total or "comprehensive" peace is quite rare. We usually find some elements living in peace and others in conflict or alienation.

2) *Conflict*—All or some of the four people in the room are waging a struggle of forces, each trying to vanquish or neutralize another or others. The elements collide, intermingle,

and obfuscate their boundaries. Each tries to dominate the others and confusion is sown among them. When one element grows beyond its basic-potential boundaries, or is massively present within another element that does not interface with it, it cannot help but crowd out the other element. This induces constant struggle between conqueror and conquered, dissipating much of the person's energy.

Such a conflict may be temporary, as when people devote themselves to the actualization of one element at the expense of others. During a period of intensive study, for example, the air element may take up a relatively large space and suppress the articulation of emotions and basic needs. A woman's earth element may transcend its boundaries in the first years of motherhood, in which case the other elements will weaken for lack of use. This is a temporary state that may pass and change.

Chronic patterns of dominance may take shape over time. This happens when one element is expressed more emphatically in the individual's life, and the others submit to it and lose some of their potency. If, for example, a person is preoccupied for years with constant action to the serious detriment of his or her emotional articulation, the fire in this person's foot will have come to dominate water so strongly that the relationship between these conflicting powers will have become permanent. Water will have lost most of its power, and fire will have entrenched itself in the occupied areas so strongly that the prospects of change are slim. Whenever an element weakens or surrenders, another element begins to invade its territory. There can never be a vacuum.

In certain situations, an element is compressed and pushed into a corner, resulting in a large surplus region within this element coupled with deficiencies in the others. This condition is common with earth. In other situations, the element seems to disappear but actually continues to bubble under the surface. The moment it is given the slightest opportunity, it rebels and erupts. In any case, a repressed element never disappears completely; there is no life without the presence of all four elements.

3) *Alienation*—This is a state characterized by elements that do not interact, that ignore each other. One element fails to acknowledge the other's presence. In the foot, this manifests

itself in sharp, clear separations of the alienated elements—abrupt change in texture and color, furrows, or dividing lines.

People with this condition cannot invoke the alienated qualities simultaneously. People whose fire and water fail to communicate, for example, may be either emotional or domineering. When they are emotional, they completely disregard the existence of their egos and personal strength. When they are preoccupied with action or control, they forget that they have emotions.

Alienation between elements, or within one element, indicates that the individual is not in touch with the quality represented by the affected element. When people's earth and water do not communicate, for example, they may be unable to experience their latent violence and, for this reason, cannot recognize the possibility of letting it flow or channeling it by choice. They are at risk of a violent eruption with which they cannot cope. Alienation is a dangerous state; the elements neither communicate nor access each other. It is often harder to modify than a state of conflict.

When we reexamine a person's feet a year after the original analysis, we usually find significant changes. A previously passive element may have risen to dominance. The greatest tragedy to afflict human beings is a static state—a state of degeneration—in which one element remains dominant for a long time. Where there is no change, there is no vitality.

The individual's age, of course, is an important factor. The older we get, the more the relationships among our forces create chronic patterns that become entrenched with the passing of time. Insofar as a mature individual's internal relations have ossified, it will be hard to effect change or create a dynamic.

Interactions among the elements also show us how individuals interact with their surroundings. The attitude toward a given energy quality manifests itself in the attitude toward the same quality in someone else. For example, those who repress their power of thought and whose air element is controlled by other elements cannot tolerate the presence of intellectuals. The analogy of four people in a room helps us understand both the interaction between people and their egos and reactions between themselves and others.

THE RELATIONSHIP BETWEEN ELEMENTS

We will always work with the symbolism of the four elements, and each part of the foot is governed by an element. In addition to this, the elements can combine in numerous ways in any area of the foot. For example, when fire qualities are manifested in the heel (an earth element), it will look red and hot, and the person will have hypertensed muscles. The heel is naturally the area of the earth element, but the qualities can be overruled by any other element, and it is this interrelationship that creates the infinite numbers of possible combinations that merge to create the many individuals that you may someday meet in foot analysis.

I am unable to detail every possible element combination in this book. To aid the student who wants to learn about this energy, I have described fifteen possible combinations (or relationships) and provided an analysis of how one can interpret the energy that arises out of the existence of an element quality located in another element's territory. Because we are limited by space, I will only describe the situations that are extreme, so that you can make adjustments as you learn to combine less strident mixtures of energy. Here one element will disappear because it is invaded by the other; or there will be a complete separation between two elements. For example, a complete invasion of water in earth would mean that the earth element (territory) has been taken over by the qualities of the water element (see p. 52). This means that the earth element *function* (practical) has been invaded and is now operating out of a water (emotional) context. To give a mundane example of this—a person cries over money, dealing with money as though it were an emotional issue—or a person cries in the middle of a crisis instead of trying to solve the problem (such as crying while the house is burning, rather than calling the fire department).

Most people have points or areas on the feet where this invasion has taken place. Usually an element invasion doesn't involve the entire territory. But we are looking at extreme situations so we can understand the implications of invasions to the fullest. Then, when you are looking realistically at someone who has had a minor invasion, you can adjust this information back down to size so you can interpret the energy correctly.

OTHER ELEMENTS
WITHIN EARTH TERRITORY

Water in Earth—Water is the element that penetrates earth most easily since it is always striving to descend. Both water and earth are passive, thus giving water relatively easy access. Water in earth creates a "swamp." A heel in this condition becomes moist, light-colored, and soft. It may be bloated and edematous, usually in the area of the ankle. People whose emotional energy has overtaken their instinctive strength construe emotional situations as existential threats. Their hysteria is much greater than the actual menace. The feet of such a subject are prone to cold and trembling. If sexually assaulted, a woman with a strong earth element will respond with "fight or flight"; if water is present in her earth, however, she will be unable to act, becoming a victim.

Water in earth means that the subject will respond to various situations through their water. For example, if duped in financial matters, such people become insulted, angry, and so forth, rather than properly addressing themselves to the issues. Encountering highly difficult life situations, such people tend to fall apart.

People whose water has occupied most of their earth who have cancer, have a slim chance of being cured. They haven't the energy to emerge from their situation; they see and feel, but lack the energy they need to sustain their existence. Water equals fear. Water-dominated people succumb to fear without trying to overcome it. Cancer is a situation that pushes people to the wall. It turns some (those with fire in earth) into strong fighters, and drives others (those with water in earth) to panic and paralysis.

Fire in Earth—The heel is hot and red. The skin is dry and tough, but not cracked, flaky, or peeling. There are red blood vessels and spots at the ankles. Our capacity for self-control keeps our instincts under tight rein. Consider, for example, a woman who encounters a rapist after having conducted herself "properly" (fire in earth) all her life. To flee, she feels, would be inappropriate and vulgar. She becomes a victim because she doesn't know how to act spontaneously.

Pulled lower-back muscles are a classic symptom of fire in earth. Men are stiff around the pelvis. There is a feeling of shame and the inability to act on the advice of others: "People will get the wrong idea about me!" Fire in earth causes lower-back pain and a constricted anus. This state of the elements is more common among men than women, because of a combination of physical phenomena and ethical-cultural norms.

When sexual energy is aroused in the male, particularly in the adolescent, it is obvious. The shame and the need for concealment begin in adolescence and persist into adulthood. Ethics, as they refer to sexuality, indicate the presence of fire in earth. Such a state decreases spontaneity. The stronger a man's desire, the more he controls his muscles, holding them rigidly not to lose control, and the sooner he will ejaculate. The greater his attempts to control his ejaculation, and his lower body as a whole, the more problems are created in this area. The state of fire within earth is evidenced in people who experience an ego problem related to sex. A man so affected may not actually meet any women, instead masturbating without enjoyment. Such people attain material and other kinds of success, which are concepts related to the ego. We speak primarily of men as having fire in their earth, since fire is a masculine element that they take pains to cultivate. Religious women, educated in the traditional manner that proscribes sexual desire as sinful, become adept over the years at repressing these needs so as to repress all sensation in their earth.

Sexuality is only one of the aspects of earth, along with other basic drives such as the need for money. People with fire in earth have difficulty asking for money when they need it. Earth that is dominated by fire points at compulsive tendencies. Any area in which a person is compulsive is probably related to earth in some way, e.g., cleanliness. We may infer that compulsive cleanliness is a substitute for some sexual need. (Nymphomania suggests the presence of excessive qualities of both earth and fire in the earth element territory, since it is a condition to which the ego must acquiesce. The state of a subject's elements depends on the origin of the crossover.) Fire dries up earth, thus decreasing its fertility. When fire is present in earth, responses will be carefully considered rather than instinctive. The button-down, starched-collar type is the embodiment of fire in earth.

Air in Earth—The heel is small, empty, weak, and light-colored. The tissue is thin, making the bone easy to feel. The foot is dry. Water and earth are clearly demarcated.

Air in earth is characteristic of people whose intellect dominates their earth forces. They are repelled by their bodies and "turned off" by anything physical. Such people neglect all their basic needs, to their bodies' great detriment. Air and earth are diametrical opposites. The presence of air within earth is akin to a clash between matter and antimatter, the worst possible invasion of earth. People in such a state treat their bodies with utter neglect, denying themselves food, drink, and any form of comfort. Ascetics are such people, rejecting their bodies and all earthly concepts in favor of spirituality. If they succeed in preserving their energy and refrain from forcing air into their earth, they experience their sexual needs in a different way. Tantra yoga, for example, is the art of elevating sexual energy to the head. Its practitioners allow their sexual energy to flow without engaging in sexual relations. Such people, rather than having an air-dominated earth element, approach a state of balance. A monk who attempts to repress his sexual energy because of his religious proscriptions, by contrast, allows air to penetrate his earth.

Air-dominated earth may, in its extreme manifestation, produce multiple sclerosis. Here, the central nervous system begins to shut down, the person deteriorates, and certain body parts "die" (usually starting with the extremities). When something takes place that is related to earth energy, such people respond by the application of intellect and fail to address themselves to the basic things in life. They are always duped on money matters, since they don't act to protect their wealth. They treat sex, too, as an intellectual act, an expression of unconditional love.

Dissociation of Water and Earth

Dissociation of water and earth is an indication of a split in the person. In terms of their passive energy, such people live in two worlds while being capable of occupying only one. Their emotional world, for example, is disengaged when they engage in sex. By the same token, their sensuality fails to penetrate their emotional world, which, in turn, may be wholly divorced from reality. The earth element represents family, a basic cell. The separating of water and earth signifies an emotional world divorced from the family. The earth element represents the mother who, in turn, represents emotion. At some stage in these people's lives, an event somehow related to their mother disengaged them from their earth. These people withdraw from or are repelled by their mother, or more precisely their own passive energy, which does not necessarily emanate from the mother. We should physically examine the area of the foot where water and earth have separated. If the site corresponds to the ovaries and fallopian tubes, for example, we find a woman who has difficulty conceiving.

OTHER ELEMENTS
WITHIN WATER TERRITORY

Earth in Water—Among the indications of earth in water are subjects who stride off the water region of their feet. Diabetics, for example, display a "picture" of earth—dry, tough, cracked skin within all the water zone.

Earth in water is characteristic of people who have sacrificed their emotional world for the sake of such corporeal attributes as a rigid framework and material wealth. Earth rarely usurps the entire area reserved for water; rather it takes over an enlarged band more than one-third the width of the water region where the subject strides (see figure 41). Such people are "dry," leading lives of inferior emotional quality. Before taking any action they ask what good it will do them rather than whether they will enjoy it.

What counts for these people is money, security, the framework, and the family. They interpret warmth as an invitation to sex. Their relationships are materialistic. They get themselves into a rut and stay there out of fear that they won't be able to manage financially on their own; the longer they remain, the "drier" they become. If their framework is jarred, they lose their ability to cope, since their place in life means everything to them. Such people build strongholds and defenses in order to avoid experiencing the contents of their lower water region. They forfeit their lower water so their earth may protect them; if their earth is shaken, the content beneath can destroy them.

Earth that dominates water blocks a highly dynamic element. By introducing a static quality to what should be dynamic, we end up with people who wish to do nothing new,

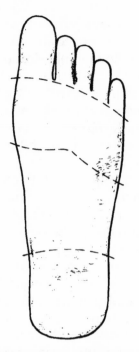

Figure 41. Earth in water. Dry, rough skin crosses the border of the water element region, indicating that this person puts most of his or her weight on this portion of the foot. As a result, there is the presence of strong earth energy in the water element and a weakness of water energy.

preferring to repeat the same things ad infinitum. These people are stubborn, stuck, frozen in place. They are unable to build emotional relationships, confining themselves to the construction of secure frameworks that will meet earthly imperatives. Their own emotional world having dried up, they cannot perceive that anyone else feels anything. People with earth-dominated water may encounter exceedingly emotional people without even noticing this trait. They cannot realize that in the course of erecting their own framework they are inadvertently trampling others' domains. Here our reference to earth alludes to violence, the commitment to personal needs irrespective of the consequences. Such people are slow to form relationships; the relationships they do succeed in establishing are very formal. Since slow, heavy earth has penetrated the swifter element of water, their emotional responses are sluggish too.

Earth-dominated water points to an arrested digestive process—people who need time to absorb things. When earth is present in water, the following physical problems may occur: loss of limb functioning, calcification, adhesions, skeletal problems, gall and kidney stones; all of which indicate a surplus in earth and underactivity of water. In women, such a state signifies an overdeveloped maternal instinct, as in the case of an older housewife whose children are grown, leaving her with nothing to do but clean and tend to the house and cook for them when they visit. In men it indicates stubbornness, an unwillingness to budge, unless their basic energy is passive, in which case it points to a type of motherliness. Such men offer warmth only at home, within a defined structure, and nowhere else.

Fire in Water—Fire and water are diametrically opposed. When fire is present in water, we encounter a very large fire area. The areas of the body corresponding to this entire area of the foot are hypertonic, marred with red spots and other markings. When fire dominates water, the latter may try to ascend to air, since fire turns water into steam and causes it to ascend rather than descend.

People whose air element functions properly do not permit their water to rise. It then tries to descend; if this proves impossible, it gathers itself into one small area. Fire in water is an indication of control of emotions. These subjects feel and experience only those things that pass the censorship exercised by their control mechanism. People whose feelings are centered in their chest have fire in their water element. Their water has diminished; fire has usurped the role of emotion (see figure 42).

People with fire in their water relate to others in terms of power, not of emotion; they attempt to dominate relationships. They perceive the world as a struggle for strength and power. They want slaves, not servants. The stereotypical "*macho*" is such a person, striving to bend others to his will. People who treat themselves in such a fashion possess an internal moral code that tells them how to behave. They repress emotions related to anger, guilt, fear, and so forth, feeling particularly threatened by their own potential emotional weakness. Some of these people persist with their stubbornness until it breaks them. They play strictly to win, unable to entertain the possi-

Figure 42. Fire in water. The foot is characterized by strong muscle tissue and an enlarged fire area that invades the water element region. This indicates the presence of strong fire energy in the water element and a weakness of water energy.

bility of "living to fight another day." They are extremely weak emotionally. (Otherwise, their fire would be unable to dominate their water.) Lacking emotional strength, they go to pieces if something emotional happens to them.

Instead of the normal dynamism of the water region, we find a toughness or rigidity at this site. Such people are workaholics, feeling that a work setting offers them an opportunity to exercise control. They tend to be independent and need to be constantly occupied. Retirement is a death knell for these people; their fire, deprived of its outlet, consumes them. They have neither hobbies nor anything else that might fill them emotionally. Such people can be highly creative but only in a technical sense; they do everything exactly right but with an absence of inner feeling. They are artisans, not artists. Their hands are very important to them. They show only those "cards" that they wish; all their external behavior is tightly controlled. They need to have things "just so." These are extremely proud people who try to knock the world into shape rather than flow with it. They neither forgive nor forget. They attempt to dominate all situations even if they have no idea what to do.

Air in Water—In such a situation, the water becomes light and dry. Where air occupies the entire water region, people replace their emotions with cerebral, analytic processes. They only think that they feel. This state is especially characteristic of psychologists who tend to interpret events instead of responding to them emotionally. Such people always have explanations for everything.

The foot exhibits a malleable layer of skin with emptiness beneath, and there is little sensation in the region. Such people's emotional world is dominated by the head. They feel what their head (their air) tells them they should feel in a given situation. They attach a reason to every feeling and consider it necessary to run through multiple interpretations before they can marshal any emotion. Air in water may indicate people who are brilliant and self-confident in their thought processes, but who lack the inner security to say: "I'm sure that what I feel is what I feel, and it's all right for me to feel this way."

People with air in their water are generally very intelligent. They hide behind their knowledge, aware at the same time that something's missing. They realize there is an entire world with which they are not in touch. These are intellectuals who feel isolated in an ivory tower; they see the "other" world from above, explain it, but never touch it. Nor does it touch them.

They eat quickly, swallowing a lot of air that subsequently churns in their stomach, causing flatulence. Air diminishes all activities of water and can lead to constipation. Weakness, anemia, and impaired liver performance all signal the presence of air within water. In cases of hepatitis we find yellow coloration in the air element, pointing at liver malfunction.

Dissociation of Water and Fire

This is the most common type of disengagement, since the opposing natures of water and fire create a struggle between the two energies. Water is an uncontrolled energy that flows on its own, as opposed to fire that represents total control and will not permit things to happen on their own. People generally veer toward one or the other of these extremes. A dissociation of water and fire indicates that water does not achieve any form of control; on a conscious level, subjects are lacking an emotional world. Such a state may occur when the dominant hands and feet are opposite. Subjects such as these inhabit two different worlds—one of action, one of feeling. When this separation occurs in a person whose dominant hand and foot are on the same side of the body, it indicates the absence of any sort of emotional world. We expect to encounter this form of detachment in people who are highly active in pursuits that have no connection with the world of emotions. Examples are people who work with computers (see figure 43 on page 132).

In the feet, the dissociation of water and fire manifests itself in one of two ways: a salient indentation (deep line like a fissure) along the line of the area corresponding to the diaphragm, or a blatant disparity in the qualities of the two elements. For example, a clearly red and hot fire element area, bordering a white, cold, and wet water element area, will indicate a person who can quickly jump from one type of experience and behavior to another. Because the qualities of these elements are contradictory, the absence of demarcation between fire and water is characteristic of people who mature steadily and pursue a process of growth. This is an inner dynamic; they experience things and avoid stagnation. Dissociation of the two elements points at people who are "in a rut"; they forfeit their lower elements and remain fixed in the upper ones. These are people who relegate their emotional world and its needs to the margins of their consciousness.

Such people are predisposed to physical conditions typified by diminished mobility in the lower body, i.e., digestive problems, sexual and fertility disorders, coupled with states of surplus in the upper body, i.e., localized accumulations of fluids and a tendency to heart attacks. Such people can not become true artists, since true creativity cannot come from fire and air alone but must emerge from an inner conflict, a struggle, a mysteriousness, from the striving for the unknown embodied in the work of art.

All these traits apply more to men than to women, both because men are drawn toward employing the energy of fire and air, and because our culture teaches that men do while

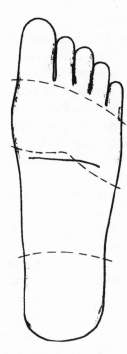

Figure 43. A line separating the fire and water element inhibits balance between the two qualities.

women feel. To be sure, some women's water and fire elements are dissociated; these women exercise control with fire and air. Observing people with a clear and blatant separation of fire and air, we may assume that they are negating their entire emotional world. Such a separation is usually even more pronounced in women, since it is contrary to their basic energy.

When people decide, "I'm not willing to suffer pain any longer; I don't want to be sad anymore," they are cutting themselves off and therefore forfeiting the positive along with the negative pleasure and pain, the joy as well as the sadness. This disengagement may take place even in the absence of emotional trauma; people erect it because their egos are unwilling to accept anything emanating from the element of water. Let us consider, for example, a man who has undergone surgery along the width of his abdomen. Both the scar and the shock may trigger a separation. We must verify whether there was a pre-existing separation that was merely given physical expression by the operation.

Our external reactions to various life situations reflect what is happening to us internally. People incur injury where they are weak, where their equilibrium is not maintained. There is no point in speaking to people whose emotionality and creativity reside only in their upper elements. The two lower, passive elements energize and strengthen one another. If one of these should be taken over by another element for a lengthy period, we will see damage throughout the passive energy. An example of fire occupying water arises in people who hold in their stomach muscles very tightly, thus producing constipation, which in turn leads over time to the formation of hemorrhoids—i.e., damage to the earth element, too.

OTHER ELEMENTS
WITHIN FIRE TERRITORY

Earth in Fire—Various qualities of the earth element may smother the fire region totally or in part. One example of earth extinguishing fire is angina pectoris, a condition characterized by blockage and impaired flow. Victims of angina pectoris have a gray area on the foot and are themselves gray in color; they exhibit neither life nor liveliness. These are people who have forfeited their hearts in deference to primary needs. Examples are people who hate their work and do it only because they need the salary. For them, a fixed structure is more important than creativity; their elemental needs cause them to forgo the love of others and the pleasure of doing, or creating. Most people do things because they must, not because they want to or love to, but because they have an obligation. They forfeit their fire for a more solid commodity: earth. There is no balance here. Nothing is built on the earth element; it actually becomes a prison and people with this combination find that everything—work, performance, career, creativity—is lived through the earth element rather than from the fire excitement they could experience.

The phenomenon of earth within fire is present in most older people. Since fire represents breathing, a physical manifestation of this state is the impairment of lung functioning. Our culture does not speak of love among the elderly; they are permitted to love their grandchildren but not each other. This is not only because of prejudice. These people do not demonstrate outward signs of love; their attitudes toward themselves discount the possibility of their "having a heart." The earth-within-fire syndrome is a manifestation of people who die while still alive. They show no spontaneity, which is a quality of fire; their every action is slow and heavy.

When one's earth ascends to fire, it usually ascends to the air element too, causing calcification of blood vessels of the brain. Earth in fire is a sign of people who are unable to love because of the difficulty and pain involved, preferring instead to hide behind a fixed structure.

Signs of earth in fire in the foot—along with a dry, cracked, and deep separation mark—characterize people who have given up on love after having been deeply hurt by separation. These are people who love frameworks; their hearts seek all the attributes we associate with earth. They strive to control their setting. The intensity of their need to exercise control originates in the "double dose" of earth in their feet. The element of fire represents the muscles, which are designed to have tone and flexibility, to contract, relax, and extend. The presence of earth, by contrast, points at rigidity and immobility of the muscles.

Young people's earth generally occupies only portions of their fire. Common examples are:

1) A callus under toes 2 and 3, which signals an inability to accept warmth and love. Being unable to take also means being unable to give. Such a condition indicates a combination of control and fear. Such people are afraid to love; the only energy they summon is that motivated by needs. This could be the profile of a terrific family man who provides for his family with great devotion but does so without any love. Afraid to exhibit love, he provides a secure framework in its place. Women in this condition invest all their energies in the family, leaving no room for their own, personal love, e.g., for a hobby or another individual.

Dominated by the attributes of earth, they maintain the frameworks of their lives but avoid real love and emotion that surfaces in higher energies. Such people have "frameworks" within their hearts. "I love this framework," you'll hear them say. "I'm comfortable and content at home." These people, however, do not come home with fire in their hearts. Long-term smoking causes a similar condition. Both kinds of people—heavy smokers and those who do not place what they love in their hearts—kill themselves.

2) A strip of dry, tough skin on the area of the foot corresponding to the bronchial tubes indicates problems of the esophagus, trachea, or bronchi, in the region where we let things "in" and "out." The structure of the earth element creates a blockage that exercises strong control over what people release vocally.

3) A callus on the boundary between fire and air, on the site corresponding to the thyroid gland, means a lump of earth has settled in. Instead of letting their self-expression and creativity flow, these people opt for passivity in order to safeguard their security.

4) Dry, tough skin in the area of the foot corresponding to the shoulder region indicates problems in the shoulders coupled with aspects of fire—of doing, of activity—whose outer manifestations are being impeded. Something in the flow of "doing" is obstructed by the presence of earth. Earth, striving to be secure, protected, self-enclosed, has ascended and blocked the fire. This description is applicable to button-down, straight-and-narrow types of people who make no sudden moves. Figure 44 on page 136 illustrates these four examples.

Water in Fire—The fire element shrinks, because the adjacent element has usurped some of its territory. In this state, people lose their self-confidence. Their sense of self, of "who I am," is uncertain as their feelings vacillate and oscillate from one moment to the next. This description fits people who undertake things easily but are unable to complete them, whose enthusiasm flares quickly then subsides. They cannot decide on a given course of action and stick with it until the end.

Physically, this condition is manifested in respiratory problems: fluid in the lungs or bronchial tubes, asthma, pneumonia, chronic bronchitis. People whose water has penetrated the upper band of fire are not in control of their actions. As they articulate and act on their emotions, sometimes involuntarily,

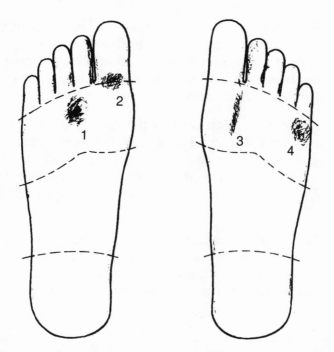

Figure 44. Four examples of earth energy invasion in the fire element area. Example 1 indicates a person motivated by needs rather than by love; examples 2 and 3 indicate blocks in the ability for self-expression and creativity; example 4 signifies a person blocked from taking action.

they sense, helplessly, that they are out of control. Instead of expressing the desires and needs of their ego, they give vent to their emotions. In most cases, however, they do not display the full range of emotions, for they haven't the strength to artic-ulate the intensity of anger. More frequently they manifest fear, anxiety, guilt, and the like.

This condition reaches its zenith in people whose water has quenched their fire altogether. They are highly prone to eruptions of hysteria, warranting hospitalization in extreme cases. People who have no fire at all have absolutely no control over themselves and are not responsible for their actions. In a word, they are insane. They do not control their fears; their fears control them.

Since one of the characteristics of fire is a preoccupation with oneself and how one is viewed by others, people with water in their fire region are exceedingly concerned about others' feelings toward them; they seek constant reassurance and demonstrations of these feelings. Such people smother those around them with their surplus of water. Lacking sufficient ego strength, they perpetually search for reinforcement from others. They do things that command a maximum of attention while ostensibly trying to avoid being focused upon. When arriving late for a concert, for example, they make such a show of unobtrusively tiptoeing in that they cause more of a distraction.

Water obfuscates the boundaries of the ego, boundaries that show who we are and how far we go. When they are obliterated, we undergo emotional experiences that do not belong to us, i.e., overemotionalism. When such people do something for themselves, for their ego, they feel guilty. They feel as if everything is in constant flux, since "real" water is always dynamic and people contain a great deal of water. Such people cannot sustain their creativity; they create impulsively and fail to control the form and substance of this outward manifestation of their inner selves. Art created by people who merely "eject" their inner brainstorms irrespective of order, structure, or discipline, is incomprehensible to others.

Water in the fire region is characteristic of people with weak egos, who are easily influenced by others. They lose their sense of boundaries and cannot restore it by saying, as they should at times, "I don't want this." They are too concerned with what others will say about them. Such people are easy candidates for alcoholism and drug abuse, tempted by the peace and security that addiction appears to offer. They find it hard to gain weight because their water, with its dynamism, does not accumulate in one location.

When water ascends to fire, the immune system is placed at risk because an internal accumulation of diverse forces ensues. People who suffer from cancer may lose their will to fight, their fire extinguished. Those who can defeat cancer are the ones whose natural fire has only been repressed temporarily, following a shock such as the death of a spouse or loss of employment. Such people have a chance of recovery. When fire is submerged by water and becomes passive, unexpressed feelings of anger and guilt accumulate in the body; these people succumb to their cancer. Strips of water on the boundary between air and fire (moisture, eczema) represent energies, such as emotional intensity, that ascended from water and lodged themselves there. Such a state is a signal of throat conditions such as laryngitis. Fire-driven energies that dissipate due to the presence of other elements are characteristic of people who lose their ability to protect themselves from invasive, harmful agents.

Air in Fire—Although air is supposed to fan the fire, an overdominance of air within this element extinguishes it. A fire region occupied in large part by air acquires a white, flaccid appearance, a very delicate texture, and an absence of warmth to the touch. Such a state is indicative of people who prefer thinking to doing. Action is displaced by thought, in the form of extensive rambling, fantasizing, explanations, and so forth. These are people who are so crammed with unimplemented ideas that they have no fire left. Since fire represents muscle, and air signifies skin, such people have loose, hanging skin and lack muscle tone. They avoid activities that entail physical exertion and sweat. Such a state is not encountered frequently.

Fire is generally penetrated by elements lower than air because people must be practical. People whose air has invaded their fire manage to survive on words and explanations rather than acts and experiences. Theoretical psychologists can be such people, people who are divorced from "doing." They do not perceive the ego and its boundaries in others. For them, "I think, therefore I am" is sufficient.

Air within fire diminishes ego strength, meaning that even bright people find themselves unable to progress in life. Only a proper combination of fire and air carries people to positions of power; those lacking fire are totally uninterested in achieving leadership status. When people's air descends into an element of control, they try to exercise that control through the attributes of air, attempting to rationalize everything they or others do. These are people who use displays of intellect when they try to present their egos and thoughts. Since they lack fire, they whisper rather than shout out their truths: "I think that . . . " In such clients we expect to find a sunken chest, hypotonic muscles, and an absence of visible indications of strength. Other physical manifestations include a weak heart, collapsed valves, muscle weakness, hypotension, fainting, and an overall tendency toward weakness.

Dissociation of Fire and Air

On the boundary between the fire and air elements lies the area corresponding to the thyroid gland, the throat, and the vocal cords. Fire and air have a natural affinity for each other; the one stimulates the other. If they are kept apart, a natural integration of active and receptive forces is violated. Such a client may have problems in two areas: self-expression—the ability to do, to create, is stymied—and the selection of one element at the expense of the other. For example, such people may choose intellectualism and neglect the possibility of taking action in their lives. Alternatively, they may concern themselves only with doing rather than thinking.

This particular type of dissociation between elements is very common. Few people reveal the true contents of their hearts as they would if there were an unimpeded flow between fire and air. Obvious signs of a dissociation of fire from air are bouts of laryngitis, nodules on the vocal cords, hyperthyroidism, or hypothyroidism. The thyroid gland regulates the exchange of various bodily substances; when its level of activity deviates from the norm, so does the activity level of the entire internal system. People suffering from hypothyroidism are generally overweight and weak, with a slow heart rate; those with hyperthyroidism are overactive and prone to attacks of anxiety. People in the latter group persist with actions that they know to be harmful. Both of these conditions are symptomatic of a dissociation of fire and air.

The damage is not necessarily caused by the material things that enter our bodies (food, alcohol, tobacco). What truly affects us is how we perceive, act, experience, and coexist with events in our lives. We, as foot analysts, should view alcohol consumption, smoking, and so forth as pernicious only if we see or feel signs of imbalance in the foot. An indented line underneath the big toe points to an interruption of the subject's studies or career. When people undertake something, fire ascends to air in order to stimulate the process of doing. But if, for example, their studies are abruptly terminated in their final year, due either to their own actions or to external circumstances such as money trouble, their ambitions, too, are cut off in midstream. The same indicator is found in creative people who have brought their own creativity to a halt, who had something to give others from their fire and failed to do so. If such people resume their earlier endeavor, the mark on the foot disappears. The related symptoms surface long after the mark does, generally one to two years after the initial event.

OTHER ELEMENTS
WITHIN AIR TERRITORY

Earth in Air—Air is an element that seeks to expand and fill a vacuum; earth, by contrast, seeks to contract. Earth within air produces people who say, "That's how it's done," and who try to impose their perception of things on others. They are immovable, stubborn, and implacable; they say that things have always been and will continue to be just as they are. (*Always* is a word associated with earth.) They are the sorts who, when confronted with"Why" questions, answer "Because!" Earth within air smothers their thinking processes; they do not attempt to consider the possibility of there being something to think about. "Because!" is enough of an answer. That's what there is and that's what there's got to be.

Earth in fire causes people to tread the straight and narrow path. There's nothing new under the sun; faith is preferable to evaluation. Such people have one-track minds and believe that every situation has one and only one resolution (whereas in real life there's always more than one). Only considerations of basic existence and the survival instinct move such people to thought.

People with earth in their air use their mouths as weapons and believe themselves to be the victims of this treatment by others. This is because they perceive things not through air but through earth. The most extreme manifestation of this condition is psychosis, in which one engages continually in a fight-or-flight response. Such people, having lost their humanity, their spirituality, their very minds, act on their instincts alone. The abilities to learn, think, remember, and concentrate are all impaired. Memory is reduced to an instinctive rather than a verbal or visual process; it is equipped with only the most basic tools of survival.

Our examination of such people shows an air-dominated foot with thickened, calcified joints and some loss of mobility. This description applies to people who have long been preoccupied with survival; they have not had time to think. General manifestations include problems of concentration, learning, and exercise of the intellect; migraines; shortness of breath, and forced breathing. Some people are born with earth in their air; they are prone to brain damage and epilepsy. In children, earth in air is strongly suggestive of some type of impaired functioning in the head.

Water in Air—Emotions displace thought. People let things slip out—things they would not have uttered had they stopped to think for just a moment. People who are very angry believe they are right. It's enough to say "I'm angry"; they owe no one any explanation as to why. When water remains in its natural state, it does not ascend to air: we only feel things. But when water ascends to air, we concoct explanations and justifications of why it's OK to feel the way we do. People on the receiving end of a burst of water emerging from air have the feeling that someone has thrown his or her garbage onto them. Water in air produces people who cannot think clearly because there's "fog" in their heads; they never know if what they're seeing is real or if they are merely imagining their worst fears.

Physical manifestations include conditions involving bodily fluids: infections in the area corresponding to the air element—the sinuses, eyes, and throat; and a tendency toward tears. Allergies are frequent. These are people who, while claiming to explain and analyze others' feelings, are really describing their own. When water is present in air, the air becomes "waterlogged" and less able to permeate the body. This, in turn, elicits the respiratory problems typical of this state. Children cry easily, constantly creating emotional scenes to have their way. They secrete water everywhere—from the eyes, the nose, and the mouth.

The foot shows a surplus in water and a deficiency in air. Toes 3 and 4 are unusual: pale, flexible, and peeling, with soft toenails. Eczema or mycosis (athlete's foot) is evident. Water does not ascend to air in the first place unless it is exceptional in some respect. In some cases this uniqueness is created when fire usurps the territory of water, thus leaving the water no choice but to rise. People in this condition are very tightly controlled but are not thinkers; all their thoughts are emotional. They reach a certain perception or belief that is not based on thinking, choice, or decision; something has "spoken" to them on an emotional level, and this suffices. The presence of water in air is the root of much prejudice. Preconceived notions caused by this combination form a basic part of our world view, even though closer examination would probably expose them as based on emotion rather than careful thought. Those whose heads are filled with water-based perceptions forfeit their intelligence.

Fire in Air—In this state, one's air is permeated with notions of control, the right way to do things, and "what will others say," in contrast to the emotional qualities described above. Fire is outwardly directed; it focuses on how we appear to others. The more fire penetrates air, the more control people exercise over their actions. It is for this reason that the behavior patterns generated within air reflect how we "should" act. We tell ourselves, "One shouldn't say such things, so I won't say what I'm thinking." Those with an even higher degree of control suspend their thinking altogether, lest they think the wrong thing. The toes of such people are hot, red, muscular, and bloated (filled with tissue).

Fire in air is associated with learned behavior. It is characteristic of people who strictly follow popular doctrine not because earth has blocked their air, but because they have been brought up to think and act in a "proper" and controlled way. Fire signifies the force of opposition: the more opposed we are to something, the more we come to resemble it. For example, people with fire in their air may say, "I'll never be like my mother," but the very vehemence of their objections causes their fears to come true. Such people jump the gun and listen later. Their responses, verbal and otherwise, are shot from the hip. These people are hotheaded; things slip out before they can stop them. They invoke the first person singular constantly (I, me, mine) because their heads, i.e., their egos, have climbed into their air, which represents outward expression. They tend to suffer from headaches accompanied by a feverish sensation.

Physical manifestations include digestive indications appearing within the air region, i.e., a bad taste or odor in the mouth and frequent gum infections. The jaw muscles are tense and sore from the effort of maintaining a stiff upper lip; control, after all, means no change. Were one's air region to be filled with air as it should be, one would not be so rigid about self-control.

People in this state must be right because their pride is always put to the test; to be wrong is an affront to their ego. They tend toward superficiality, believing they know everything about a given subject after only a short time. Such people cannot admit their mistakes, defending themselves even when they are wrong lest their strength, i.e., their fire, be broken and their pride hurt. Wounded pride can trigger very serious conditions, such as cerebral hemorrhage, in which a great eruption of fire consumes the air element so devastatingly that the person can no longer function. No few subjects have described feelings of anger or insult just before experiencing a cerebral hemorrhage.

• • •

In this chapter we viewed four basic energies (or qualities) and how they intermingle. Each has a space (or territory) where its qualities and functions are dominant. Each energy also appears in the other three domains—but not in a dominant form—and when balanced, all four qualities exist in all four domains. What appears strongest and clearest in each of the four domains is the element that belongs to the territory. The number of possibilities for some of these qualities gaining force in others' domains or losing force in their domain to other qualities, is what defines our individuality. This is the balance, or lack of it, that demands change and growth because of the constant personal struggle to regain the balance.

7

DIVIDING THE FEET

By examining the feet we may learn how people relate to aspects of themselves that are not evident to the outside observer but nonetheless form the basis of their personalities. Various types of feet demonstrate the discrepancy between the "face" people present to others and the way they feel about their own inner world.

Occasionally we encounter feet that look older or younger than they "should" in view of the subjects' age. This points to differences between the subjects' internal and external selves, and may indicate whether or not the "child" within them still lives. A foot that seems youthful in comparison to the body as a whole shows that the subject has taken a relatively easy path in life to date. It may also suggest that he or she has learned little along the way and may take life a bit too lightly. A foot that seems older than the rest of the body may be indicative of a person whose travels through life have been difficult, held back, heavily burdened, or tested in the crucible of war. Along the way they have learned lessons but not necessarily the right ones.

In principle, dissimilarities between the foot and the rest of the body teach us a great deal about people's attitudes toward themselves and about disparities between their inner and outer worlds.

The right-left division is important in determining differences between left and right states. For instance, passive and active energies are divided in two different ways. First, division between left and right, with the dominant foot being active and the other passive. Second, division according to elements—air and fire active, water and earth passive. Three possible states arise from these two divisions:

1) When the dominant hand and foot are on the same side, the active energies are present on the dominant side, and the passive ones on the other.

2) When the dominant hand and foot are not on the same side, there is a split between the subject's active and passive energies, a break between fire and water. (In such a case, we must explore the possibility of a "mechanical" origin such as injury or amputation.)

3) When there is a dominant hand but no dominant foot, we identify the foot on the side of the dominant hand as the dominant foot.

Subjects with a dominant right hand and foot have their active energy in their dominant right side, where it is most clearly manifested in the elements of air and fire. Their passive energy is manifested on the left side.

Subjects with a dominant left hand and foot have the zenith of their active energy on the left side, with the passive energy on the right.

Right-handed subjects with dominant left feet, and left-handed subjects with dominant right feet, must be "bisected" into water and fire; their active and passive energies are in a state of basic conflict. In their active sections (fire and air), which represent "doing" (the hands), their dominant energy is on the right side. In their passive aspects (water and earth), which represent "experiencing" or "passing through" (the feet), their dominant energy is on the left side. Such people are indeed split in two, each side pulling in a different direction. This type of conflict is not necessarily bad for a person; in certain cases, it may even be helpful.

In the foot we have identified as dominant, we encounter both the active and the passive elements at the zenith of their respective levels of performance. Passivity comes in many gradations. It is less passive, or more active, within the dominant foot, where the dominant, active, outward-directed elements are in control. In the nondominant foot, by contrast, the passive elements reign supreme and operate at a maximum of passivity. By the same token, activity is manifested in its most passive form in the nondominant foot.

When we speak of active and passive, we are referring to our most basic energies, and our tendency to control and drive our lives rather than being controlled and driven by them. In every area of human functioning, we may observe which of the above is holding sway. "Driving" signifies an excess of effort; "being driven," insufficient effort.

Between the active and passive energies is the tension within which we live. Our essence is neither active nor passive; rather it is the outcome of the tension between them. People grow through the struggles they experience between these two energies throughout their lives. Equilibrium between these forces is a static state that does not exist; change takes place constantly. Chinese philosophy speaks of the moments before and after equilibrium, for equilibrium itself can not be addressed. One who achieves such a state is no longer part of this world. Throughout our lives we experience only fleeting moments of equilibrium.

The foot informs us of people's experiences in the struggle between their active and passive energies. This ongoing process also operates outwardly, in terms of people's relations with their environment, spouse, parents, and so forth. In this chapter what we mean by saying surplus or deficiency is a way to simplify all the combinations of elements out of their territory.

When opposite hands and feet are dominant, we have a state which is characterized by a boundary (a line or a sharp change between the water and fire elements in texture or color across the foot from side to side) forming a complete break between water and fire. A partition of this sort is rarely encountered.

We have already described the mutual attraction between the active and passive worlds, pinpointing various types of connections and relations between them. When the opposite hand and foot are dominant, the active and passive sides of a person are dissociated from one another. The world of feeling and emotion exists but is not connected with the world of expression, action, and thought; they are two completely different universes. Such people may be highly "cerebral" at work, for example, but concerned at home with emotion only, to the total exclusion of the intellect. This kind of partition between active and passive generally takes place during childhood. It may be caused by adults who force left-handed children to write with their right hand, since handedness is a feeling (water) whereas forcing is fire; such people have no choice but to separate their water from their fire.

When such a state is present, we must analyze each foot separately, first with an eye toward the active elements and then the passive ones. If we want subjects of this type to understand and absorb what we say, we cannot insert a sudden reference to something passive in the middle of a discussion of their active attributes. Since these people cannot draw connections between these two worlds, we surely cannot.

In the case of a left-handed person with no dominant foot, we treat the left foot as the dominant one; in the case of a right-handed person with no dominant foot, we treat the right foot as the dominant one.

• • •

All the above states provide us with information that we attempt to verify during the first stage of our examination. By placing our subjects in one of these categories, we are better equipped to know how to address them, what words to use in order to get our message across. We need to determine which of the four elements should serve as our starting point. Coming from the direction of earth would mean speaking on a physical level, discussing the subject's physical problems; if from air, we would speak of intellectual qualities; from fire, the subject's creativity, the things he or she does; and from water, what happens to him or her in the stomach—not necessarily from the physical standpoint.

8

THE SPINE
AND THE FOOT

The spinal column as reflected in the foot is very similar in form to that of the column itself, in terms of the arched and rounded portions of both (see figure 45 on page 150). For purposes of foot analysis the spinal column is particularly important because it passes through the areas of all the elements. Therefore, special conditions of the spinal column indicate connections or separations between the elements. The main flow within the spinal column takes two forms: descent from above, and ascent from below. It represents the body in all phases of development from conception, pregnancy and birth.

In any analysis conducted through examination of the feet, special attention must be paid to the spinal column, including the mapping of areas of surplus and deficiency, observation of the movement of the arches as these mirror parts of the spinal column, and comparison of the feet. Lower-back problems are indicated, in accordance with their severity, by cracks or swelling in the region. Upward, downward, and sideways movement of the big toe will show the state of the small arch at the nape of the neck. Comparisons of the angles of the big toes in a state of rest, indicate a particular side of the back of the neck that is more strained and problematic. Any internal state, such as constipation, is manifested in the appropriate region of the spinal column.

Within the area of the foot corresponding to the spinal column, one may observe the area that denotes the moment of conception, the period of pregnancy, and the birth of the client (see figure 46). The highest area on the back of the neck represents the moment of conception; it is indeed here that we begin, as a cluster of cells. The process ends at the center of the heel on

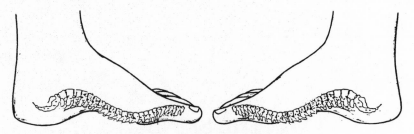

Figure 45. Spinal column as represented in the feet.

the inner side of the foot—corresponding to the base of the spinal column. In terms of the distribution of the elements, these two extremes represent the zenith of masculine energy in air, and of feminine energy in earth. The male is active at the time of conception, his energy penetrating and actually energizing the air element. Here we observe the father's role in creating the energy that affects the person. In the region of the heel, which corresponds to the uterus (earth), we view the site where the mother's energy reaches its climax as she brings a new life into the world. The line between these two points denotes the nine months of pregnancy extending in an imaginary line.

THE CREATIVE ENERGY OF THE FATHER

This is an element of air and fire. The exact location of the high point of the father's energy is the site that corresponds to the end of the toenail on the inner side of the foot (see figure 46). If this site is in surplus, the masculine energy that formed the person was and remains a compressed, hard, dominant energy, with qualities of surplus in the air element.

Air in balance usually means that the father had no repressive or "negative" influence, and that relations and communication were balanced. In general, the relationship with the father is comprised of these two elements, fire and air, through which communication with another masculine energy is generated (in women as well). Thus these two elements may give us a deeper view of the relationship between the father and his newly created offspring.

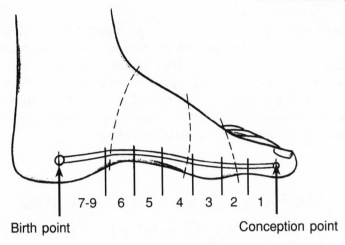

Figure 46. Nine months of pregnancy shown in the foot.

Severe surpluses and deficiencies along the line that passes through fire and air (see figure 47) give us insight into the state of the masculine energy that affected conception and early pregnancy. The paternal element is highly important to us, for it shapes many of the person's masculine energy states. In specific cases where the strength of the mother's masculine energy exceeds that of the father, the appropriate regions of the foot change, so to speak. This is because we view the father and

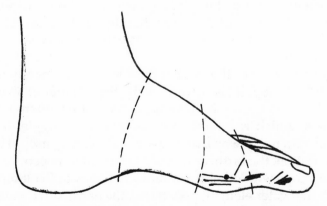

Figure 47. The progress of your fetal development can be seen in your foot. The imbalances that will affect the active, masculine energy of an adult started to develop in the early months of fetal growth—or in the early stages of the mother's pregnancy.

mother not in sexual terms, as complementary opposites, but rather in terms of the strength of their respective energies. In other words, the client's "father figure" masculine element does not necessarily reflect his or her real father (although it usually does); it may instead reflect a mother figure whose powerful masculine energy serves as the strongest source of influence on the person's masculine energy.

THE PASSIVE ENERGY OF THE MOTHER

The element of the mother is composed mainly of earth and water. During the final five months of pregnancy, we see the effect of feminine energy on the subject, as well as the nature of his or her relations with the figure who provided this feminine energy. For example, if we find many indicators referring to the process of pregnancy in the water region, while the earth region is clean and balanced, we may say that in general terms—stability of the relationship, basic trust—the ability to derive security and warmth exists, but emotional complications are present, as is a problem in establishing a deep emotional connection with this figure. An ambivalence that actually separates the two elements may be present. These months tell us how such people were maintained in the womb; how they feel in the present when faced with situations that require them to develop and grow; to what degree they accept their own feminine energy; and to what extent it is complex and problematic.

The element of the mother does more than merely maintain and develop; it also produces the first separation in a person's life. It is from this element that an independent energy emerges, which will have to wage its own struggle for balance and, in many ways, will have to take care of itself. The act of separation, the birth, often sheds light on how people carry out and cope with other separations in life. A difficult birth, in which the water element penetrated the earth, often indicates the early formation of patterns of dependency, departure, and abandonment in that subject. A cesarean section is treated like any other birth, since the markings on the foot will show how the person experienced the birth process; it is not necessarily more traumatic or problematic than a regular birth.

CONCEPTION—CREATING LIFE
FROM PASSIVE AND ACTIVE ENERGIES

The masculine element reaches its apex here, where sperm and ovum come together. The location of concern to us is the point where the toenail of the big toe joins the lower inside part of the toe (see figure 46 on page 151). Markings here indicate states of surplus and deficiency in this energy. Beauty marks and birthmarks point to genetic states that suggest problems, genetic diseases, or special genetic phenomena. Other conditions of the toes, such as webbed feet or special malformations, also indicate a genetic transfer through the masculine energy that created this person. If you encounter such a condition, and find that a similar state exists in the mother or father, you can determine which of the parents possessed the stronger masculine energy.

Often such states are evidence not of illness but of the individual's unique makeup, which can definitely serve him or her in a positive, healthy way.

PREGNANCY—THE NINE MONTHS

Pregnancy is an important process for foot analysts to observe, since injuries or disharmonious energies at any point in the pregnancy may leave physical evidence of disrupted fetal development (corresponding to the particular stage in the pregnancy when the imbalance occurred). Thus we may discern the fetal origins of behavioral, emotional, and other adult patterns. Numerous psychological theories and psychotherapeutic techniques have been formulated to try to liberate us emotionally from traumas suffered during pregnancy and birth; hypnosis and rebirthing are only two examples. In foot analysis, we concern ourselves not only with the emotional element, but also with the physical states that emotion may cause and, of course, with the way that emotions affect relations among the elements.

The nine months appear on the spinal column region of the foot, which develops throughout the pregnancy. Old markings in this region indicate an event that occurred during a particular stage of pregnancy; by correlating these with the organs that developed during that period of the pregnancy, we may determine the origin and the early patterns of a current problem. Such influences on the fetus might include a mother who did not want the baby, an unsuccessful effort to abort, medications taken by the mother at a particular stage of the pregnancy, and hunger. If, for example, one of these situations appears in the area corresponding to the month when the lungs develop, this would provide an explanation for the subject's breathing problems.

The distribution of the months on the feet is asymmetrical, since each individual experiences time differently. The fetus may experience some of the months of gestation as passing very quickly, and others, slowly. If we observe small regions of air and fire, we may infer that the beginning of the pregnancy passed very quickly, meaning that the influence of the masculine energy was short-lived and less significant relative to the duration of the experience. Physical growth takes place in the first six months, followed by emotional growth when the baby moves and feels.

Month 1—The fetus begins to develop. The circulatory system begins to function. The two hemispheres of the brain are formed. The first signs of the spinal column emerge. The muscles, liver, digestive system, face, and neck start to form. Markings that interrupt the flow indicate the possibility that damage to the head, heart, spinal column, neck, and circulatory system occurred during this formative period. Most spontaneous abortions occur during the first and second months because, if the head is injured, the fetus cannot survive.

Month 2—The face, limbs, brain tissue, skeleton, and spinal column develop. The toes and ears take shape. Muscular mobility and interaction between muscles and nerves begin. This is the month when the element of fire originates. A miscarriage at this stage indicates that the feminine energy had not succeeded in absorbing the masculine energy. A marking on the corresponding site will show difficulty in the absorption of masculine energy by feminine energy. A woman with markings in this region finds it hard to receive masculine energy, to accept men. Markings in the region indicate problems with the muscles, the tendons, and the interaction between muscle and nerve. Significant trauma in the region would cause early injury to the structure of the subject's personality, since this is where the ego resides.

Month 3—The fetus becomes more mobile. It swivels its head and controls its hands. The body is sensitive to touch. The first stage of the sucking reflex emerges. The facial muscles arrange themselves in a hereditary pattern. Fire reaches its apex during this month. We attribute markings in this area to states related to the subject's personality. In the modern era, this month is the point at which women decide whether to continue or terminate the pregnancy. Signs of the mother's indecision sometimes appear at this site. This ambivalence affects the fetus, as evidenced by extremely insecure adults, unsure if they were wanted. Such vacillation is a trauma to the person's ego.

Month 4—The nerve tissue is formed in the cartilaginous structure of the skeleton. Differences between the sexes become evident; the genitals take shape. This is the first month inside the water element. Feminine elements begin to operate. Masculine energy is no longer as strong; feminine energy begins to predominate. This is a month when the fetus has some choice as to its future. It constitutes a transition between fire and water, points of balance, a choice to survive. Near miscarriages and preventive measures (complete bed rest, stitching of the cervix) are visible in this region. The diaphragm and the upper water region are physically affected. This is a point of transition in the pregnancy from the influence of masculine to that of feminine energy, and there is a strong possibility of a clash between these energies. In such a case, there would be an indicator on the region.

Month 5—The skeleton coalesces. Fingernails, toenails, nipples, and hair are present. The length of the fetus is approximately ten inches. This is a month of water. Strong markings in this region signify fears and other emotional disturbances. (Lines flowing into the lower arch indicate fears.)

Month 6—The fetus closes its eyes voluntarily; the grasping reflex becomes stronger. The fetus' formation is nearly complete. (Some premature infants born at the end of this month survive.) This month constitutes a boundary between water and earth, indicating the connection between them. The region corresponding to the sixth month of pregnancy affects the bladder, the lower back, and the small intestine.

Months 7, 8, and 9—The fetus does little more than gain weight. The hair grows; the fetus practices sucking. In month 8 it gains at least two pounds. Starting with the middle of month 7, these are the months of the earth element. Indicators on these sites are related to problems with the lower back, fertility, and sexuality. The mother is again the predominating influence; the fetus receives most of its energy from feminine energy. These months are very significant; the symbiotic bonding of mother and child is established at this point.

BIRTH

In the region of the heel, below the ankle joint, extreme signs of surplus or deficiency indicate a specific trauma during birth. For example, an asthmatic who exhibits a birth region with a surplus in water may have swallowed amniotic fluid during birth, become entangled in the umbilical cord around the neck, or experienced breathing problems in the last month before birth. The indication of an accumulation of fluids suggests any of these.

Any marking that is not new (deep lines, beauty marks, freckles) (see figure 48), indicates events that are long past. The same is true regarding the structure of the foot. We look at the spinal column, observe indicators, and deduce what sites may have been affected by them. We examine the corresponding areas of the foot where we would expect to see signs of such influence. If indicators are present there as well, we diagnose by

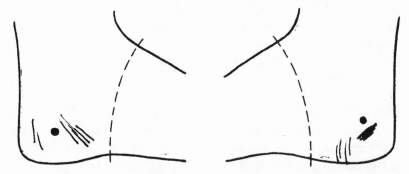

Figure 48. Signs of a difficult birth are jagged vertical markings in the region of the woman's heel. If the markings appear horizontal in the region corresponding to the uterus, it is an indication of a spontaneous or induced abortion.

inference a chronic pattern that originated very early—before the subject's earliest memories. Such indicators are difficult to interpret. Thus, to treat such conditions, we must divorce the subject from his or her conscious state (through hypnosis or rebirthing), in order to bring him or her back to the period of gestation and birth.

Pregnancy and Birth—Signs on the Foot

In women who have been pregnant, have undergone a spontaneous or induced abortion, or have given birth, foot analysis will indicate by way of markings the states of conception, pregnancy, and birth in the same regions and the same order as those relating to the woman's own period of gestation (see Figure 46 on page 151). Unlike her markings as a fetus, which appear old, the above indicators—if the pregnancy and birth were relatively recent—will appear sharper, newer, and fresher. These signs show the state of the fetus and indicate problems, illness, or other injury during the pregnancy—conditions that may correspond to the state of the mother's spinal column and the organs involved in the development of the fetus. Women often experience the same pregnancy and birth that they themselves underwent as babies, and the markings connect with each other. Signs of a spontaneous or induced abortion appear in the form of a horizontal indicator on the region corresponding to the uterus, in the earth element, that interrupts the natural flow (see figure 48). A difficult and problematic birth appears as a jagged, vertical marking. In principle, an experienced foot analyst can identify the markings of several births.

9

ENERGY PATTERNS

By carefully observing the lines on the feet, we can discover the direction of the energy flow, as well as any states of imbalance within the flow (see figure 49 on page 160). In the region corresponding to pregnancy and birth, we see lines that signal an excessive and/or interrupted flow. Lines that indicate an interruption of flow are characteristic of some aspect of energy that did not develop properly, hence obstructing the development of the fetus. A "dissociation line" of this type in the area of the fourth month suggests that masculine energy was obstructed and engaged in a struggle with feminine energy. A "flow line" signifies excessive energy flow. Such a line in the region of the third month points to danger, fear, or a desire to abort the fetus. A length line in the region of the fourth month indicates a triumph of masculine energy over feminine energy; such lines in the region of the last months of pregnancy show an excessive flow near the end of gestation, and may indicate an acceleration of the development process and the subject's premature birth.

Since water naturally tends to flow downward, transverse lines or folds in the water region indicate an interruption in the flow of water energy, a classic sign of constipation. Such people are emotionally constipated as well. Length lines in the water region point to an excessively swift or otherwise exceptionally strong flow, and are characteristic of people with diarrhea and tendencies to hysteria. Vertical and transverse lines in the water region point to a combination of hysteria and emotional blockage, coupled with chaotic physical symptoms in the abdomen. Most people display a combination of this type.

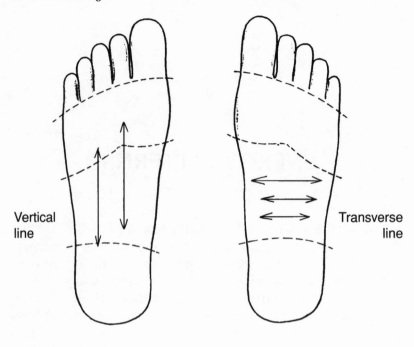

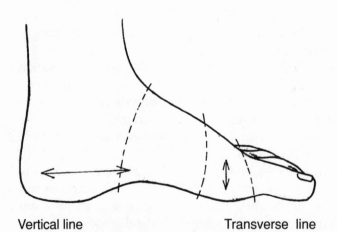

Figure 49. Two typical lines found on the foot—transverse lines (lateral lines) block the flow of element energy while vertical lines (that run the "length" of the foot) are indicative of an excessive flow of energy.

Sexual Flow—the Wave of Sexual Energy

Equilibrium in the flow of sexual energies is indicated by a gradual shifting of colors from the earth region to the head with no flow interruptions along the way. Although sexual energy is represented by the earth element, sexuality is composed of all the elements and must flow upward to the air. When people's sexuality resides in their air element, they have earth in their air and can neither think nor exercise control. A moment occurs during orgasm in which the earth energy drains away, causing an altered level of awareness and perception as a state of ecstasy takes hold within the air element. This sexual energy must then return to earth along the pregnancy/birth line (see figure 50 on page 162).

Sexuality embraces all the elements in all the sexual contexts: the sex organ, the emotions it arouses, the performance of the sex act, and the individual's perception of sex. When earth and water are dissociated, a subject may have sexual relations but fail to experience these relations in the other elements. If the dissociation falls within the water region, some aspect of the subject's emotions prevents the ascent of his or her sexual energy.

A dissociation in the fire region is characteristic of people who cannot relinquish their self-control. The more pronounced this dissociation is, the harder it is for them to "let go" and the more vigorously they try to control their sexuality.

A dissociation with air is indicative of inhibitions connected with perception, thought, critical faculties, and social norms. Such people rarely "lose their heads." Intelligence correlates with sex. "Primitive" people experience much less sexual satisfaction, engaging in sex for the purpose of procreation only. Animals know nothing of sexual enjoyment; they recognize need only. Indeed, the earth element represents need. While man can meet this need on levels other than earth alone, some people experience sex strictly on the earth level. The adherents of some religions, for example, practice sex for procreation and nothing else; enjoyment, pleasure, thought, and actions exceeding the necessary minimum are proscribed.

Our use of the term *orgasm* embraces not only the male ejaculation or the woman's experience of the sex act, but a mingling of all the elements. People inhibit their sexual energies

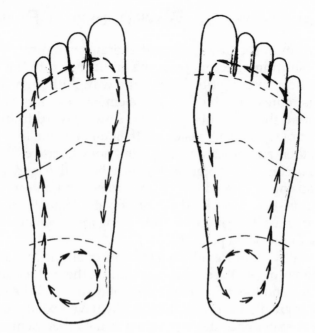

Figure 50. The flow of sexual energy progresses from the heel to the small toe, then on to the big toe, down through the spinal column area and back to the heel.

in an area in which they are already experiencing trouble. Wherever we see a problematic element, we should expect to encounter sexual problems there, too.

Sexuality is a passive energy that flows into active energy and then returns to its passive state. Strong-willed people inhibit the ascent of their passivity lest this cause them to lose control. The greater his need for dominance and control, the poorer the male's sexual performance will be, since sexual energy is a passive energy. When the flow is harmonious, the sex act is long and slow; a faster flow signifies control and much nonpassive activity.

The little toe is an indicator of sexual flow in the head; its appearance tells us how the client's head is dealing with sexuality. If the toe is enlarged and swollen, sexual energy is obstructed inside the head, indicating a problem in the subject's perception of his or her sexual energy. The absence of a striding mark on the foot indicates a lack of sexual flow. We encounter this condition in children, women who reach old age without engaging in sex, persons who remain celibate for religious reasons, and people who have planted their sexual needs in the earth. Unaware that these needs are present in every other element, such people experience difficulties in the earth region.

Subjects whose sexual energies are in equilibrium should have a striding mark spanning roughly one-fourth the width of the foot. If it is larger, earth or fire (depending on the color) has usurped territory belong to water. If it is smaller, then water has ascended to and usurped the space where fire and earth meet. Most blockages occur between earth and fire, because our education and culture do not permit a smooth, uninterrupted flow.

FLOW FROM MOUTH TO ANUS

This term refers to the flow of energy that enters the body. It embraces food, water, the air we breathe, comprehension, and insight (transcending mere thought, which does not involve all the elements). The larger category of flow from mouth to rectum contains numerous subcategories.

Breathing

This is a bidirectional flow between air and fire and, in part, to water as well due to the movement of the diaphragm (see figure 51 on page 164). Any interruption of this movement causes a disruption of breathing. We see this most clearly in toes 1 and 2 (air and fire) and in the region corresponding to fire. An asthma marking indicates excessive flow as well as blockages. Stridor (breath stoppage in infants and young children) appears only in the form of blockages.

Digestion

This flow moves from air to fire (the stomach), passes through and commingles with water, and exits in earth (the rectum, situated on the boundary between fire and earth) [see figure 52 on page 165]. Any sign of blockage in this region points at a dis-

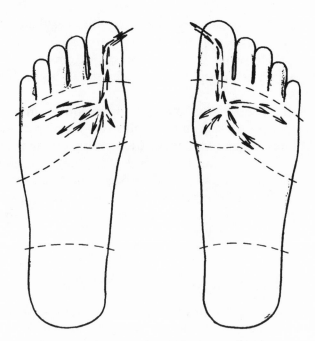

Figure 51. The flow of the breath through the big toe in the air element into the fire area. This flow is bidirectional.

ruption of the digestive process. An ulcer appears as an indented line on the part on the foot corresponding to the stomach, since such a condition is characteristic of a blockage between air and earth. Lengthwise lines in this area point at overly rapid digestion; the body has insufficient time to take advantage of the nutritional value of the food ingested.

This observation applies not only to food but to anything we experience. Learning, for example, must be digested. We absorb material by way of the air; material becomes stuck at the site where we ourselves are already "stuck," i.e., in the water region for people lacking in self-confidence, and in the fire region for those who cannot master the material. People who do not understand what they learn are considered stuck in their air; others, who are stuck in earth, never even reach the point of learning.

The digestive process is completed when water is absorbed into earth; any unimportant or irrelevant material is expelled via the rectum. The problem is that many people disregard what

1 MOUTH	10 TRANVERSE COLON
2 THROAT	11 DESCENDING COLON
3 ESOPHAGUS	12 RECTUM
4 STOMACH	13 ANUS
5 DUODENUM	14 ILEOCECAL VALVE
6 DUODENUM	15 APPENDIX
7 LIVER	16 KIDNEY
8 SMALL INTESTINE	17 URETER
9 ASCENDING COLON	18 BLADDER

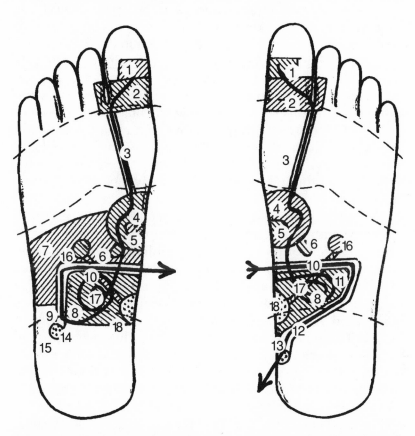

Figure 52. The flow of digestion. The movement of energy through the digestive system as expressed through the feet. Includes digestion through extraction.

counts and retain what doesn't. Everything that happens to us in life undergoes a process of digestion. For example, most of us review the events of the day before falling asleep, paying particular attention to what we consider important. If we become "stuck" at a particular incident, we cannot free ourselves of it in the morning. If we are able to get past it, it forfeits its hold on us. When we allow our active energies to rest, thus giving the passive ones room to function, absorption takes place in all the elements. Our passive energies are meant to operate at night and our active energies by day. When obstructions exist in water, we experience constipation and cannot sleep well since our active energy fails to "shut down" as it should, leaving our passive energy unable to realize its full potential.

For the process of absorption to be complete, everything we absorb must pass through all the elements on its way to earth. People with transverse indentations in the water region have slow instinctive responses, since their digestive process is slow. This observation applies to both the physical process of excretion and to the speed of their other responses following absorption and digestion. Transverse indentations in the water region of the foot reveal things that we have always found hard to digest, while lengthwise markings in the same area point to things we have digested too quickly. An unsuccessful attempt to pass things through ourselves at excessive speed elicits crisscross indentations.

What we wish to see is a cycle formed by the subject's sexual and mouth-to-rectum flow patterns. Wherever this cycle is broken, we encounter a chronic problem that has become "stuck" at the site. The earth-to-air and air-to-earth flows take place concurrently at all times. In order to know the cause of a disruption, we attempt to find the place at which the flow was interrupted. Alternatively, indicators related to the direction of flow can help us determine why the flow has been speeded up. For example, a blockage in the fire region is indicative of people whose ego stifles their ability to digest things. These people are so burdened with theories about what is permissible and how things should be done that they deny themselves the ability to feel many things. By contrast, allergy lines signify a spurt of water, an excessively rapid flow. Lines flowing upward from the earth region (over the spleen and liver) indicate a highly intensive earth element, possibly an indicator of arthritis.

SPINAL COLUMN FLOW

An additional type of flow is connected to the central nervous system. It manifests the kind of control exercised by an air element that rises to all parts of the body. Its focal points are the cranium and the spinal column, since these are the centers from which the nerves governing all sensory and motor activity, as well as communication with internal organs, branch out to every part of the body. Accordingly, these pathways intermingle not only in fire and air but also within the other elements (see figure 53).

The air element, by way of the head and spinal column, is able to clutch the other three elements in its own embrace. If we view the spinal column as a large pipe from which many narrow pipes branch out to all parts of the body, we can differentiate between two patterns of flow, one within the "main" and another in the smaller pipes. The flow of energy between the two kinds of pipes takes place in both directions simultaneously. We also know of an ascending and descending flow within the "main" or the spinal column; it manifests itself in the way we load and unload this energy through a constant cycle of action and reaction. In other words, when we sense something, the message reaches our air and elicits a physical response such as movement or a change in the concentration of the air element at the site. The touch of someone's hand, for example, creates a localized concentration of the particular

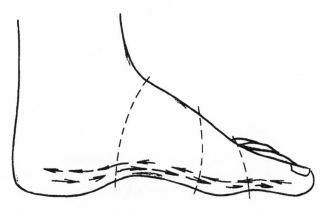

Figure 53. The flow of energy in the spinal column. This flow is bidirectional.

sensation produced by the contact. When a stranger touches us by accident on a train, this creates a state of dissociation from the point of the contact.

Lengthwise lines along the region of the foot corresponding to the spinal column suggest the presence of a stepped-up, excessive flow in this area (similar to the lines indicating diarrhea or fear in the water element). Such lines signify a surplus in a particular region, manifested by localized sensitivity and hyperactivity. When we examine the client's spinal column by studying the transverse bands dividing the foot, we may find lengthwise lines superimposed on one of the bands. This indicates a strong surplus flow of the specific energy located in that band. The physical manifestations of this condition might be a nerve disturbance at the site, causing hypersensitivity (see figure 54).

Transverse lines signify an obstruction of the flow of the spinal column; the subject's energy is "stuck" and cannot reach its destination. For example, an indication of blockage in the area corresponding to the lower back may signify a ruptured disc caused by intravertebral pressure. Such a condition creates pressure on a nerve, interfering with its proper functioning. Sciatica is an example of such a condition. These lines, depending on the bands in which they are situated as well as the part

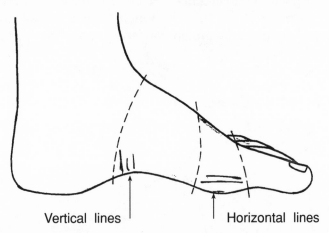

Vertical lines   Horizontal lines

Figure 54. Lines on the region of the foot corresponding to the spinal column. Vertical lines indicate blocks relating to the spine. Horizontal lines indicate an excessive flow of energy in the spine.

of the body served by the nerves branching from this particular point of the spinal column, indicate a decline of flow, weakness, and loss of function at a given site. In any such instance, we may encounter pain or impaired functioning in those parts of the body corresponding to the entire width of the band where the symptoms occur.

Since this energy emanates from air, which intermingles with the other elements and strives to energize and sensualize them, we observe the elements and bodily regions in which our subjects' natural intensity is amplified or diminished. In this fashion, too, we may verify conclusions previously reached in our examination of the four elements on the underside of the foot; we may also double-check the presence of the conditions we identified there. We usually find a perfect correlation between the spinal column and the four elements. When discrepancies arise, we must examine the markings carefully for two possibilities that distort the picture: they may be old scars on the region corresponding to the spinal column, or they may reflect an injury on the underside of the foot.

FLOW TO THE ARMS AND LEGS

This rubric embraces two kinds of flows: that emanating from the spinal column to the limbs and those of the specific element from which the limbs supply fire to the hands (see figure 55 on page 170), earth to the legs. In other words, the entire element of fire and part of air flow through the hands; the feet contain the flow of the entire earth element and part of water.

Examining the condition of the limbs, we must first observe the transverse bands related to them on the feet, i.e., all of fire and the lower band of air, and all of earth and the lower band of water. The qualities we identify in these elements give us an indication of the type of energy flowing through the arms and legs. This alone, however, is not enough, since the arms and legs themselves may be in states of imbalance (other element energy is manifesting). We therefore examine the limbs themselves, as reflected in the foot, to locate lengthwise or transverse indicators (on the spinal column, for instance) or other signs of another element.

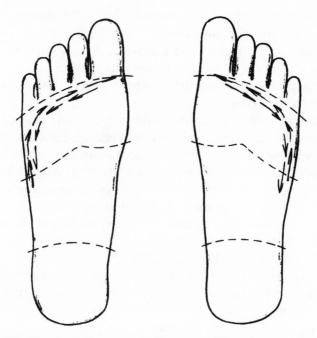

Figure 55. The flow of energy to the arms. The energy moves from the spinal column at the joint of the big toe, underneath the toes and down to the arm area located below the big toe. The flow is bidirectional.

The arms and legs, by permitting us to act and to be mobile, constitute our interface with the world. Our examination tells us, literally, how people "stand on their own two feet." Injury to the feet signifies damage to the earth element and to the lower portion of water. Problems on the foot are frequently byproducts of trouble elsewhere, e.g., in the lower spinal column. Circulatory disorders in the foot may arise from problems in lower water and the entire region governing sex hormones.

The hands reflect what people do with their lives; they express people's creative power, charisma, and ability to construct reality out of ideas. Injury to the hands impairs all those things and points to a problem in the flow of these forces. Usually we can see very clearly the decline in quality and balance of the lower fire and air elements on the underside of the foot.

10

EXPRESSING TIME

It is their personal histories that make our subjects what they are; hence we should view their lives as a process unfolding through time. A chronic pattern is something that people do repeatedly throughout their lives. Marks on the foot, such as lines of parting, lines of surgery, and the like—remnants of all those unresolved traumas that created lingering imbalance—represent attempts by the subject's energy to reinstate equilibrium. It is important that we note these markings when presenting subjects with pictures of themselves as reflected in their feet. By understanding how patterns build up over time, we may show our subjects how they repeat the same actions, and experience the same feelings, throughout their lives.

Physically speaking, it is easy to see how an existing pattern coalesced over the years. The order of events composing the pattern is also important for us. For example, a five-year-old boy with severe chronic earaches may have developed the habit of raising his shoulder in the direction of the afflicted ear in order to mitigate the pain. This shrugging motion, repeated over a lengthy period of time, creates a pattern independent of the earaches, a pattern that persists even after the earaches have ceased. If the shoulder is continually held in this position the neck is also thrown off kilter, and the body becomes especially susceptible to lower-back pressure. As an adult, the subject may suffer from chronic headaches originating in the nape of the neck or radiating upward from the lower-back region.

Most chronic patterns are formed by the end of physical maturation (age 20–25). The passage of time is manifested on the foot starting from the edge of the heel and continuing toward the toes. This picture mirrors the subject's development

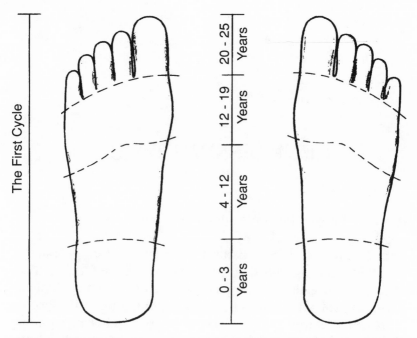

Figure 56. Time as expressed in the feet. The earth element represents 0–3 years of age; the water element age 3–12; the fire element age 12–19; and the air element age 19–25. This is the complete cycle of a fully developed person.

and patterns from birth to age 20–25. The locations of markings along this continuum are indicative of the age at which a given pattern took root. The element in which the marking is found indicates which energy was dominant during that period; by observing the change in the quality of this element, we can predict the type of pattern that may appear (see figure 56).

Within the earth region, we may identify signs of patterns that became entrenched up to age 3, since earth is the most intensive element during the first three years of life. The passive energy that typifies this period usually emanates from the mother, although there are cases where the father is the stronger source. The passivity of these years is reflected in the fact that children at this stage of life give nothing to the world; they merely receive. They require a maximum of security, support, and satisfaction of basic needs. Most of their activity occurs on an instinctive level. An imbalance that hardens into a pattern at this age determines how people relate to their earth energy and that of others, how they construct the frameworks of their lives, how they treat their own children, and how they develop sexuality and sensuality.

Since the earth element reflects our physicality, signs of weakness here may be indicative of individuals who were very sick during this period of their childhood and who suffer from general weakness even today. Something in the quality of this basic energy was degraded. This is usually visible in the overall shape of the heel, its size and texture, all of which point to weakness and deficiency in the earth element.

The closer the markings are to the water element, the closer our age of reference is to 3 years. This is because water is the element that typifies ages 3–12. Although children are still primarily influenced by and dependent on their mother during this period, their emotional world is beginning to take shape. They are preoccupied with emotional energy—fear, anger, irritability, jealousy, frustration, guilt. These forces are highly visible during this period, and imbalances unresolved at this age create permanent patterns connected with these forms of energy.

As we approach the fire element, the point where passive and active energies meet, we pass through the area of puberty—the stage at which most cultures celebrate rites of passage—marking the transformation of boys and girls into men and women. This is the time when the menstrual cycle usually begins and sexual hormones become active. Voices change, behavior clearly shifts, breasts and pubic hair begin to appear. The longer the stage of adolescence is extended or delayed, the longer the dominant influence of the mother persists. In the foot, we see evidence of this in the larger area occupied by the water and earth elements.

During the difficult years of adolescence—ages 13–17—there is an attempt to strike a balance between the entrenched passive forces and the active forces that have just begun to develop and gain strength. It is at this age that the conflict between the internalization and externalization of emotions surfaces, in keeping with the structure of the individual's self-image and ego. It is a difficult struggle, one that often causes teenagers considerable agony. In cases where a permanent pattern has developed, markings on the boundary between fire and water indicate how harsh a conflict it was.

The fire region embraces the years between puberty (12–14) and approximately 19 years of age, during which the masculine energy becomes dominant. It is in the fire element that patterns of behavior and bodily movement are formed, the self-image is established, and the ego begins to take shape. Although the ego often retains its original structure, it may continue to change throughout life due to the basic active nature of fire. This is an age when we are exceedingly preoccupied with our appearance. As our identity begins to coalesce, there is a tendency to become caught up in various beliefs and ideals that guide what we do and how we act. Many people make choices during this period that will affect the course of their lives—choices of occupation, areas of interest, pastimes, and pursuits. The patterns governing our social relationships and interactions are also established during these years, as are the traits of courage and daring that mark the rest of our lives. The fire element is the most important component of creativity, and it is during this period that most people choose between a creative and a "routine" way of life.

The time frame spanning 20–25 years of age is reflected in the air element. The patterns in the other three elements are largely entrenched by now; they virtually dictate individuals' ways of thinking and perceptions of the world. For example, people with a pronounced pattern of anxiety can hardly be expected to become cognitively and ideologically receptive to new horizons. People controlled by their basic needs are unlikely to take the time to cultivate the qualities of thought or spirituality. It is during these young-adulthood years that people shape their world view and the direction in which they learn and develop. It is a rare individual who modifies his or her world view after this stage; in fact, most of us attempt to defend it at all costs.

It should be noted that imbalances may appear and leave their mark in any element at any age. However, the period in which a particular element is dominant marks the stage when the pattern related to that element takes root. Signs of imbalance in a given element before it has reached its peak put the development of that element at risk. This point should be brought to the subject's attention during the reading, lest the pattern in question become entrenched. For example, pronounced markings in the fire element of a boy of 3 suggest a difficulty involving his active, masculine energy, as well as a problem with the ego, that marker of individual identity. If the state is not modified or resolved, chances are strong that this pre-existent pattern will intensify and coalesce during adolescence, thus ruling out the possibility of future change.

An alternative way of reading the time dimension is through the nine months of gestation. The markings we observe on the spinal cord (representing the period of gestation or the area of the foot corresponding to the spinal cord) generally correspond with chronic patterns that we identify on the foot in the same transverse strip. A connection exists between fetal experiences and postnatal events.

How do we know the age of a marking on the foot? In all signs of surplus and deficiency, some may be characterized as old and others as new. The following list indicates markings that are new (3–6 months):

- Red blotches;

- Delicate, wet peelings;

- Blemishes;

- Strong, red markings in the water region;

- Deep, red grooves;

- Extreme sensitivity to touch;

- Hypertonicity without lumps or rigidity;

- Changes in epidermal texture;

- Old beauty marks. (Generally indicative of a congenital or longstanding imbalance);

- Thin, white, indistinct grooves that start to resemble the texture of the surrounding skin.

Markings older than six months are as follows:

- Calluses or structural changes that cannot be restored to their original state. (Strong indications of earth in fire and air are very old, since it took a great deal of time for the region to acquire the attributes of an element originally alien to it);

- Very dry, deep, white-colored groove, lighter than the colors of the foot but evidently part of the foot;

- Crystals;

- Numb sensitivity. (Dull pain is an indicator of a longstanding, chronic problem);

- Tough calcified "stone" that "cracks" but is not a crystal. (Hypertonicity that has hardened into a lump);

- Changes in the texture of underlying layers of skin.

The more embedded an indicator is within the structure of the foot, or the greater the structural modification it has caused (e.g., deformed toes or rigidity/immobility in any joint), the more longstanding the condition is.

The structure of the foot is a function of bone and skeleton; it provides information about a subject's potential. Structural changes are determined during gestation or early childhood. Problems or symptoms may appear at advanced ages only, even though the structure of the foot indicates they are a result of an earlier imbalance. In young people who have not yet completed their growth process, signs on the foot appear more dynamic and changeable than those of adults, since they are not yet indelible.

To learn how time leaves its mark on people's feet, we select several common indicators that represent states that have immediate, nonrecurring effects. These might be separation, surgery, death, or fear-induced shock. (The latter manifests itself in a line on the kidney-pancreas strip; if the fear is associated with a sexual incident, it appears closer to the earth element.) We then ask the subject when the aforementioned events took place. Once we know how old these markings are, we deduce the age of other indicators.

The feet may reflect the subject's actual chronological age or they may appear younger or older. Senescence (old age) and youth are functions of a person's energy. Young people with old feet burn their energy very rapidly. They live intensely and may have undergone many strenuous experiences that they took badly. Such people view themselves as older than their age. Older people with young feet may view themselves as younger than their age; alternatively, life has simply passed them by. Senescence is a state of steadily declining energy. The less energy there is, the harder it is to restore balance; consequently, seniors take longer than younger people to convalesce after an illness. Old age manifests itself in tissue loss, general deficiency, cold, dryness, stiffening of joints, and calcification of bones.

The age of a given indicator on the foot is highly significant because it shows us how long the problem we are addressing has been entrenched. Does the problem originate in a chronic pattern of long standing, or is it the result of a recent situation? Such precise pinpointing is less important among the very aged, since five years more or less is insignificant when speaking of patterns that date back twenty-five years. In general, the advice we offer our subjects is influenced by the duration of a particular pattern. If the pattern has very early roots, we refer the person for treatment; here we may play a useful role by preparing him or her for protracted therapy. A current pattern may be related to aspects of life style, in which case immediate changes may be possible.

Remember, the process of reading periods of time on the foot is highly important to our work; it may elevate the results of our reading from a mere collection of details to a life history.

11

THE TOES

The Western perspective regards the head as the most important and complex part of the body. We tend to believe that since the head houses the brain, it controls the entire body. This is not true. The brain controls the nervous system alone; its domain does not extend to the energetic quality of each element.

In search of information about the state of the air element, we examine the toes. Air is typically all-embracing and all-encompassing; as such, it contains all the other elements. The toes exhibit indicators of the subject's intelligence: IQ, conceptual and learning skills, organization, memory, creativity, and processing of information. The state of the air, i.e., of the toes, tells us how people use their intelligence, how they learn, and so forth. It should be stressed that intelligence is not necessarily related to formal study and information gathering.

In order for a person's intelligence to be balanced, it must contain all the elements. It must be rooted in earth, meaning that the subject must be on the earth in order to be capable of, and receptive to, new learning. The water element must be present both for the purpose of digesting things and as a characteristic of fear. Fear forces us to grow, gain strength, overcome; it is what causes us to grow and develop (as long as it is not overabundant). Fire gives us the impetus to learn. Potential without motivation is not enough; without the ambition to transcend our limitations, we do nothing with our potential. (For example, long toes containing a small fire element are indicative of people who fail to put their intelligence to use.) The air element points at intuition; it shows how capable people are of acquiring new knowledge and transcending the limits of their old information.

In order for intelligence to find expression, the remaining elements, i.e., those other than fear, must approach a state of balance. If the potential of air is large and the other elements are out of balance, the latter will thwart any efforts by the subject to realize the potential of his or her intelligence.

Intelligence is not defined by one element alone; all the elements play a role in its utilization. A certain degree of ambition and strength is needed, as reflected in the fire element of the foot. (Fire heats the air, allowing it to rise.) Water plays a role in the digestion and processing of information absorbed. Earth sustains the connection with reality, the frame within which the subject acts, the organization of material, and the acquired confidence that provides the freedom to develop.

Like any other potential, intelligence can be in deficiency or in surplus—unrealized or overemphasized. Such states may be permanent or variable. Intelligence and curiosity correlate; the more curious people are, the more they ask, investigate, and know. The tendency toward specialization has created a culture that often asks questions that lead in one direction only. There are fewer people whose questions take them along multiple paths. (Their toes are splayed; each is different in appearance.) Such people harbor many conflicts; they possess a readiness to ask and struggle, coupled with an ability to relate to different things that are not part of their customary perspective.

Intelligent people are aware that they know only a small proportion of what they are capable of knowing. With regard to over 90 percent of a given subject, they don't even know how much they don't know. Something about knowing is an obstruction to learning; one's readiness not to know makes one capable of learning more. The learning process integrates all the elements; the state of each element tells us how an individual goes about it.

Since everything is represented in the toes, they provide us with an opportunity to verify what we have observed on the foot as a whole. The toes are not a striding region. Since air has to be free, the toes must be easily raised; they must not be stuck in the earth element. Orderly people have neatly arrayed toes; the toes of the absent-minded are splayed. When one strides, the foot is raised and is located entirely within the element of air. At this stage it must be relaxed. If it is kept in this elevated position, we may infer that the head is putting out a high level of effort.

When we observe the toes, we first examine whether their state corresponds to the subject's original potential. Do the toes stride or don't they? Are they straight, crooked, cramped tightly together, or loosely relaxed? Are they arrayed harmoniously? In a balanced state, the toes will decrease in length progressively, without deviations of size, length, or form. Such a state indicates highly developed intelligence and basic potential.

People whose air is in balance do not overstep their boundaries. Their thinking or intuition lacks uniqueness; they get along just fine with what they've got and are disinclined to develop anything new. Air in balance tells us that the subject is not engulfed in struggle and does not attempt to advance. Such people are in a rut; there is nothing to push them forward.

Elements that penetrate air are indicative of the subject's way of thinking. An invasion by earth is a sign of practical, organized thought. Such a person craves order and has a need to solve problems. Water in air points at emotional thinking, a person beset with "fear." Fire in air is a sign of thinking related to doing, implementation, command, and control. Air in air reflects clean, lucid thought. The exact location of element surpluses in the toes is significant, too. We will treat this matter at greater length later. Air is partitioned in the following four ways:

- By the toes
- By the eyes and ears
- By lateral division
- By lengthwise division.

PARTITIONING BY THE TOES

Each toe illustrates how the head relates to each of the elements, how it regards sexuality, emotions, and so forth. The head is only our instrument of observation; it is not our vehicle for experiencing things. The state of the toes corresponds to the state of the elements; when a toe has an unusual appearance in its air element, we expect to find something unusual in the element itself. See figure 57 on page 182.

Toe 1: Air (the toe of thought)—This toe shows how we perceive ourselves and external objects; it manifests the articu-

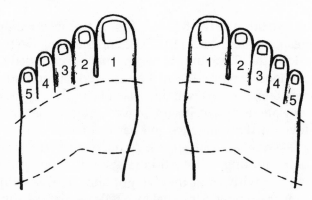

Figure 57. Toes and their corresponding elements. Toe 1 corresponds with air and signifies the head, thinking and perception; Toe 2 corresponds with fire and signifies the chest, heart, courage and charisma; Toe 3 is the boundary between fire and water and signifies balance and the diaphragm; Toe 4 corresponds with water and signifies the liver, spleen, and emotiveness; and Toe 5 corresponds with earth, signifying the uterus, prostate, sexuality, fertility, and money.

lation of our masculine energy. It indicates thinking; information that enters by way of the eyes and ears becomes organized in the big toe. The size of this toe and its pad are highly significant. The larger the toe pad, the more room there is for thinking. Where the pad is huge and the rest of the toe small, we may infer that the subject's thinking is strongly dominated by air. When such people think, that is all they do; no other element is allowed to intrude.

A small, conical big toe is a sign of a manic-depressive state—either a predisposition or the real thing. People experiencing an attack of depression do not exercise their processes of thought and control. The place they describe is gloomy and unlit, since thinking is a form of light. The less internal light there is, the smaller the big toe. People who tend to depression prefer not to think. Thinking depresses them; they would rather act and experience. They are capable of thinking but not of building thought or a lasting thought process. People entrenched in a familiar, well-ordered world fail to absorb new things and cannot transcend the limits of their thoughts. In both cases, the process of reception and the use of information do not reflect intelligence.

Let us observe through the following examples how the square-shaped big toe relates to the other toes. People whose big toe is square and whose other toes descend in a harmonious and balanced fashion are "square" thinkers. They let logic dominate; they do not break down barriers. We would not expect them to be trailblazers or inventors. A square big toe with a longer toe 2 is characteristic of people in conflict. On one hand, they are "square" thinkers. On the other hand, when they comprehend they do so in a manner that oversteps all logic and order: consequently, they are confused. They can't help perceiving things beyond the constraints of logic; once they've done so, however, they have to press what they've absorbed into tidy, square frameworks (ideal for a foot analyst).

Framework and intuition have to strike a balance. People who absorb by intuition only cannot communicate their findings to others. This is not intelligence.

Toe 2: Fire (the toe of action)—This toe connects with our faculties of communication, sight, empathy, extrasensory perception, perception of others, and sensitivity or insensitivity to things outside the subject's own boundaries. While the length of toe 2 has no appreciable affect on intelligence, it is significant as an indicator of the subject's ability to transcend the boundaries of his or her "I." If the toe is long and crosses the boundaries of the head, the subject is the kind of person who can act without thinking. These are emotional, intuitive, empathetic people. Those who cannot contain their ego (fire), whose emotionalism has damaged their ego, curl the toe into a tentlike shape, causing their air to lose some of its airiness. They literally walk on air, creating a striding zone, which in turn allows earth to invade.

Children whose second toe is shorter than the other toes may have a cerebral problem. In adults, the syndrome may point to a family problem (perhaps connected with one of the children) or insensitivity to others. Toe 2 represents action; it is the one we observe if the subject asks us to tell him or her how to behave in the future. Space between toes 1 and 2 indicates a discrepancy between action and thought.

Toe 3: Balance Between Water and Fire (the toe of balance)—This toe tells us about the subject's equilibrium. Genetic illnesses that affect general equilibrium show up here.

If toe 3 is much shorter or much longer than toes 2 and 4, a basic disequilibrium of some kind (emotional, motoric, mental, and so forth) may be present. If this syndrome is coupled with beauty marks on the region connected with fertility, we conclude that the source of the imbalance lies in a genetic problem. This indicator may point to a family member's imbalance rather than one affecting the subjects themselves. Anything unusual in toe 3 points at an imbalance; this, coupled with additional indicators in other regions of the foot, such as the example provided above, leads us to the source of the condition.

This toe is connected with the kidney—to fear, the emotion that safeguards us. Fear strikes a balance between our drives and the need for caution. Toe 3 is also associated with sight. To discover what people do with their fear in their thought processes, we note the element that reigns supreme in this toe. Fire is a sign of control of one's fear; dominance of water indicates that the subject treats fear by repression.

Toe 4: Water (the toe of emotion)—Toe 4 corresponds to the liver in the right foot and the spleen in the left. This toe is connected with blame, guilt, and anger, as well as hearing, attention, and inward absorption. Intelligent people acknowledge the existence of their feelings even though they are not obliged to let these emotions control them. Unusual markings on toe 4 suggest a problem with air and water. The subject may have hearing problems (since toe 4 corresponds to the ears). People who are filled with anger (water) are incapable of listening (ear = air); they cannot let things enter.

Toe 5: Earth (the toe of needs)—This toe reflects the state of the earth element as it occurs within air. Sexuality is one of the aspects of intelligence, and toe 5 indicates how people perceive their sexuality. Intelligent people acknowledge that they have needs that must be accorded due importance.

Toes 4 and 5 tell us how people obtain information through their ears. We needn't do anything in order to hear; the act of hearing is a passive one. Information absorbed through our faculty of hearing has to activate the air and form a link between our thought processes and the sound received. People are capable of hearing and thinking at the same time, even if the message heard and the substance of the thought are unrelated.

Toes 2 and 3 indicate how people receive information through their eyes, how things "enter" them by this medium.

Eyes can be opened and closed, making them an active form of reception that entails control and muscle activity. Absorption by way of sight is active in an additional sense: we have something to say about everything that we see. Visual reception is always related to analysis, explanation, the assignment of names. These toes signify judgment and critical faculties, since we critique what we see.

Most people have separate and unequal aural and visual capacities. To determine whether a subject absorbs more by way of sight or by hearing, we compare the height of toes 2 and 3 with that of toes 4 and 5. Those who favor hearing have stronger passive energy and tend to passivity; those who prefer the visual sense possess a stronger active energy and tend to be active, to participate, to speak, and to initiate action. Different combinations of toes indicate how our subjects' sight and hearing interrelate and how they process what they absorb through their senses.

Adjusting to a completely new place is a very difficult process because it is an encounter with the new and the unknown. It forces us to catalogue and assign names to everything we absorb (much as we had to do in our infancy). To determine the subject's ability to adjust, we connect toes 4 and 5 with toes 2 and 3 and the big toe. Toe 5 reflects earth, toe 4 water. Since the elements of water and earth are dominant in our first three years of life, we may regard them as mirroring the childhood process of learning. These are the years in which we learn by listening, imitation, and mimicking. Sight is less crucial in this kind of learning process. Our examination of these toes shows us what kind of child our subject was during these years. These are the years in which warmth and basic self-confidence ("I am wanted") are inculcated and the capacity to cope with fear is built up; it is then that our subjects construct a realistic basis for life. If they experienced trauma during these years, we encounter weightier evidence of subsequent listening problems ("listening" being the ability to absorb external information quietly). Such people are filled with fear; so acutely does their fear preoccupy them that they cannot pay attention to any other endogenous or exogenous input.

Any combination of overlapping toes indicates an interplay of elements. One toe above another signals that the higher one has assumed an active, dominant role, and that the one

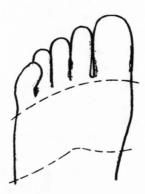

Figure 58. Toe 5 is curled under toe 4, indicating the domination of emotions over earth energy.

underneath has given up, forfeiting its strength. By observing which toe has overlapped which other toe, we may understand what people do to themselves. And, by direct extension, to others.

If toe 5 is curled under toe 4 (see figure 58 above), water has penetrated and dominated the earth element in the foot. This signals the presence of acute fear centering on survival, sexuality, and the power of the emotional past over this person.

When toe 2 is overlapping toe 1 (see figure 59 below), the energy of fire (of control) has taken control of the subject's thought. When such people process data, they tend to think subjectively rather than objectively (how they wish things to be with respect to their ego). These are people who hear what

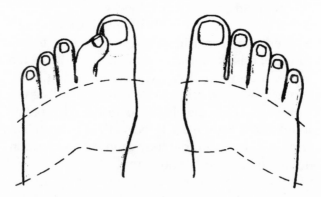

Figure 59. Toe 2 on toe 1 indicates action dominating thinking.

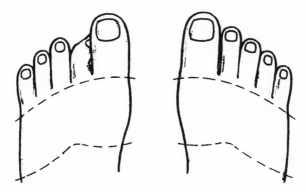

Figure 60. Toe 1 on toe 2 indicates ideas dominate action.

they want to hear. Their verbal responses to others' stimuli are sharp, dominated by fire. Such people typically suffer from heartburn and migraines originating in the stomach.

Toe 1 overlapping toe 2 (see figure 60 above), indicates people who control their egos and actions by ignoring the fact that their egos also have needs. Such people's activity, creativity, self-expression, and ambition are impaired, since all of these pass through a filter of criticism that generally prevents their exit. Since the toe representing outward-directed sight is hidden, these people are preoccupied with thoughts of how they view others and concern themselves greatly with how others view them. At the same time, their ability to perceive themselves and others is nil.

If toes 1 and 2 are very long (see figure 61 on page 188), and the other toes are short, the air energy expresses itself through a strong masculine element. We expect to observe a very low level of passive energy in the foot, but some people ignore this energy, believing it is needed for comprehension and thought only.

Overlapping is not the only indicator of such conditions. A subject's toes may be crowded together, signifying elements in conflict, or spread widely apart, indicating a separation between adjacent elements. Western culture stresses the primacy of thought and action, represented by toes 1 and 2, over emotions and unspoken needs. Few people take account of their needs; many engage in pursuits they don't like and that don't feel right to them. Not enough people treat their feelings about

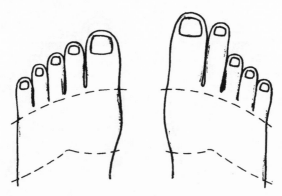

Figure 61. Toe 1 and 2 are very long. This indicates a strong potential of active intellectual and empathic abilities.

what they must do with the importance they deserve; few permit their needs and emotions to play a role in their decision making.

SEEING AND HEARING IN THE TOES

The toes are the foot's "antennae," representing the senses of sight (toes 2 and 3) and hearing (toes 4 and 5) [see figure 62 on page 189]. Visual perception signifies active energy—fire and air. A process of investigation and emanation is at work; we see something "over there." Sight permits us to control our surroundings. Once we see, we can respond. Our eyes can emit messages that attract people or repel them, obstructing entry. The opening or closing of our eyes is voluntary; we may consciously select what we admit and what we emit.

Aural reception, by contrast, represents the passive energies of water and earth. Our ability to listen embraces not only the intake of information from the outside but the emanations of our inner unconscious world—our emotional qualities—as well. Introspection is not as prone to selection and control. Even if we close our ears, we cannot block out all sounds. And were we able to obstruct all outside auditory stimulation, we would still have our inner voice to occupy our attention. The messages that we hear are less clear than those we see. Since they provide no immediate explanation, their connections with prejudices and stereotypes are more tenuous.

Western culture is far more strongly oriented toward and supportive of visual perception than aural reception. Most of the arts are built on the sense of sight; listening is connected with emotions and needs that have to do with the world of mystery and, therefore, with the frightening and the unknown.

Children's ear problems are usually related to fluid in the ears (water and air). Children respond to emotional tension within the home. They hear things that frighten them, things they cannot understand. Thus water (fear) ascends to air. As the acuity of our hearing fades in old age, our ability to hear internal voices also diminishes.

Human suffering is often connected with internal messages that repeat themselves ceaselessly, like broken records. Many emotional problems originate in relentless inner voices that evoke uncontrollable fears. Phobias stem from fears that have no rational basis; the subject is beset by nothing but that same inner voice reporting the presence of something fearful and life threatening (water and earth). Our ears warn us; our eyes permit control. People who "listen with their eyes" also listen very well with their ears. The ability to listen—to hear and think at the same time—allows us to keep our outward and inward attention in balance.

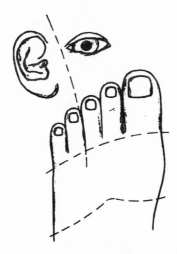

Figure 62. The division of the toes into seeing and hearing. Toes 4 and 5 represent hearing and passivity. Toes 2 and 3 represent seeing and activity.

The condition of the toes, their length, interrelations, structure, and the proportions of their area occupied by sight and hearing, all combine to show which elements are relevant for the individual at hand. We may encounter receptive and enlightened intellectuals, people aware of the external world, whose internal listening abilities point at a state of detachment or acute inner suffering. Others, preoccupied with their inner world only, are divorced from their surroundings.

People who are exceedingly preoccupied with their appearance or their emotional world are deeply concerned about the way others perceive and think of them; paradoxically, the internal messages they receive generate never-ending concern about externalities. These are people whose water and earth have ascended to the air. People who were born deaf find it hard to develop the ability to listen; their warning mechanism is impaired. People who are born blind find it hard to deal with the world of thought and abstract concepts. The divide between the eyes and the ears is the place occupied by masculine and feminine—active and passive—energies in a person's life.

PARTITIONING BY LATERAL DIVISION

Just as the foot is partitioned into element zones, so is each toe.

- Earth—From the junction with the foot proper up to (but not including) the lower joint.

- Water—From the lower joint (inclusive) up to (but not including) the upper joint.

- Fire—From the upper joint (inclusive) up to the toenail.

- Air—The toenail and the flesh above it on the top, and approximately half of the toe pad on the underside (see figure 63).

According to this scheme, toe 5 (representing the earth element) contains mostly earth. The toenail is very small and has almost no air. This is the least important toe in terms of intelligence. The big toe represents the air element and con-

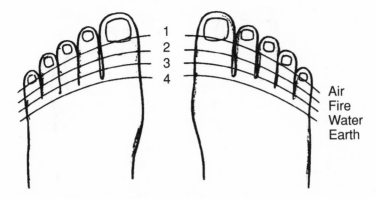

Figure 63. The lateral division of the air element. The four elements as they are divided in the air element.

tains the greatest amount of air. By observing each toe, we see which element it represents and which elements within it have gained or lost strength. Thus, by addressing the qualities of each element represented by a particular toe, we may diagnose the elements that are dominant and those that have been suppressed.

If toe 5 has no toenail, the toe that represents the earth element has no air. Such people never take any initiative that transcends the tried and true; they bring nothing new to their sexual relations (see figure 64).

When toe 2 is very long (see figure 65 on page 192), that is indicative of a great deal of air. We may infer that their actions, too, are abundantly influenced by air. These people are "full of

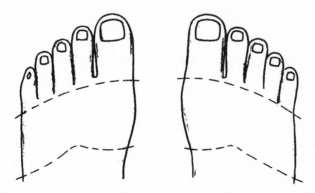

Figure 64. Toe 5 without a nail indicates an imbalance in air.

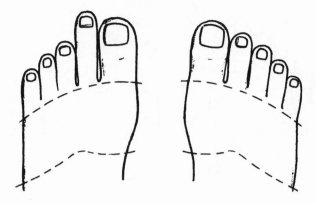

Figure 65. A long toe 2 allows for more space for the fire element in the air area.

hot air"; they absorb things from the air but find it hard to bring them to fruition. We expect to find a surplus of air within the fire element of their feet.

The presence of a bunion indicates an abundance of earth in the air toe (see figure 66). The thoughts of such people are limited to practical rather than abstract matters. Their clarity of thought and the degree of awareness of why and how they think, are affected by the elements that dominate air. As air gives way to earth, awareness and clarity diminish.

- Air within air is indicative of very lucid and conscious thinking.

- Fire within air suggests a lower degree of consciousness and lucidity in the thinking process.

- Water within air creates fog.

- Earth within air stifles visual perception.

In Indian and Chinese thought, air within air indicates a region of high chakras—an area of sublime spirituality, a gateway to God. So pure is this combination of elements that it touches upon the "fifth element." Air with air—the air element in our toes—affects memory, our ability to recollect past events. People with difficulties in the air region of their toes

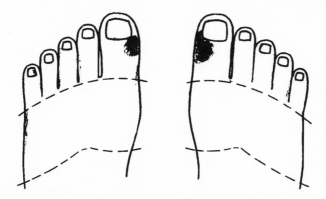

Figure 66. A bunion on the air toe indicates a person who is overly practical in matters of thinking.

have problems with recall. If toe 4 carries indicators in its air element, we may deduce that the subject has difficulty remembering matters related to the emotions.

When testing intelligence, we observe the subject's ability to listen, visualize, and conceptualize, and we assess the quantity and quality of each element in the toes. For example, toes with a lot of earth and a large air region separated by a small partition indicate that fire and water have little to do with the subject's thinking. Such people's thoughts lack the concepts of digestion (water) and perseverance (fire). By examining the structure and tissue of the foot, we may assess the subject's potential and what he or she has done with it. Observing all the toes in this fashion, we draw conclusions as to the functioning of the ear, the eye, and the thought processes. For each toe separately, an element in deficiency indicates underuse and an element in surplus points to overuse.

PARTITIONING BY LENGTH DIVISION

Lengthwise, the toes are divided into two sections. The upper external section of the foot, the part that faces upward, embraces the active elements—fire and air (see figure 67 on page 194). The lower section, that used for striding, includes the passive elements—earth and water. The two sections are separated by an imaginary divide running laterally through the middle of

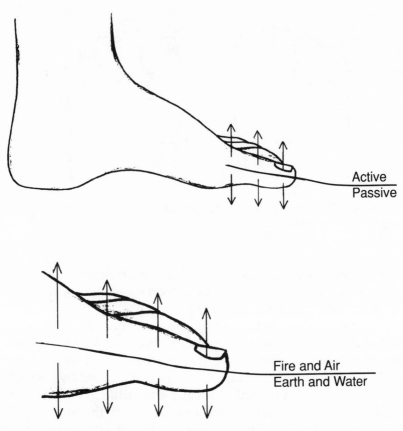

Figure 67. Horizontal division of the toes into the active and passive elements.

the toes. This partitioning allows us to observe the characteristics of people's thought processes: how they learn, where they are strong, and where in the learning process they are liable to become stuck. The ideal state is one in which the passive section is larger in the lower elements, and the active section larger in the upper elements.

People's views are more easily modified in youth. The older we become, the more rigid and fixed our thoughts and views are. Indeed, our toes tend to become more curled and less pliable as we age.

Intelligence contains both active and passive components. Active intelligence is typical of inquisitive people, those who constantly ask what is missing and strive to venture into new areas. These people learn and absorb quickly. They grasp things "on the fly" and tend to let matters slip through. People with passive intelligence, by contrast, have to digest thoroughly anything that enters. (In the final analysis, people of both types may be equally successful, however different their paths may be.)

One aspect of intelligence is learning ability. Those with learning disabilities display various patterns on their toes. A surplus of fire in air, for example, suggests a learning impediment to which we should address ourselves, since people must break the bounds of their ego in order to learn something new. Fire in earth within air points at difficulty in coping with frameworks. Water in the earth region of the toes suggests a fear of frameworks. In order to learn, one must be capable of coping with frameworks.

To view people's natural aptitudes, we examine the potential of the toes by stretching them. How did our subject learn in the past—by sitting and listening or by hands-on activity? Once this question has been answered, we observe what the subject has done with his or her potential. The dividing line is an axis of sorts; people tend to raise and lower some or all of the toes, or part of an individual toe. A toe that is unconnected to the earth element signifies detachment, hovering, "spinning wheels," whereas a toe that presses, pushes, or bends in the direction of earth is an indicator of stagnation, dryness, and inactivity.

If all the toes cross into the upper section—rising to the active region—we infer that none of the subject's thought and cerebral activity is planted in earth. The subject is floating, bursting with ideas that are not fulfilled. He or she has a "good head" that is divorced from the here and now. Such people always have fleeting thoughts and shifting ideas. For example, they may be full of bright ideas about what type of shoe to manufacture, but they'll never produce anything on which someone might take a single step. They fantasize and allow themselves to be swept up in their ideas, but insofar as it depends on them, even the most original and fascinating notions will not come to pass. Such people cannot be relied on to consolidate their thoughts into something "real." They must work in a setting that requires nothing more than brainstorming and developing ideas.

People whose five toes are under the divide are short-sighted. They are always preoccupied with what is happening at the moment, and show no interest in building for the future. Count on them to perform effectively but without investing much thought in the process. They are people who have to be shown what to do. They are artisans who do their jobs well, succeeding at tasks that demand diligence and consistency. The corner shoemaker is an example.

Toes that rest on the divide belong to people who perform well in both realms: coping with the here and now and thinking ahead when the situation demands it. People with toes in this position have the potential for an unobstructed flow of creativity. (The toes serve as conduits through which creativity emanates.) If the toes rise above or drop below the line, the flow is impeded in some way.

The condition of the toes is generally not as extreme or uniform as the examples presented above. In our examination, we ask ourselves the following questions:

1) Which toe lies above or below the divide? Is it related to hearing, visual reception, or thinking? To which element does it belong?

2) Which part of the toe is above or below the divide?

3) Do our findings with regard to the toes correspond to the state of the elements in the foot as a whole?

If we see a toe that first rises and then drops, we examine which part of the toe rises above the line and which falls below it. The part that rises is generally that section of the earth element situated near the water (using the transverse division), along with the water and some of the fire. The part that drops represents the edge of fire and air. This description fits people who do not truly think; their thoughts are adulterated by needs, emotions, and ego. They seek ways to avoid fear. Such people "walk on air," allowing earth to penetrate their air element. Their thinking becomes exceedingly dry and rigid. Their thoughts never change; nothing new is admitted. They find learning a very difficult matter. "Seeing is believing," they'll tell you. Lacking all imagination, they accept information only when it is accompanied by hard and fast proof.

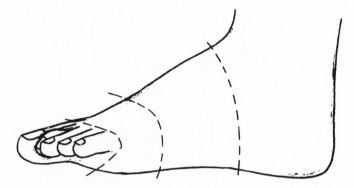

Figure 68. Toe 2 dropping into the passive region indicates a loss of active energy in expressing thoughts and ambition.

The part of the toe that rises above the divide represents the active facets of the subject's intelligence. If the ascendant elements are water and fire, we can infer that the form and substance of this person's thoughts are shaped by his or her emotions and ego. Such people are willing to accept only those things that pass their ego's muster; anything else is "in one ear and out the other." If we observe a great deal of fear in the foot, we infer that the subject's "head" is seriously preoccupied with its fears. Such people avoid thinking about certain things or contrive ways to escape the object of their distress.

When toe 2 (fire) falls into the passive region (see figure 68 above), this represses the subject's creative abilities. Such people's preoccupations diminish their creativity and self-expression.

Each toe has an under pad. If the pad is large and robust, the subject's air is obstructed and heavy. Water churns in the subject's head, obstructing lucid thought processes. Bloated and swollen toe pads are strongly characteristic of sinusitis.

If the toe pad contains a tough callus (earth) instead of a soft protrusion (see figure 69 on page 198), and the toenail is damaged, the subject has a deficiency on the active, airy, flowing side that permits deep thinking; the passive side becomes even more passive as it gravitates toward the earth. When this condition occurs in toe 4, the subject cannot comprehend emotional qualities and possesses only "beliefs" connected to a framework of earth.

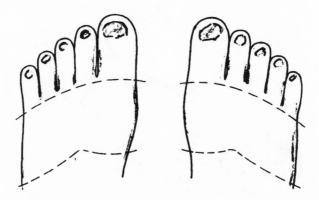

Figure 69. Earth in air. The presence of strong earth energy in the air area may create strange, horn-like shaped nails. It indicates that needs influence a person's thinking.

When the passive side of air in toe 3 shows signs of surplus, the active side is in deficiency. Such people cannot think in stressful situations. If the passive side is dominant and the air in toe 3 is problematic (in terms of both the lateral partitioning of the toes and the lengthwise division into active and passive zones), we infer that the subject is so beset with fear, so terrified, that he or she cannot think. We recognize this fear as a disruptive force because toe 3 represents the kidney. Its effect is evident in the dominance of the passive side and the presence of a problem in the air needed for thinking. If we also observe lengthwise lines in the area of the water element of the toe, we realize that the subject suffers gravely from the fear-of-tests syndrome.

When people are so preoccupied with money that they give no heed to their actions and feelings, toes 1 and 5 rise into the active area while toes 2, 3, and 4 drop into the passive area (see figure 70). Such people treat their feelings, emotions, and creativity with neglect.

If the passive side of air within air is absent and the toe pad is flat and sharpened, we infer that the subject lacks imagination. Unconscious thoughts fail to rise to the level of consciousness. Such a person's thinking never transcends the ordinary, and thoughts that have fallen into the passive zone fade from consciousness. Such people may walk around with strong guilt feelings deeply buried in their unconscious, of which they are altogether oblivious. This applies to any of the toes in keeping with its function (sexuality, emotions, and so forth).

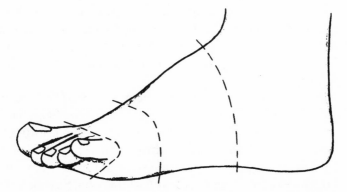

Figure 70. Elevated toes 1 and 5 indicates a preoccupation with physical needs (such as money or sex) without considering feelings or the effects of his or her actions.

In an extreme situation of treading upon earth, the toes rise upward at a ninety-degree angle, signifying a complete dissociation of air and earth. Such a condition points to an extremely serious emotional problem.

TOENAILS

The toenails represent the zenith of air within air, the highest point in both the vertical and lateral divisions of the toes. The toenail indicates how people activate their thought processes. Imperfections in the toenails reflect problems of concentration and thought. Vertical lines on the toenails are typical of people whose thoughts "escape" them, vanishing too quickly to be retained or recalled. Transverse lines on the toenails are characteristic of people who are "stuck" in their thinking, who suffer from "constipation of the brain."

Since pure, unpolluted thinking is a rare occurrence, most people's toenails are problematic: ingrown, crooked, mycotic, unusually thick or unusually brittle, and so on. To draw conclusions from the toenails and to appreciate the significance of air within air, we must consider the toe as a whole, its position relative to the lateral divide, and any surplus or deficiency of air within air reflected in its state.

For example, earth in the toenails (tough, brittle, cracked nails with a tendency to form transverse lines) tells us that the subject's air element contains no freedom of thought. The dynamism and activity of air has been replaced by the stagnation of earth. Farmers often have such nails, because their lives, at one with the earth, extend to their heads as manifested in their preoccupation with their own needs and those of their crops.

Another example would be watery toenails (flexible, soft, mycotic). We often encounter one mycotic toe (i.e., afflicted with athlete's foot) alongside four healthy ones, indicating that the affected toe has water within its air element. This condition mirrors a client who focuses on his or her emotional world to the exclusion of other considerations. Such a subject is unaware of this pattern (as shown by the absence of air within air).

A toenail with an inverted-cone shape and a tendency to grow into the flesh is characteristic of special problems affecting the head: ringing, fainting, dizziness, migraines, and so on.

Toe 5 demonstrates how people handle external stimuli (hearing, touch); toe 4 tells us how they cope with internal stimuli (thoughts).

EXCEPTIONAL PERCEPTIVE ABILITIES

Every exceptional manifestation of intelligence, aptitude, or ability finds expression in some unique property of the toes. The toes may be oddly hinged, mounted sideways, misshapen, punctuated by beauty marks, and so forth. What we look for is something unique in the structure of the toes, something that reflects the subject's basic potential rather than the distortions created over the course of his or her life.

Exceptional perceptive abilities usually manifest themselves in toes 1 and 2; sometimes they appear in toe 3 as well. This is because these toes represent the active elements. For example, toe 2 slanting on its axis toward toe 5 is indicative of a subject who receives outside information in some special way. If it slants on the divide toward toe 1, a special form of introspection is evident. If toe 2 is positioned higher than toe 1, the subject is able to empathize, i.e., to know what is happening to someone else without knowing how he or she knows.

Spots on the toes suggest the presence of exceptional abilities because they point at our basic potential. Unusual attach-

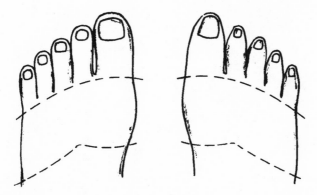

Figure 71. Cone-shaped toes indicate a tendency for manic-depressive moods.

ments of toes, such as skin (air) joining toes 2 and 3, indicate a special ability to adduce connections, to perceive.

A structural abnormality in toe 3, which represents balance, suggests the presence of something exceptional in the physical and/or mental balance of the subject or of members of his or her family. When toes 2 and 3 are nearly equal in height and slightly shorter than the big toe, the subject is a logical thinker. Seriously marred toenails that "climb" over the toe may be indicative of brain damage. When one of these states is coupled with a hot, red, swollen region around the toenail, a certain form of autism may be present.

Psychotic states may evince themselves in the toes in various ways:

1) All the toes are cone-shaped (see figure 71 above). The air element within air has been badly damaged and is deficient in its base—a state manifested in the subject's original potential.

2) In the case of chronic psychosis, we find extensive differences between the state of the toes and the markings warranted by the subject's potential, e.g., striding on the toenails, raising all the toes, toes climbing over one another, or skin disorders between toes. When one of the elements—in this case earth— achieves total dominance over the air element, a state of psychosis originates in calcification. This condition may occur in the very elderly.

12

EMOTIONAL POTENTIAL

Water is the element with the weakest connection to our lives in the here and now. It does, however, contain much of our history. Water is an element of fear, the basic, primal emotion of humankind. From the moment we are born, there are always things that threaten us. Water occurring in various combinations—fear in combination with other elements—shapes the parameters of our range of feelings: shame, frustration, anger, terror, and so forth.

People without chronic patterns in their water element mold their fear into a different emotion every time it is aroused. When people are willing to experience emotional energy without creating a scene, to let their "waves" rise and move on, their water flows. In other words, when the fear is allowed to flow, the feeling passes. Those with chronic patterns have learned to respond the same way every time fear arises, thus acquiring a predisposition to irritability, anger, guilt, and so on.

The water element reminds us that we can neither initiate nor determine our feelings; we can only let them be. We can watch the waves rise and let them flow. Constant emotional tumult points at a lack of balance. Hence all our basic emotional patterns originate in the way we've chosen to handle fear over the years.

Raw fear is the basic fear of death. It has nothing to do with the survival instincts associated with earth, the element that reminds us of the possibility that we may cease to exist, that we may die. Neither is it connected with the choice between fight and flight. Rather, it is a fear that we may experience even when we face no real threat. Fear protects us and keeps us alert; it reminds us that we are not omnipotent. Fear shows us our limits. When we experience something new, venturing beyond our normal boundaries, the fear we feel prevents our doing things that may harm us. We fill the space of our new boundaries with water, with fear.

Water does not act on its own; it fills an existing space. When people's water element is pure and balanced, they experience not only fear but the full spectrum of emotions. They feel afraid when they're afraid, angry when they're angry, and so on. All these sensations, however, are transitory, for water moves on. People with entrenched emotional patterns, by contrast, always experience the same feeling and respond in a set way. We may discern an emotion on the foot only if such a pattern exists, in which case we find indications of surplus or deficiency in the regions corresponding to this emotion.

Emotionally balanced people have no such indications in their water region. Because their water flows as it should, they are capable of feeling fear, sorrow, anger, guilt, and the like. When the water element is not in balance, it imprisons rather than safeguards us. Fear can be an excellent teacher. How sad

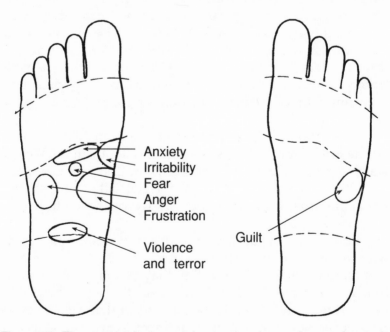

Figure 72. The areas where certain emotional energies are located in the water element.

it is that instead of learning its lessons, we learn only that one must not fear (see figure 72).

FEAR

We must undergo fear in order to internalize new experiences. Without fear we learn nothing; there is no excitement, no enthusiasm. Fear makes our lives at once pleasurable and tortuous.

Pure fear is reflected in the kidney, a focal point of the water element. Its corresponding site is the softest and deepest point on the foot, and generally the wettest and most light colored as well. One hardly ever encounters a foot with no markings at the point corresponding to the kidney.

When the water element is in balance, the region should be light in color, cold, wet, and insensitive to the touch. Since most of us have experienced fear, we generally strive to get along in life without fear and avoid making waves.

TERROR

The lower portion of the water element houses fears connected with existence, basic physiological needs, and other imperatives related to growth. Terror occurs when water commingles with earth, producing mud. When the lower water region is marked and the earth element looks odd, we are alerted to the presence of fears flowing from basic needs that were not satisfied in the past. Insofar as the subject's individual needs as an infant were not met, we find a fearful and underconfident adult today. Such people are insecure, beset by unexplained fears emanating from their distant past. They may not be aware that their earlier needs had not been fulfilled, since they usually have no linear or theoretical recollection of the time of occurrence. This is a genuine, primeval, existential fear. It resides in the section of our psyches that is farthest from comprehension and awareness, the oldest and deepest level of all.

While some of our subjects can perceive only the tip of this iceberg, others may be able to plumb the depths of these fears. If the indicated region is heavily marked, the subject suffers from many irrational fears and uncontrolled terrors—a state that elicits the signs of a chronic pattern. When we observe indications of such fears on the subject's passive foot, we expect to find the fears in his or her deeper psychic levels. This is because these are emotions we tend to hide, even from ourselves. They are associated with needs related to our passive energies. People attempt to repress such a lack of confidence by disregarding it. They waste energy that might be invested in action to cope with the situation. Repressing the feeling only magnifies its strength as it meets with the subject's inner resistance.

A consistently wet foot signifies a devastated earth element that has become soft and spongy. Classic water-dominated feet are exceedingly wet and cold; the ankles are swollen, their entire lower portion occupied by water. Such people live in constant terror. When the tide of terror rises, fire responds by attempting to reach its optimum level (tense, taut muscles) and counter the fear. This is how such people survive their terror attacks. If the fire is not strong enough, its response fails and panic ensues. After a trauma such as combat syndrome ("shell shock"), we may find that water has invaded earth, eliciting terror of a directly existential nature—the most basic fear that we possess. Terror seats itself firmly at the base of the spinal column.

The presence of lengthwise lines on the foot, ascending from the earth toward fire, suggests easily aroused feelings of terror. Such subjects tend to hysteria, broadcasting their fear through their actions. Hysteria signifies a tremendous emotional force—primarily fear—that ascends toward the realm of outwardly directed action. If the lines cross into the fire region, we may observe loss of control, panic, and paralysis, since earth has ascended to a place where it does not belong and quenched the fire. The subject drowns, gasping for breath.

VIOLENCE

People who cannot cope with their terror convert it into violence. The indication of this condition on the foot is an invasion of water by earth in the center of the heel, rather than an invasion of earth by water. This violence is not existential. Such people, perceiving certain emotional forces as life threatening, respond with violence against anyone associated with that emotion. In other words, this violence erupts not for self-defense but in order to eliminate a perceived threat.

Signs of earth in water tell us that the subject will respond violently when feelings of jealousy evoke a spate of terror. The presence of water in earth tends to dampen one's response, and people in a state of balance are jealous simply when they're jealous. For example, most people who act violently during an attack of jealousy have been on the receiving end of violence.

As a rule, violence is evident on the dominant foot since this is an outwardly directed action. Indicators of violence on the passive foot are characteristic of people who, incapable of harming others, turn their violence upon themselves. Signs of violence on both feet indicate the coexistence of both syndromes.

ANXIETY

Anxiety is indicated on the area of the foot corresponding to the kidneys. It is the fear of fear: a manifestation of our resistance to fear and refusal to experience it. Our fire deserves the credit for this.

Anxiety represents a struggle between water (upper band) and fire. Water in surplus attempts to rise and escape. We try to stop it because we are afraid to fear; our egos do not permit us to fear. Those who manage to curb their anxiety show indicators of anxiety in the center of the upper water region (transverse dissociation lines), coupled with indications of the penetration of fire into the area. Such people suppress their attacks of anxiety. Striving to distance their anxiety from elements related to consciousness, they deny these attacks and insist that they have "overcome" them. People vanquished by their anxieties exhibit lengthwise lines in the upper water region, pointing at an invasion of fire by water in a state of surplus. They manifest their anxiety in their behavior. They are conscious of its existence, since it has ascended to the elements governing consciousness. We often find both scenarios within one individual, who sometimes controls and represses his or her anxieties and at other times yields to its domination.

Physical manifestations of anxiety include rapid heartbeat, dry mouth, contractions of the diaphragm and skeletal muscles, dilated pupils, and shortness of breath. We ask subjects to breathe deeply in order to stimulate proper diaphragm functioning, thus restoring the connection between fire and water. They experience genuine fear, ascending from water to the area of awareness, rather than the fear of fear experienced generally. Anxiety inhibits breathing, thus diminishing people's energy, whereas fear causes them to gulp more air, which augments their energy. There is no need to make people in a state of fear breathe deeply since they will do so naturally.

IRRITABILITY

This trait appears on the area of the foot corresponding to the stomach. It reflects an attempt by fire to dominate water by drying it up. An inwardly directed action (the subject has "swallowed" something) is followed by an outwardly directed motion (an attempt to express it). People's egos, culture, and education seek to block these articulations; fire imposes itself vigorously on the attempted flow, thus preventing outward expression. Fire tries to take the act of expressing and freeing this emotional energy upon itself, to dry it up and release it through itself by means of nervous stimulation of the muscles. Such a state produces fire in the stomach area, reflecting irritability ("irritable bowel syndrome" in medical terminology) and ulcers.

An ulcer is indicative of a concentration of fire within water and is characterized by high acidity and intense stomach activity. Its victims feel as if a fire is raging inside; if this is because they are trying to hold back something that should be let out, they literally eat themselves up. They are usually unaware of their irritability and fear, and, if asked, would deny their existence.

Fire and fear are incapable of understanding each other. People who cannot bring them into harmony "consume" themselves or others. Irritability represents an attempt to control something that wishes to ascend; in order to fear, we must stop being irritable.

Physical indications on the foot, in the area corresponding to the stomach, exhibit bold indented lines coupled with signs of surplus in the fire element. Outwardly directed irritability is manifested in the dominant foot; inner-directed on the passive foot.

FRUSTRATION

Frustration reflects disparities between the aspirations of the ego and actual events. Either the fear posited between fire and earth prevents the fulfillment of these hopes, or the subjects' fear keeps them from doing what they want or need to do. In both cases, water that has ceased flowing and become stuck now obstructs the flow between fire and earth (upward and downward). Indeed, frustration is indicated by transverse lines that cut off the flow at the site of water's apex. (These lines run from the area of the spinal column representing months four through six of gestation, extending into the water element.)

Frustrated people are stuck; they are afraid to do what they should be doing and what's right for them. They feel they are not fulfilling their potential but offer myriad excuses instead of simply admitting that they are afraid. Rather than experience their frustration as fear, they repress it. Fear is a dynamic force, generating the energy with which we cope with new experiences and extend the boundaries of our "I." Frustrated people neither take initiatives nor apply anything new.

Signs of frustration on the foot tell us that, because of fear, our subjects have not dared to do the things they wanted and loved or needed to do. In other words, their fire and earth, respectively, are being stifled. The way out of this frustration is to go ahead anyway, even while afraid. Frustration emanates from an unfulfilled desire or need. Buddhism solved this problem by encouraging us to want and need nothing. The story of Siddhartha encapsulates this attitude. This extremely poor man wanted everything. At the height of the realization of his dreams, when he was a prince, he turned his back on everything and became Buddha—not out of perfect renunciation but out of perfect fulfillment.

People who cease to want and need are not people. If we give up before we even begin, frustration will ensue. But if we have everything and then relinquish it, we can rise to a higher level. It is our choice. Frustration and confusion collaborate to guard the gates of the palace of wisdom. They are a sign of learning, for anything new in our lives represents a step beyond the customary parameters of our "I." If we do not experience the fear generated by something new, we become stuck, frustrated.

Conversely, this fear can be used as a motivating factor, expediting our movements and urging us to transcend our usual limitations. Because most people prefer to avoid experiencing fear, they become frustrated when confronted with new knowledge. Frustration blocks absorption and halts the flow; things are *ingested* but not *digested*.

Our initial encounter with something new causes confusion; we want more than we can achieve. To extend our boundaries and welcome the new into our lives, we must allow our feelings of confusion and frustration to ascend and flow freely. They represent growth and development, processes which are at odds with feelings of security, protection, and perpetuation of the tried and true.

ANGER AND GUILT

Anger and guilt walk hand in hand. Since they represent opposite poles of the same spectrum, both are manifested in the same area of the foot but on separate feet. Both are connected with external influences; guilt is aroused by something outside the person, while anger attempts to flow outward and demands articulation. Consequently, we find the signs of guilt in the passive foot and those of anger in the active one. Both kinds of patterns are related to the people with whom we grew up. Most are entrenched by the end of adolescence. That is a time of life in which guilt and anger figure very prominently, since young people lack the self-control to channel their feelings. At a later age, a small and unimportant stimulus can trigger patterns of guilt or anger rooted in matters that had been genuinely important in the past. The emotional intensity of the present experience is wholly disproportional to whatever triggered it. At the site of the foot where anger and guilt appear, we observe patterns connected with the subject's emotional relations with others.

Anger

Anger is an energy of the liver, a site that houses a combination of water and fire. This is where fire is at its strongest within the water element, generating an energy that acquires heat and ascends easily. Fire heats the water, which then rises as steam. (Hence we speak of "hotheads" and people who "see red.") Underlying this anger are feelings of fear and threat, which we attempt to keep under control. People become angry when frightened; eruptions of anger are their way of coping with fear. Although anger is meant to flow outward, most of us try to stifle its articulation because our culture does not legitimize such manifestations.

Most people do not know how to harmonize their anger, and respond by displaying one of two behavior patterns. The first is a state of chronic rage. Their overuse of anger is evidenced by lengthwise stripes in the area corresponding to the liver, indicating vigorous upward movement. No matter how much anger they express, they cannot liberate themselves from its clutches. They are vindictive, they bear grudges, they know no peace. Any emotion they experience is accompanied by a demonstration of anger. The liver region on the foot is in a state of surplus; it is swollen, red, and hot. Fire and water rush to join.

Lengthwise lines at the site are characteristic of people who cannot stop being angry. The fire region is in a state of surplus. Fire blocks all other emotions; only anger manages to ascend. Physical manifestations include a tendency toward hypertension, liver trouble, gallstones, and high levels of cholesterol and other fats in the blood. Lengthwise lines on the site of a liver in deficiency point at an abundance of anger that remains unexpressed for lack of energy in the subjects' fire element. Their water, unheated by fire, ascends as cold energy, thus producing the classic symptoms of allergy. Instead of an eruption of rage, their ascending water generates coldness and alienation. Such a state is generally accompanied by a strong sense of frustration.

The second behavior pattern is characteristic of people who try to repress their anger. Although the fire in the region indicates that anger is present, the transverse indentations and surplus in the area show that this anger is not being expressed; it is not allowed to flow outward. In cases where the dissociation lines are closer to the fire, the subjects are aware that they are restraining their anger but feel that this is the right thing to do. If these lines occur at lower points, the anger is obstructed on a completely subconscious level. Such people insist that they are not angry; it never occurs to them that they are beset by unexpressed anger. An extremely low line is displayed by people who deny ever getting angry at all.

A surplus of anger is manifested by a wide red connecting strip between fire and water. People who block their anger near the fire region regard this as an affront to their ego; this is where they get stuck. Anger that is allowed to flow is not felt at the time of its occurrence. It comes and goes, rising and falling, on its own. When it is in a state of balance, the region will be slightly lighter in color than fire.

Guilt

Guilt is an energy that appears in the spleen. Underlying guilt is the fear of losing something on which we depend. People opt for the "easier" of the two emotions, choosing to feel guilt rather than fear of loss. People accumulate guilt from the many occasions on which they regard themselves as being deemed guilty by others. It is the manifestation of a fear that has been "swallowed" instead of outwardly experienced. Since guilt (or its twin, regret) is a passive emotion, we would expect to find a surplus of water in the water region. People who try to repress their guilt feelings exhibit a surplus of fire in the region corresponding to the spleen, as indicated by hot, red skin. The harder people try to contain their guilt, the more it affects their actions. Suppressed guilt emerges in the form of accusations aimed at others.

Anger and guilt are two types of feelings that can bring people together. It's easy to unite around something external to us. After banding together because of our guilty or accusational emotions, we turn these into a collective feeling. Religious dogma is built, in part, upon guilt. It prescribes the performance of certain acts and instills guilt in those who do not comply.

People acting within these frameworks have no fear of loss. They "have to," it's legitimate, and therefore they feel no guilt. The option also exists for individuals to develop apart from the group, choosing their own path.

Lengthwise indentations on the site corresponding to the spleen, as encountered in cases of arthritis and asthma, indicate guilt manifested in the subject's actions. Arthritis usually appears as fire that has penetrated the spleen region, signifying an attempt by fire to conquer fear in order to stifle its expression. Allergies generally reflect an admission of guilt; such a subject is constantly apologizing. These people exhibit a surplus of water in the spleen region and a fire element invaded by water. They are always guilty.

Guilt resides in the passive foot, beneath the line of consciousness where we toss anything we don't want to see. Pure guilt is manifested in a surplus of water in the water region. We need guilt feelings, for they drive us to seek something new in order to rectify the old.

Anger appears in the dominant foot and guilt in the passive one. In a left-dominant person, the region corresponding to the liver reflects guilt and that of the spleen reflects anger. Physiologically, it makes no difference whether either of these energies is seated in the liver or the spleen. If there is confusion between the left and right sides, there will be confusion between anger and guilt.

JEALOUSY

Jealousy is a hybrid emotion composed of frustration and anger. It signals its presence by leaving marks on regions of the foot that reflect frustration and anger, coupled with transverse lines connecting the two sites. Jealousy is indicated more clearly on the right foot than on the left since it usually contains anger, but the left foot too may be marked because jealousy contains guilt.

People tend to choke on their jealousy; it becomes stuck inside them. (Notice the transverse lines.) The fear that underlies their jealousy remains unexpressed. There is a feeling of loss, caused by the disruption of emotional relations with the object of their jealousy.

When both length and transverse lines are present on the site corresponding to the liver or in the central water region, we realize that the subject expresses feelings of jealousy in the form of anger or emotional outbursts (attacks of envy).

PANGS OF CONSCIENCE

Pangs of conscience are manifestations of the control of air over water. They reflect thought; the head has something to say to the heart. Air descends to the region near the boundary between fire and water on the foot, producing an empty, light-colored area with folds in the skin, located very close to the site of consciousness.

Pangs of conscience are generally preceded by feelings of anxiety that are transformed into what we call conscience by the intrusion of "logic." Air "donates" the qualities of comprehension and organization. Pangs of conscience are easier and more acceptable to experience than feelings of anxiety, since the former are related to something we have actually done, not just felt. There is a progression beginning with fear, advancing to thoughts about fear, and culminating with pangs of conscience.

On the foot, pangs of conscience are indicated in the area usually marking anxiety, but with the addition of various signs of the air element: skin that is very light in color and easy to lift, indented lines, and a more delicate texture than the rest of the area. While we all experience pangs of conscience at times, these indicators occur in people who have such feelings constantly. These are the ones who often begin their sentences with "Oh no," as in "Oh no, how did I forget?"

Emotions may be manifested in completely different ways in the dominant and passive feet. People who repress their feelings have indications of imbalance in the passive foot; those who punish themselves emotionally show markings on both feet. People with strong dynamics in their water element are emotionally unreliable; they are in a perpetual state of flux. If the condition of the foot changes repeatedly during the reading, e.g., from hot to wet to dry to cold, the water element is playing a strong role. Such people, controlled by their emotions, never know what moves them.

The emotions described above relate to different kinds of relationships between fire and water. Since the energies of fire and water differ so strongly from one another, we must have "good fire" in order to have good water. The converse holds true as well: no ego is strong enough to function when the ground underneath it is muddy. Fire rarely admits water. People who cannot vent their emotional intensities have entrenched ego patterns. Their ego sets the boundaries, barring anything it is unwilling to accept. The subject is unaware of these boundaries since they originate in the lower water, the point farthest from our consciousness.

The character trait most directly related to water is fear. In its balanced state, fear manifests itself in inaction; the subject accepts the fear for what it is and simply lets it be. Most people do not know how to fear, preferring instead to wallow in anger, depression, self-pity—anything but fear. They worry that their egos would disintegrate if fear were to penetrate their consciousness. The only people with true courage are those who dare to feel their fear, courage being the strength to take action despite fear of the action. Such people summon their energy from the lower parts of their bodies, elevating it to the level of action.

People who devote their energies to control of their fear have no strength left for anything else. Having lost the energy of the fear itself and having sacrificed the energy used to subdue it, they fall into a rut and remain their for lack of strength to do anything new. Animals do not suffer from this syndrome. Danger lurks, fear is aroused, and they become alert; when the danger passes, their fear subsides. Once we learn how to fear, we find ourselves much better able to cope with our other emotions.

People with a strong fire element and problematic water may attempt to solve their emotional problems if we appeal to their ego in such a way that it is tempted to fight for control of water. Such clients accept this and try to change, thus giving their fear a chance. In some cases (e.g., chronic blamers), we ask the air element to do battle. If we appeal to their air and show them what they are doing, demonstrating that they— and no one else—are responsible for their situation, they will be able to cope with the problem. But first their air must be brought into balance.

In addition to indications of surplus and deficiency in various areas of the foot, we look for grooves or deep lines that tell us about the subject's emotional flow. Lengthwise indentations indicate a rather intense flow of emotions, surfacing even when the subjects would prefer to keep them hidden. Grooves at a specific site point to a surplus in the expression of the relevant emotion. Lengthwise grooves throughout the water element indicate an all-embracing emotional force on the ascent; transverse grooves are indicative of an emotional blockage. Grooves in the lower water region point to an emotion far from the subject's consciousness, while higher grooves, closer to the fire element, show a greater proximity to awareness. In the latter case, people realize that the emotion is present and try to inhibit it, but it is so close to the point of consciousness that they manifest it through their actions.

We generally expect to observe grooves following one direction throughout a region. In the case of fears originating in the lower water—the point farthest from consciousness—the subjects have probably never experienced their fear and are completely unaware of its existence; they are embarrassed. Such people may exhibit a problematic water region containing many inhibited emotions. Several parallel grooves emanating from earth and rising toward the extremities, i.e., the hands, suggest the presence of emotional energy that subconsciously affects what we do, how we behave, and how we articulate ourselves (no flow to the head) as manifested in our body language.

Blood belongs to the water element. People whose fire controls their water (i.e., who are unwilling to experience their fear) may suffer from vascular obstructions in the chest, causing angina pectoris. Fire dries up their water, causing it to thicken and clog up the vessels. Without a free flow of water cleansing the fire element as it passes through, the fire will consume itself. In such cases, the problem is not with the heart muscle but with the blood vessels that surround it, i.e., not with fire but with water (the blood vessels). At a subsequent stage, the fire may become so dried out that it turns into earth.

Cholesterol is another cause of vascular obstructions. Compulsive eaters generally behave as they do in order to stifle their feelings. When the water region of the foot is compressed and dry, we observe a groove running from the kidney region to the bladder, a classic symptom of insufficient fluid intake. Such a state is most common in people who have undergone an intense bout of fear and have drawn themselves tightly around it, locking it into their body.

Drinking is connected with fear; people engulfed in terror are disinclined to drink. Women who have low blood pressure (hypotension) and cold feet with signs of dryness are unable to imbibe large quantities of fluids. The way they cope with fear is to quarantine it and bury it deep in their psyches. (This applies primarily to women or to men whose passive energy is dominant.) Such women suffer from problems involving the navel and ovaries as well as the kidneys and urinary tract—the region of the water element—due to the pressure they exert on that element. Children exhibit signs of insufficient fluid intake after an acute episode or a prolonged period of intense fear. Fear dries up the mouth.

People who do not want to drink show that they are unwilling to experience their fear; they don't want the water. Such people usually have some kind of complex involving water, pools, the ocean, or the bath. Often there is an obstetric problem involving fluids, such as fluid on the lungs or a sensation of strangulation or drowning.

Fear and the energy consumed during an episode of fear show up on the pancreas. People have been known to contract diabetes in the aftermath of an incident involving intense fear. By reexperiencing that situation, we may free ourselves of such a trauma. Signs of the earth element on the site of the foot corresponding to the pancreas, point at fear linked with survival.

When there is a strong connection between water and fire, we often do something without identifying the inner force that motivated us to do it. People with a dissociation between fire and water forfeit much of the mystery of their lives, the ability to ride on a "gut feeling," to act spontaneously. Everything is controlled. Spontaneity is a manifestation of an energy that emanates from below and can cross from water to fire without any difficulty. A "gut feeling" is a concept involving water and earth. We cannot think about or understand water, we can only feel it. We cannot speak about emotions; when we do, it is our judgment or notion of comparison talking, not the emotion itself.

Water does not require action in the wake of feeling. Those who are unwilling to feel their water are not creators of new things (which come from below, from water) but rather technicians who do only what they already know. Such people do not develop.

By contrast, people with strong connections between fire and earth are willing to fear, innovate independently, and create. For this to take place, people's active and passive energies must interface so that their actions (representing the active aspects) tie in with their unconscious psyche (their passive aspects). One way to solve a problem is to avoid thinking about it for a day; after this respite we often find that we know more about the matter. By refraining from doing something, we give water a chance to flow; our "inaction" is a form of action. To permit our intestines to work well, we must do nothing. If we do something, e.g., generate internal tension in some way, they will not function properly. Hence the "action" in the head is related to the "inaction" in the water.

The problem is not the energy itself (anger, guilt, and so forth) but what we do with it. The overabundance and ceaseless gushing of water—the drama—no longer represent the emotions themselves. They are open-ended, for they are not truly resolved. This is the "flip side" of keeping everything bottled up within, a form of behavior that produces similar results.

We need water (fear), for it sustains us. People swamped by their fears are hysterical; they are the victims of their fear. Their feet are flooded by water. Others, who are unwilling to feel, allow their water element to evaporate altogether, thus forfeiting the latent energies of water.

As we analyze their feet, we strive to present our subjects with a mirror through which they can view what they have done with their emotions, which of their feelings predominate, and how these emotions affect their lives. The element of water has far-reaching importance for our bodies. It cleanses us and, when we leave it undisturbed, it flows and cleanses itself as well. People who "collect" unresolved situations and keep them inside, by contrast, flood themselves with poison.

13

THE TECHNIQUE
OF FOOT ANALYSIS

A foot analysis session usually takes one to two hours. In the time available to us, we must remember to focus on the important things. Optimal conditions include no one in the room but ourselves and the subject, a quiet setting with no disruptions (such as telephones), and the full concentration of both parties. The material discussed is written down or taped, since most people, faced with the sheer volume and scale of the information presented, forget more than half of what they are told. The content of the session should be recorded and played back two weeks later and again in a month. Some of the points that may have evoked resistance or misunderstanding may become clearer further down the line. With respect to chronic patterns, we presume that previously misunderstood material can be rediscovered on the tape even after a lapse of two years.

The subject should sit comfortably, with his or her feet protruding beyond the armchair, table, or examining couch. The analyst, too, should sit comfortably, preferably in a swivel chair on wheels so he or she may examine the feet from all possible angles. Keep a towel handy; if the subject is highly agitated, the feet may perspire heavily and be hard to palpate. The temperature in the examining room should be pleasant, not too hot or cold—70 to 75 degrees. For the upright examination, ask the subject to stand on a flat, hard board that provides an accurate view of his or her posture.

Foot-reading is an intimate act that should preferably be conducted in the presence of the subject only, unaccompanied by friends or relatives. For the sake of confidentiality and privacy, the subject should be given all written or recorded material. The reading is an act that "bares" the subject; any information we obtain must be kept secret and not revealed in any way, shape, or form. Subjects should pay for the reading rather than accepting the service as a gift, thereby taking full responsibility for the act and getting more out of it.

Upon entering the room, subjects are asked to provide all the technical details referred to on the analysis form. The analyst asks them to remove their shoes and socks and stand on one foot, then to take one step forward several times in succession. After observing the feet in a standing position, we ask the subjects to climb onto the examining table. We continue to fill out the relevant sections of the diagnostic form, verifying the data by empirical observation. The reader identifies classic symptoms of various conditions where present. Completion of the form marks the end of the physical portion of the examination.

Even as it provides a firm basis on which to build the foot analysis, the body offers us a great deal of additional information. We observe characteristic indicators and pronounced signs of surplus or deficiency, and question the subject to confirm whether the problems indicated are actually present. For example, we may encounter an indicator of allergy coupled with markings on the airways and sinuses; subsequent questioning reveals that an allergy manifesting itself in the airways and sinuses indeed exists. The presence of an allergy tells us that the water element has "migrated" into other elements, on which basis we may conclude that water has penetrated the subject's fire and air.

All chronic physical problems point to a chronic imbalance that manifests itself in the subject's life in some way. If we treat bodily symptoms as our point of departure, we will be able to reach other levels as well. A chronic physical imbalance leads us to related findings. An unbalanced menstrual cycle, for example, indicates that we should address ourselves to the subject's sexuality and fertility. A marking on the liver indicates the presence of a special emotional condition. Chronic emotional conditions have physical manifestations. A chronic state of fear is reflected throughout the body and is indicated on the foot in particular.

The holistic approach affirms that the body and the soul are inseparable. Where a physical problem exists, we must examine the organ involved, the element, and the significance of both.

Our entire diagnosis will be built upon our physical findings, for this is the type of examination that gives us a picture of the subject as a whole and permits insight into what is happening in his or her life. Moreover, our subjects know that we are really seeing them, thus creating a sense of trust on their part that leads to greater openness. During the physical examination and completion of the diagnostic sheet, a bond has been forged with our subjects. We have learned "where they're at" and how to speak with them. The basis for the foot analysis is now firmly in place.

At this juncture, we must decide where to begin. We choose as our starting point that which is most blatant and external-ized, and progress slowly toward aspects of the subject that are more hidden, internalized, and passive. Among other things, we look for sites where tension has accumulated. All people are tense; everyone lives under stress. However, this tension accumulates in the parts of the body best suited to the indi-vidual. When we identify the element that is most sharply out of balance, we are shown the spot where the subject's func-tioning is impaired and where tensions have accrued. We focus on this region (i.e., "I see you have a lot of pent-up tension in your stomach," or, "I see you internalize things in your stom-ach") since this is the site of all the real and relevant things in the person's life, the place where he or she is usually "located." Physical problems are centered here; it is the subject's battle-ground where the real struggle is waged.

At this point, we examine the overall state of the feet, gen-eral states of surplus and deficiency, the foot as a whole. Is this foot dominated by a particular element? After covering all chronic patterns in evidence, we turn to the area of potential, of basic abilities. To what degree is each aspect of the subject's potential actually being realized? We review each of the ele-ments, observing whether it is over- or underutilized.

It is important for us to observe the state of the fire ele-ment: do our subjects push their lives along, or are they pushed around by them, i.e., are they victims of their situation? We then probe their relationships with others and with their own occupations. The answers to these questions will tell us how to approach our subjects and, ultimately, what direction to point them in. Using all our findings, we present our subjects with a picture of their lives and of how they have "walked" through them. Then we ask the subjects to present us with questions on issues not dealt with or not completely understood.

At this point we summarize the reading and terminate the session. In our summation, we should discuss what our subjects do with themselves and how they do it. Are they wasting themselves? Are they or are they not where they ought to be? What are their weaknesses? How do the difficulties of their lives manifest themselves? What are their pernicious habits, the things that get them "stuck"?

We address important facets of their history: is there something important about their gestation and birth, relations with parents, partings, losses (a marking indicating death)? There is a potential connection between the death of a loved one and physiological problems that surface after the death—a connection that we can point out to our subjects. If, for example, we have a subject who lost a loved one seven years ago and tends to "lock" things away in his stomach, we would draw a connection between this loss and the terrible stomach pains that originated six and a half years ago. Personal history is important because our lives don't unfold by chance; things happen to people because of the way in which they "walk" through life, because something that accumulated in them reached a flashpoint.

Just as people change, so do their feet. Foot analysis conducted at six-month intervals allows us to observe movement and change in people. A subject may come for an analysis to discover and change aspects of his or her life, and return six months later to reaffirm and reinforce the process. As hard as it may be to believe that feet can change so drastically over six months, it is true. When people transform their lives, their feet change from one extreme to the other.

Each foot analysis is a one-time act. The more important it is to our subjects, the more likely it is that this one hour will truly alter their lives.

HOW AND WHERE WE LOOK

The goal of foot analysis is to show subjects a picture of themselves that embraces aspects they have ignored, aspects they have forgotten, aspects they are not interested in seeing, aspects of which they are totally unaware, and aspects with which they are in daily contact. When we try to communicate such a picture, however, various difficulties arise.

Language

Because we use the same phrases or terms to portray completely different things, we must rely upon descriptions rather than terminology to gain the subject's comprehension. People who do not know the correct names of things tend to misinterpretation, especially with regard to emotions such as fear or anger. It is important to remember not to speak in terms of elements but in a language that the subject can comprehend. If we invoke a certain term, we must make sure our listener actually understands what we're talking about. Real-life examples should be provided, especially historical events that can be viewed without excessive involvement on the subject's part, thus allowing him or her to understand a recurrent pattern. This being the case, we must check and recheck whether the subject has truly understood the reader's references.

Intelligence

The first stage of the diagnosis relates to physical characteristics. Through conversation, we are able to form an impression about our subjects' ability to understand and absorb, and to verify the level on which they perceive things. We then seek ways to communicate messages so they will be listened to and heard. The state of people's air element, rather than their level of formal education, may provide an indicator of their ability to grasp complexities.

If the air element is well-developed (attractive, long, almost perfectly balanced toes), strong intellectual ability is indicated. In those cases it is preferable to conduct the conversation on a higher level and avoid oversimplification. If the air element is problematic in some way, one should keep things clear and simple enough to understand, avoiding entanglements in complexities. Our subject's intellectual level should determine the rhetoric of the session ("street talk" vs. "professorial" language). Bear in mind that highly intelligent subjects may be in such emotional turmoil that all their intelligence vanishes.

Resistance and Receptivity

People have various traits that they deny or resist. For example, some people regard fear as a state that they can not and will not countenance; they will avoid any situation likely to generate fear—either internally or externally. When we attempt through our reading to present our subjects with aspects of their personalities that they generally repress, suppress, or otherwise ignore, we may meet with a refusal on the subjects' part to discuss or acknowledge these aspects or an unconscious resistance to hearing us out. This is why we tape-record our sessions; subjects who listen to the tape one or several times may hear all sorts of ostensibly brand new things that their resistance had previously obstructed.

Determining Style and Direction

When we examine new subjects, we must decide how to approach them in such a way that they will truly listen to us and see themselves. It would prove highly problematic if we were to take subjects whose personality was built mainly upon self-control and immediately launch into a discussion of the very things that lie beyond their control, thus arousing the full force of their resistance. Such would also be the case if we were to talk with acutely fearful people about their abilities without addressing ourselves to the fear that prevents them from fulfilling their own potential.

A general examination of the foot is necessary to ascertain the presence or absence of a dominant element in the dominant foot. This would be the element that immediately surfaces in our meeting with the subject, the one most outwardly visible. Such an element, if it is present, should be our point of beginning, since we attract our subjects' attention at the point where they are focused in the here and now. We must address this element in a fashion that suits it and will not evoke resistance. For example, in cases of people with a dominant water element in the dominant foot, we should address ourselves to the anxiety and pressure generated by the analysis itself, and calm such subjects enough to enable them to listen. Otherwise we may "lose" them to their anxieties.

Another example might be a subject with a dominant fire element in the dominant foot. Here, it would be necessary to appeal to the element itself, demonstrating that it still has control over the situation and need not resort to resistance. This is accomplished by "stroking" the element and being extremely careful not to injure its pride in any way. Should we fail to do so, the subject will stop listening.

The first stage of the session is devoted to an encounter with the subject's most blatant, most externalized trait. Once we have established an atmosphere of trust, confidence, and interest, we may turn to the more passive, subsurface aspects of personality. By way of the element through which the subject listens, we are also able to address the diametrically opposed facet of his or her personality. With an air-dominated person, for example, we may descend to earth through the language of air, i.e., discussions of existence and existentialism. By philosophizing with such people, we can demonstrate that they are neglecting a part of themselves.

At the end of the session, we should fashion our summary to match the strongest and most prominent force in the subject's life, since this is the element through which he or she will attempt to comprehend and utilize the reading. For example, if the air element exerts a high degree of control over an individual's life, our summary should be cerebral, sagacious, precise, and clear—however complex the subject matter may be—since people with such leanings will try to view whatever we say through the prism of their intellect.

Achieving a Working Context

The analyst must adhere to certain strictures. It is not advisable to analyze the feet of relatives or others with whom one has a close relationship because our hopes, expectations, and foreknowledge of these people combine to create a distorted picture of the feet. Even if we feel we're being objective, we can't do it. Our very manner of speaking already demonstrates a closeness, knowledge, and feeling of comfort that blocks the formation of an accurate picture.

Before any analysis we should strive to create a calm, focused ambiance free of any distractions. We should be ready and willing to reflect any picture through the lens of our own being; to accept aspects of the subject that we find repulsive in ourselves; to refrain from passing judgment on others' behavior, ideals, or feelings; to merely observe, without measuring our findings against any moral yardstick whatsoever; and to bear in mind that people may conduct their lives in infinitely varied ways, all of which may be correct and appropriate for them. Great sincerity and acceptance of others are vital prerequisites. We don't know how others should live in order to find satisfaction and contentment. It is our job to accept the fact that we cannot offer advice or solutions to others; the most that we can do is provide an accurate picture of the subject's state in the here and now. The more successful we are in freeing ourselves of any personal "baggage," expectations, values and individual perspectives, the deeper the understanding that we bring to the task of observing our subjects' lives as revealed by their feet. Thus we may describe their lives in such a way as to permit them to see the whole picture. Their various facets and strengths will then play a more balanced role in their decision making.

An obvious trap we must avoid is the desire to make people feel good. This wish may lead us to be "nice" and to cushion the impact of things that we find hard to say. In so doing, we are in effect harming our subjects by not daring to "tell it like it is."

Foot analysis should not be viewed as an act of charity. Our assistance is limited to holding up an accurate mirror in which the subjects face their own reflection. If we become caught up in our own feelings and begin to feel sorry for people, we are in essence offering them no tools beyond our pity— for which they have no need. By robbing them of responsibility for their situation, we lose respect for them. The entire reading should be conducted from a perspective that honors the right of people to live by their own lights.

It is important to be aware of any tendency you may have to always start out from the same point or to repeatedly touch upon a particular aspect of others' behavior; this may be a function of your own pattern rather than your subject's.

Referral and Guidance

Referring people onward is part of the conclusion of the analyzing process. Subjects often wish to be pointed in new directions, be they in the areas of treatment or some other endeavor. Whatever the case, we must not invalidate everything they have done up to this point; they would construe this as a denigration of their lives and themselves. If, for example, we refer a greengrocer to academic studies, we should advise him to start out by pursuing both roads simultaneously. If his studies proved sufficiently attractive, he could cease working and shift to his other area of interest. Rather than throwing away a person's past, we learn from it for the future. People do not undergo profound change overnight; this is part of a gradual process.

Change generally requires someone else's support. When people are "in a rut," they need support in order to emerge from their stagnation. Were it otherwise, they would not have come to us. A crisis is a golden opportunity for change and development; it tells us that a person's potential is thirsting for something more. We become "messed up" at the place where our potential demands the most of us, where our greatest strength lies. It is on this aspect of a subject's life that we focus in offering guidance.

Pain of any sort signals that we are no longer in a state of balance. Anything that leaves a lasting mark on the foot points to missed opportunities to restore balance. For example, the loss of a loved one gives excessively inhibited people a chance to break their pattern; the opportunity is theirs to take or leave. During our analysis, we may indicate this pattern to our subjects, partly as a way to help them extricate themselves from its constraints. People usually treat pain as something that should be eliminated rather than learned from. As long as we suffer pain, something inside is trying to urge us to get off that harmful treadmill.

As foot analysts, we should show our subjects that they are constantly repeating the same pattern, thus motivating them to ask questions. This is something they should reread periodically, in order to recall the pattern anew each time. Whenever they are tempted to return to this cycle, they will need to ask themselves whether they wish to alter it or not. When we refer people to a certain endeavor or occupation, we must observe the state of their elements. We might advise them to engage in activity A if we discover a deficiency, and to cease activity A, or do less of it, if we encounter a surplus. For some people, change might entail doing nothing, if their chronic pattern is one of abandoning things in favor of starting something new. We refer people to new areas of activity, to treatment, or to whatever else is appropriate, in accordance with their potential and the degree of its utilization. Several examples are offered below, although the possibilities are, of course, endless.

In the case of people with a dominant but underutilized earth element, we would refer them to activities involving use of the body, e.g., massage, physical exercise such as walking—in short, things that connect them with their own bodies. Those entangled in emotional difficulties would be referred to experiential forms of treatment such as psychotherapy, gestalt therapy, or psychodrama, in order to help them cope with the states that created their imbalance.

If a subject's air element is highly developed, it is advisable to combine the treatment with an aspect of comprehension and conceptualization as well, since such people are able to inform the situation they are experiencing with their own understanding, thus allowing them to cope in the best way possible for them.

When people's fire is in deficiency, we instruct them to do something they love to do, something that will satiate them. If their fire is in surplus, we advise them to halt or curtail their activity, to learn to relax by means of techniques such as reflexology, meditation, or some similar activity.

In certain situations, our advice might include a change of vocation or avocation, in which case we would direct our subject toward a field that matches the findings gleaned from the feet. A sensual, earth-dominated type might be referred to activities such as the arts and beauty, painting, art therapy, physical activity, or occupations involving money and finance. Where the foot offers evidence of deterioration in the digestive system—even if actual symptoms are not yet present—we might recommend seeing a specialist for a balanced diet, especially if subjects tell us they are not eating well.

The condition of the toes is relevant because it sheds light on the nature of our subject's perception and personality structure. For example, a square big toe indicates orderly, logical thinking; such a person has aptitude for fields such as accounting, physics, mathematics, and electronics, that do not necessarily involve working with others.

If toes 2 and 3 cross the big toe, a need and a talent for communication (on interpersonal and other levels) is indicated, coupled with an ability to perceive things beyond our own "I." These aptitudes might serve a person well in the "helping professions."

A lot of problems in the water element suggest a person with a sizable load of emotional experiences; it would be beneficial to make use of this experience through work as a psychologist or other type of care giver.

If toe 2 is on a higher plane than the big toe, a career in communications or public relations may be in the offing. Toe 2 and energy flow to the hands are connected with eye-hand qualities that are useful in photography, landscaping, painting, and sculpture.

Highly developed fourth and fifth toes indicate musical ability. A strong fire element ascending to toe 2 is indicative of people who push too much, who are always on the go. They should be advised to ease up a bit. Their area of endeavor may be highly suited to them, but they work themselves too hard. When we direct people to a creative field, we should check just where their creativity is "blocked" and use this information to refer them to a field involving this very type of block.

In referring people to various activities, we should ask ourselves the following questions:

1) What do they want? Is this truly *their* goal, not ours? Without the subject's willingness there is no point to any referral.

2) What are the individuals' basic potentials? How longstanding and entrenched are the patterns that are holding them back?

3) What are their life factors: age, general situation, family status, financial standing, environment, cultural background?

4) How willing is the subject to change and take risks?

5) How aware, attentive, and receptive are they?

6) Are they willing to push their lives along—and to what extent—or are they "quitters"?

THE MIRROR PRINCIPLE

In essence, the mirror principle is the attempt to tell subjects about themselves in such a way that they will see themselves in mirror image. The problem is that even when we view ourselves in a real mirror, there are things we refuse to see or cannot absorb, even as we contemplate other aspects of our personalities with great concentration. We are highly judgmental about what we see and are preoccupied with how we "should" be.

The goal of analysis is to create a different mirror image that truly reflects what is there, not what "should have been" or what the subject would like to see. We aim to show our subjects those parts of themselves that they generally do not examine—and to dredge up past and present issues that have been left dangling—in such a way that they will be able to view them as they are, without the resistance and judgment that generally come into play.

The very fact that a disinterested stranger manages to show me things about myself, without my providing any clues, opens my eyes in a manner that is nonjudgmental and does not obligate me to act in any way. This permits me to see myself as reflected from a different angle.

To be good mirrors, we must be certain that we reflect a full picture of all the strongest and most important forces affecting our subjects' lives. By illuminating these areas, we permit our subjects to embark upon a process of acquiescence and balancing. We have to maintain a noninterventionist posture as we work, refraining from advice or recommendations, demands or judgment. Our task is simply to describe the subject's condition as shown on the foot. Any personal involvement, any hint of condolence, pity, anger, or judgment of any sort, will obfuscate the very things we are trying to show our subjects. The idea is not to project coldness, detachment, or lack of humor, but rather to avoid any personal interest in the subject, be it positive or negative.

A subject's encounter with his or her reflection in a clear and undistorted mirror generates the possibility of a personal breakthrough and the initiation of an intense process of change and balance leading to health and freedom.

THE ROLE OF INTUITION

Thus far we have referred only to our conscious understanding, to the exclusion of that part of ourselves that receives messages in ways we do not comprehend. Intuition is defined in many ways and takes different forms in different people. Without entering into the meaning of intuition, it can safely be stated that every individual has a characteristic personal way of receiving nonverbal messages that skirt the standard "channels of information."

Interestingly, people generally absorb such material through the region where they expend the smallest amount of their energy. People who are preoccupied with thought and words, for example, somehow receive messages through their bodies rather than their heads. I believe we absorb extrasensory messages via the area or region where our attention is least focused and where, consequently, our "filters" are less active in screening the input. I believe it takes no special paranormal ability to receive nonverbal or nonsensory messages from others. The first prerequisite is that one accept the possibility that we can receive information without knowing its source. For intellectually inclined people, the problem is how to silence the inner "dialogue" of the head and listen to the messages of the body. Emotional people must neutralize their emotional involvement in matters and try to absorb the information "coldly" and unemotionally, through visualization.

In this way, an opening is created in our perception where we do not harbor defined expectations—a state of affairs that permits the unknown to become the known. In my years as a reflexologist, during which I spent thousands of hours in direct contact with subjects' feet, I found a staggering amount of intuitive knowledge to be gained. "Being intuitive" does not mean knowing what is right for a person; intuition is telling people something that we suddenly know about them.

A clear distinction must be drawn between intuition and hysteria; intuition has nothing to do with emotional excitement. It is not a burst of water spurting upward; rather, it is a state of great lucidity. Intuition arises not from thought, action, or emotion, but from the depths of the water element. It is not a process or an emotional state but a sudden flash of information.

Strong powers of concentration are needed in order to exercise control over one's intuition. We may speak of intuition and how it can be stimulated, but the fact remains that it arises from the lower water element, and even if we are able to plumb these depths there are times when nothing will come of it.

To get in touch with our intuition, we must first come to a firm decision that we are going to concentrate *now*. We also need a certain degree of inner silence—in other words, control over our internal dialogue without distracting thoughts rattling around inside our head. Once we have attained the requisite concentration and quiet, we must wait. This waiting is so silent and tranquil that it induces a state like that of a moon reflected with precision in the surface of a lake. The lake is so still that the moon appears completely unchanged upon its waters. It is during this quiet time that intuition may rise. If and when it does, we should not care exactly what has surfaced. (Neither, however, should we be cold or indifferent.) Intuition is like opening a door for something that's already inside.

The following procedure during a foot analysis session maximizes the probability that intuition will rise:

1) Make it clear to the subject that you will not be speaking to him or her for the next several minutes. Say, "I would like to observe and think in silence for a few moments."

2) Sit down, place your feet on the floor, and breathe slowly and deeply.

3) Any tension in the body blocks our concentration, since our energy is occupied elsewhere. We therefore lower the shoulders, allow the jaws and anus to go slack, and relax the legs. Thus far we have achieved outward calm, relaxation, and the focusing of our energy on what we choose to do.

4) We close our eyes and palpate the subject's feet. This "legitimizes" our action in the subject's eyes, protects him or her from feeling pressured, and avoids the introduction of tension. While our eyes remain closed, we note what's happening in our head without paying it undue attention. Rather than trying to stifle the noise in our head—a move which would only intensify it—we take the approach that the messages being transmitted by our heads are of no concern to us.

5) Amid the silence, we imagine that our bodies are a type of conduit, the lower part connecting us to the earth, the other end open to the sky. Our arms extend outward from the middle of the channel. It is through them that information enters this

passageway. We do not try to understand or feel, but only await something, feeling the subject's foot all the while. The next step is to find a way to communicate to the subject the information we have obtained.

There are myriad ways to connect with the unknown. Some prefer to picture a door being opened by themselves as they wait to see what lies behind it. Some imagine a television screen, others hear a voice, and still others see a picture. Some feel it in their bodies; others know it suddenly. Each person's intuition takes a different form.

It is always worth leaving room for intuition—giving it the option to surface, but not depending upon it. It takes practice to hone one's intuition. Our intuition and our intelligence relate to time in different ways. Intelligence envisions a linear progression from past to present; intuition absorbs things from the unknown, where past, present, and future intermingle.

A SAMPLE FOOT ANALYSIS

The subject is a 31-year-old male. We ascertain the locations of states of extreme deficiency and surplus in each of the elements; we identify these as "open" (i.e., unresolved) past situations:

Earth Element—The bottom of the lower earth band shows highly conspicuous signs of a surplus in accumulated earth energy (dry, tough skin). The thickness of the markings indicates that the condition is of many years' duration. We may infer that this is an unresolved state of energy connected with violence, survival, and instinctive responses. The specific location of these signs on the foot leads us to conclude that the condition originated at a very early age.

Dry grooves are noted in the region corresponding to the lower back, the bladder, and the spinal column. This is the boundary between water and earth, where water penetrates the earth element. It reflects a period very close in time to birth. The grooves and other signs in the region point to a clash between two noncomplementary factors. Such a state indicates a lack of coordination between emotions on the one hand

and sexuality and instinct on the other. This person has been characterized by dissociation from these drives and lack of communication with them from as early as 4 or 5 years of age. The subject informs us that a younger sibling was born during this period, which changed his status in the household. The family may have moved sometime during those years. A transition from earth to water is effected at the age of 4 or 5.

In the foot, the lines of partial dissociation in the lower water element point to fears bound up with primal existential insecurity; the subject may have viewed the sibling's birth or some other change as a threat to his own existence. To this day, any situation involving change or the creation of a new framework is experienced as a powerful existential dilemma. A state of surpluses of earth energy in the lower earth band, coupled with partial separation lines in the lower water band, indicates a problematic, unresolved situation connected with home, family, and / or money. In most of the territory occupied by the earth element, the subject's self-control represses his experiencing of basic needs; he perceives himself as being uninterested in a secure life structure or in money.

To verify our observations in the subject's earth element, we now examine toe 5. If it is small relative to the other toes, we deduce that the subject is congenitally disinclined to attach importance to the qualities associated with this element. The fire element is visible in the fifth toe, and its toenail is smaller and different than the other toenails. This toe reflects a special state in the earth element, specifically a dissociation between instinct drives, sensuality, sexuality and the other elements, or even a hormonal or fertility problem.

To sum up, it is evident that the energy of earth has been compressed into the bottom part of the element; instead of spreading out and occupying its designated area, it allows the energy of fire to reign there. Such an unresolved state prevents the subject from taking possession of all the earth energy he's got.

Water Element—This element exhibits classic signs of emotional frustration—very clear lines, mostly old, that fan out from the region corresponding to the spinal column to the entire inner portion of the water region. Such markings indicate a very long history of frustrations, dissociation of fire and earth, and an attempt to stem and control fear. The signs appear in the region that reflects the ages of 3 to 7. This period was an emotionally difficult one, leaving a heavy residue of insecurity. The indicators point to many unresolved emotional states, chiefly dating back to that period, resulting from resistance, struggle, and refusal to accept the emotional states emanating from within. The energy of water struggles vainly to rise and manifest itself. It remains inside, trapped, thus making it hard for the subject to express any emotional state. This dissociation also indicates that the subject is unaware of certain of these emotional states. He knows only of their consequences. This leaves a trail of unresolved states for many years to come.

Grooves over the region corresponding to the liver and spleen can be seen. The skin texture is rougher than the norm, and the regions are fuller and darker in color. The liver region exhibits signs of past hepatitis as well as accumulated rage and a difficulty in expressing anger. The spleen bears markings of guilt feelings that have accumulated from age 8 through 10 onward. Lengthwise lines in the center of the foot rising from the bladder region to a point approximating the kidney region point to an intermittent, rapid movement of water energy either upward or downward—a sudden outburst of emotion. The ages that are marked most prominently are 4 and 5 and 12 and 13.

Question: What do you remember from these ages?

Answer: According to what I've been told, I was taken abroad at age 3. Until the age of 5 I was in nursery school and didn't speak with the other children. From ages 5 to 6 I spoke with the kindergarten teacher only. When I was 10, we went abroad again. I started high school at age 12 and had a hard time finding my place in the new social circle.

Question: What was hard about going abroad when you were 10 or 11 years old? The time you were there or the return home?

Answer: I don't remember.

Question: Is it hard for you to recall this period of time? What overall impression do you have of that period?

Answer: A lot of insecurity abroad.

Question: Does this feeling of insecurity resurface from time to time? Do you have attacks of insecurity?

Answer: Yes.

Question: Have you experienced much fear during your life?

Answer: I haven't been afraid. I've looked for it, provoked it, and haven't been able to experience it.

Fire Element—Several signs of separation quite close together indicate that the subject does not know how to part with people; he has a history of unresolved separations. He has not succeeded in truly "closing" or resolving matters with any of the people from whom he has parted. This has caused earth to accumulate in the fire region, with a consequent attempt to repress and to avoid experiencing the pain of separation. Earth energy within fire is characteristic of a constant preoccupation with how things "should be," leading the subject to conclude that the parting was inevitable. The separations were caused by circumstances, and not by an emotional choice.

Both feet exhibit surpluses of earth in the region corresponding to the shoulder, implying that the subject experiences chronic states of clumsiness and poor coordination in activities involving the hands. Although the fire element is well developed, the presence of earth that has risen from its original location to that of fire, points to an obstruction that keeps fire from exiting through the hands and manifesting itself in the subject's actions and behavior. It is obstructed, stuck, and slow, making the subject's actions static rather than dynamic. Now it actually reflects an internal insecurity within the fire element itself—a lack of confidence in the ability of fire to act and create. Excessive control has become an existential need.

There are numerous indications of separation of water and fire, generating a state of conflict between itself and water, between control and emotionalism. Even though one of the sides prevails at any given point in time the subject is the perpetual loser, since he finds it exceedingly difficult to bring the two elements together. He tries to control, to deny, to avoid feeling the emanations of his water element, but periodic outbursts of these very emotions make him into their victim.

Air Element—The subject's air is gravely permeated by fire (as manifested by red toes with much muscle tissue); some signs of earth are present too (dry, tough skin on the side of the big toe and several stiff joints in the toes). This penetration pollutes the element and indicates that the subject's air has never fulfilled its potential in terms of intellectual, conceptual, and sensual capabilities. This is because the existence of this element is being fought intensely. In fact, the subject has spent many years living by his feelings and experiences only. In other words, he lives by living rather than by thinking, perceiving, understanding, and seeing. He lives with neither goals nor strategy; he attempts to live for the moment. He has never engaged in learning nor in intellectual struggle.

In the present, the imbalance manifests itself in difficulties with concentration, reading, verbal expression, writing, and lucidity of thought. The subject is extremely insecure about his ability to learn, i.e., to understand, analyze, and process new information. He yields to intellectual power and opts for silence in the company of people he considers smart. The gaping disparity between the basic potential of the element and the extent of its realization generates great frustration (which we observed earlier in the water element).

Relationship with Parents

The area representing the mother throughout the earth and water regions is indicated much more strongly on the active foot than on the passive one. There is little passive energy; in its place we find fire, as manifested in red coloration throughout the earth and water regions. A small amount of passive energy is compressed into the edge of the heel, appearing there in the form of dry, cracked skin. These signs point to a weak presence of the mother in terms of her passive energy and to a long-standing, difficult problem with the mother in the context of this type of energy. The subject has experienced lack of warmth and physical contact. To this day he demands constant warmth, touch, and "stroking" from those around him. Nevertheless, he finds it hard to accept demonstrations of warmth.

In the area representing the father, we observe a strong presence of earth on the side of the big toe, reflecting an unresolved state with respect to the father and a persistent problem in relations with him, dating back to a very early stage of life. The subject experienced his father as an authoritative, strong, rigid, and demanding personage, emanating powerful masculine energy. The earth element in the region indicates that the subject has attempted to resist his father's influence with all the might of his passive energy but none of his active energy. He attests to having chosen throughout his life to oppose his father's life-style. The father is an intellectual with an extensive educational background; the son shirked study all his life and chose not to think. He grew up in a home where both parents expended their active energies; he experienced this as the relegation of emotion and instinct to a less important position. It is evident that he has always neglected his passive aspects and resisted his active ones. The result is a situation marked by the recurring theme—also reflected in his feet—of perpetual frustration and a sense of impasse.

Intelligence

Observing the subject's air element, we find it to be highly developed, attractive, and possessed of impressive potential. We see a very strong ability to empathize, display sensitivity, absorb, and comprehend. This basic potential has been somewhat impaired, as evidenced by the fact that some of the toes are bent under and surpluses of fire and earth have had a detrimental effect on the quality of the element. The strong presence of fire in the toe pads points at an attempt by the subject to control his thinking, to think as he "should," and to confine his perceptions to those situations that he can control. This, in turn, points to a certain degree of impenetrability. There are things he is unwilling to accept or to understand. He thinks many things are implausible, impossible, and illogical, and he is unwilling to think about anything that he considers impractical.

The subject tells us: "For many years, I tried to confine my thoughts to 'sure things.'" (An expression of the earth element within air.) "I didn't take the risk of trying to learn anything new. I acquired rigid opinions and ideologies, and held on tight to them."

Toe 1—On this toe, which represents the zenith of the air element, we find signs of earth in the region corresponding to the nape of the neck (the same signs that we spoke of with relation to the father). This indicates a learning problem manifested in concentration difficulties, flawed memory, passive (i.e., lacking creativity and initiative) and illogical thinking. The air element makes no attempt to spread outward as it should by nature; instead it tries to compress itself by trying to make things simple and uncomplicated. The subject flinches from intellectualism and abstract concepts. For years, his high basic potential has remained unexploited in areas related to air, such as reading, memory, and the use of general knowledge.

Toe 2—This toe is bent under on both feet, indicating that the subject wishes to protect himself and to repel baggage that would be hard for his ego to accommodate. The toe represents the fire element and the subject's communication with other people; its length also shows how well he empathizes, i.e., how he shares or feels—in a way that defies logic—someone else's experiences. The bent position of the toe shows that the subject is unwilling to see and understand others' situations. The rise of the water region of the toe to the active area points to an attempt to achieve the kind of control that eradicates "gut feelings." The subject does not let himself experience others' ordeals; neither does he permit his feelings to surface, lest this bruise his ego. The bent position also points at impaired creativity (the toe of fire representing creativity), since, as we have seen, the free flow of creative forces is blocked.

Toe 3—The fire element manifests itself intensely in this appendage. The subject has again attempted to assert self-control, trying to keep his emotional power from finding expression in communication and its depth from surfacing in thought. The thought process represents an attempt to control, to arrange, to understand, and to deny as needed. We may infer that the subject does not reveal his emotional state internally (the air element), instead maintaining a "poker face" to hide his feelings from others. Toe 3 is also related to the processes of digestion and absorption. The presence of fire here indicates problems in these areas and, in fact, signs of a surplus in the fire element may be visible over the region corresponding to the stomach. In general, the toe is ramrod straight and is divided among the various elements in a very correct and healthy fashion. Signs of surplus and deficiency are few. All of this indicates that, despite the presence of fire in the toe, long-term processes of absorption and digestion—transformative processes—are taking place.

Toe 4—This toe is wider and more swollen than the other four; fire is present here to a greater degree than in the others. Such a state points to large surpluses of anger, guilt, and frustration in the thought process. The subject attempts to control them and block their manifestation in the presence of the fire element. The air region of the toe has become passive; since this toe is related to learning, we may deduce that the subject has difficulty with active learning that "pushes" and demands. His problem is how to cope not with the intellectual content of the subject matter but rather with the study framework. He chafes in the presence of authoritative teachers, since they evoke his anger, frustration, guilt, and blame tendencies. He is presumably reluctant to learn from such personalities in the future; he may have made a practice of avoiding them over the years.

Toe 5—This toe represents the earth element within air. Its own earth element is in a state of deficiency; the toenail is very scanty and the toe itself is small relative to the other toes. The fire element has taken it over. The earth deficiency indicates great difficulty in maintaining structure and obedience, sustaining consistent learning toward specific goals, creating or identifying orderly study frameworks, and organizing and safeguarding things so that they will not be lost. The subject finds it hard to persevere with a task and to carry ideas through to reality.

Our subject is a young man with very high intellectual capabilities. His difficulties in this regard are related not to the qualities and skills of the air element itself but to the presence of energy from an earlier period—primarily of earth and fire— in the region. This energy keeps his air from spreading and occupying its rightful place. To permit his intellectual abilities to find expression, the subject must "close" the unresolved situations in his life and channel his control over his intellect into cultivating that same quality. In other words, he should use his control of air for the purpose of developing it further. Appropriate steps might be deciding to read, study, or develop himself intellectually, choosing to observe the complexity of

things instead of judging them, and expressing himself emotionally and intellectually. The decision to take these steps
toward self-improvement and self-development will allow the
air element to grow, expand, and cleanse itself of the superflu-
ous elements within it.

The subject tells us: "My problem with studying in a formal
setting is something I see very clearly. I've also got a problem
with independent study and fitting into other frameworks. I
resist thinking; I get angry about anything involving thinking
and learning from someone else. I also perceive my problems
with 'digesting' thoughts, processing things, and creating something new."

When asked if he knows that he has intellectual leanings,
the subject answers: "I only know that I've always run away
from that."

Emotional World

A general examination of the subject's foot tells us that its dominant element is fire. Several signs in the water element suggest
the presence of the power and qualities of fire. The lateral walking strip (where we place our weight when we stride) is very
wide, red in color, and larger than its potential within the water
element would indicate. There are regions where the water element is dry. Many spots and red grooves are present, as are
crosswise markings that indicate obstructions in the flow of
water. The latter appear as signs of fire within water.

We pay particular attention to areas within the water element. The characteristic grooves that indicate constipation also
express emotional frustration originating in early childhood.
We deduce the exact age by noting the specific location of the
lower grooves in the water region; in this case they point at age
3 and up, meaning that it was at this point in the child's life
that the emotional pattern of holding back and controlling emotional power surfaced.

We then infer that the subject has been trying to rein in
the force of his emotions—primarily those connected with fear,
insecurity, and frustration—from a very young age. The location of the indicators in the lower water region points to an
obstruction of very low-level forces originating in the boundary between earth and water. Sexual vigor and emotional

potencies are not permitted to emerge and manifest themselves in proportion to their actual strength.

A long, old, and deep line in the center of the water region indicates a longstanding fear that the subject is repressing and containing with all his might. He has dissociated himself from it; the emotion is not allowed to ascend to his consciousness, just as the groove fails to reach the upper water region where the degree of emotional awareness is higher. The lengthwise and crosswise lines indicate emotional confusion. On the one hand, the subject attempts to prevent the ascent and articulation of his feelings; his emotional force is anesthetized or extinguished. On the other hand, he experiences periodic emotional outbursts.

The strong presence of fire within water tells us that the subject's emotional world is very significant to him. His attempt to repress and control his feelings shows that he attaches great importance to them. True, he regards this force as a powerful threat; he knows neither how to cope with it nor how to let it flow freely. His very attempt to control it, however, shows us how important it is to him.

Around the area corresponding to the stomach, we see red grooves that indicate a tendency to irritability. When the subject's emotional forces approach the level of consciousness, he loses patience with them. He wants things to happen already— to take place swiftly, not gradually. Situations that evoke irritability and demand quick response do not occur often, but when they do, he is impatient.

Red vertical signs over the region corresponding to the liver are present; these indicate outbursts of anger. The subject tends to flare up quickly, but the surplus in the region tells us that his anger is never actually expressed. He repeats the same pattern incessantly—growing angry, getting "stuck" on the anger, controlling it, preventing its ascent and articulation. When his control mechanism fails, emotional outbursts take place. (The subject informs us that he is known as an even-tempered person who never gets angry, although much of his anger comes to the fore in his driving.)

Thus far we have seen how hard it is for the subject to express emotions within the water element itself, because this element is under the control of fire. We now examine how manifestations of the subject's inner emotional world rise to the level of consciousness and how he communicates these manifestations to his surroundings.

The region corresponding to the throat shows strong signs of surplus. This suggests a surplus of earth where the head and the spinal column intersect in the vicinity of the nape of the neck; there are also crosswise grooves in the throat area. All of these indicate that the subject has difficulty expressing emotion; when called upon to do so, his throat tightens and his feelings become literally "stuck" inside. This happens because his self-control is at war with his emotional forces. When he tries to be honest and true to his emotional potencies, he comes up against all his longstanding patterns of control, of holding things in, of "how I think things should be." He feels one thing and expresses another—a situation that leaves him confused and dishonest with himself. He has difficulty saying "no" or expressing his emotional needs clearly because this disparity between thought and word shakes his confidence in his own feelings. The subject's emotional awareness becomes foggy: "Am I really feeling this way or do I only think I am?" Sometimes he feels nothing at all, because his self-control smothers his very ability to feel.

The region corresponding to the spleen—an area connected with guilt—shows a large accumulation of fire and old, deeply embedded signs. These indicate that the subject has suffered from very intense guilt feelings since the age of 6. He increasingly clamped down on his feelings as he aged, thus repressing them and forcing them beneath the surface. Much of what motivates him emotionally today are these same feelings of guilt, still residing in his abdomen. We should assume that this subject's guilt feelings are his constant companion.

Sexuality and Fertility

The state of the earth element in toe 5 teaches us about the subject's sexuality and fertility. The lowest end of the earth element area is in surplus. As we rise, the earth becomes more balanced; where it adjoins water, it falls into deficit, meaning that there tends to be more fire than earth. As for basic potential, we see that the earth element is large and attractive, although it is much smaller—and a great deal less significant in the subject's experience—than fire. In general, there is a flow of energy between the heel and toe 5. Still, there are three problematic sites: the boundary between water and earth, the region corresponding to the shoulder, and toe 5.

The subject needs to learn how to deal with his sexual energy. He disregards and rechannels this potency, thus preventing its full, direct articulation. His control represses this energy severely. It is unable to flow freely and gets "stuck" in the area corresponding to the sex organs. Markings on the boundary between water and earth indicate an interruption in the sexual flow. A very old fear—dating back to something that happened to the subject as a child, not as an adolescent or an adult—is obstructing some of his sexual energy. (The location of the marking tells us when this happened.)

A large quantity of "stuck" earth means that the ego is trying to keep the earth energy under close rein. (We see this in the shoulder area and in toe 5). The subject judges himself strictly with regard to his sexuality. When sexual energy is aroused, he "stands aside" and observes himself judgmentally, thus preventing a flow of energy that might sweep him along. Responding to fear of losing self-control, the subject builds a permanent state of overcontrol, lest this energy gain the upper hand. Even when its power is on "full throttle," something is always left behind—a judgmental observer who keeps score throughout. This is another example of the interference of fire in areas that are not its province.

Toe 5 is small relative to the other toes. Again we see that, in terms of basic potential, the energies of sexuality and fertility are not of cardinal importance in this foot. All the other elements are basically larger and more fully developed. The subject does not regard his powers of sexuality and fertility as particularly important. The notion of establishing a family is not of much interest to him.

The lower inhibition is the more problematic of the two, since it originated at a very young age and its content is unknown. At its root is a basic problem connected with physical contact. Situations involving intimacy terrify the subject, causing him to distance himself from others. The tentacles of this inhibition impose themselves on all areas of the subject's life. Since this type of pattern is so deeply rooted, it is hard to contend with.

The water element symbolizes our emotional life. It is a moving world, where shifts in the atmosphere change reality quickly and responses are not limited only to what is visible or recognizable in our thoughts. Currents of water, even in emotionally controlled people, may burst all dams and flood them out of control. In this world, fear and excitement are dominant forces that run a gamut of shades and colors and give personal reality to our emotions. Many people bury the fears of the past in this constantly changing place. Other people are haunted by emotions that they can't tolerate in themselves; others cover excitement with rigid behavior. It is hard to define the nonverbal reality of the water "world." It can only be felt as the undulating ocean of our own experience.

14

LOVE AND CREATIVITY

Since love is a state of being that embraces all the elements, it is apparent throughout the foot in the way the elements interrelate. Love is located in a place where inner balance reigns. When it is present, people's relationships with themselves and with other objects or people are tranquil; they accept the world as it is, making no attempt to add to it, subtract from it, or modify it in any way.

Over and above the picture that emerges from the foot as a whole, we learn about the role of love in the subject's life from the boundary between the water and fire elements in the region corresponding to the heart (see figure 73 on page 248). This is where a person's passive and active forces meet; at the very zenith of the opposition and contradiction between them, coexistence and balance become possible.

The encounter between fire and water is a meeting of awesome forces. Love embraces both giving and taking (water and fire). The act of love is not connected with wisdom, action, emotion, or need. Love is like a light containing all the colors from the brown of earth to the white of air. It passes through, and is experienced by, all the elements. It is present in all people, but manifests itself differently in each of us. The presence of love depends not on absolute balance but on a state approaching balance.

It cannot exist when one of the elements dominates our being, thus dictating our behavior and the way in which we experience life. Love is therefore not dependency, domination, the need to be with someone, fear of intimacy, and so forth. Most people long for moments of love—moments that bring them face to face with inner tranquility, sadness, depth, and

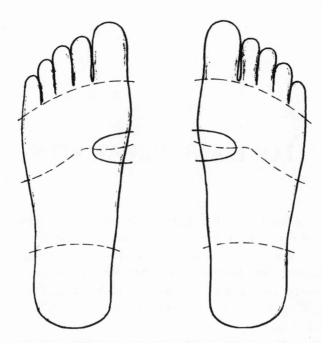

Figure 73. Love. This is the area between the water and fire elements in the region corresponding to the heart. In this region we can see which energy is influencing and shaping the person's ability to love.

pain in their most intense forms. Our culture, with its unwillingness to experience hurt or cope with pain, does not prepare us for an encounter with the potency of love and everything it expresses. We tend to dissociate ourselves from loving moments, leaving ourselves with only a vague longing for something we cannot precisely identify.

We long for love and, at the same time, are repelled by it—like the flame of fire or the depths of water. We are sad because we know that most of us will only rarely and fleetingly achieve love and, with it, a few moments of balance. We generally look at love through an invisible barrier, as if from the wrong side of a plate-glass window: we may see and know but cannot touch. To live a life of love is to live life to its fullest, with all its untempered joy, sadness, pain, actions, spirituality, sexuality, and so on.

Love is the readiness to go all the way, to experience our emotions to the utmost, by choice. Such willingness leads people to a vast space harboring uncertainty, fear, ability to learn, self-renewal, and many other things that many of us perceive as risks that we would do well to avoid.

Love cannot be judged or measured; it is neither logical nor rational. People can love someone or something even as they inflict harm on it. Our first encounter with life—upon conception—is an act of love. Love is bound up with beginnings and endings. Life is dynamic; from the moment we are formed, through our birth, growth, and eventual death, we are ever accompanied by movement and change. Every parting represents a moment of choice, whether we are aware of this or not. Most of us perform acts of development, or even upheaval, in our lives because we have lost something we loved. When life is "all right" and nothing pushes us toward change, the chances of a true encounter with our hearts become slim.

Love and pain are intertwined. When people dare to love, they must take account of the prospect of pain; this is why so many avoid love. If we accept the pain, our hearts can grow with it. This is irrational but possible, since love and pain are themselves not rational. When we choose not to run from pain, we gain the possibility of love and become "someone special" in our own eyes, endowed with great inner strength and charm.

We can reach people only if we touch them where their love resides, if we reach out to that space from the same place in ourselves. If, in the course of a foot analysis, we appeal to thought, custom, or actions, our words will quickly be forgotten. If we appeal to structure, chances for change are negligible since such frameworks are difficult to change. If we appeal to emotions, it will be akin to walking on water—a highly unstable process.

An analysis that brings together two people where their hearts live is an act of transformation. When we love people fully, we give them themselves—not ourselves. Only when love is directed toward us, and we consent to experience it and thus to love ourselves, may we be who we are. To agree to accept love is to agree that we are worthy of it. A one-hour encounter during which we love our subjects can change their lives to the point where they are ready to touch their pain, too.

A good reading must emanate from a place of balance; if we manage this, the subject will truly hear us, since this site radiates energy of great intensity—greater than the energies

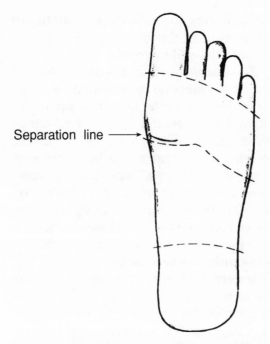

Separation line ⟶

Figure 74. Separation line. This line appears when a person has parted from a relationship and something significant in that relationship is left unresolved.

of all the elements put together. To succeed in coming from this place means that we touch people without judging them or wanting something for them; we accept them, thus evoking the same feeling of acceptance and self-love in them. Without this, the reading has no real impact. We do not truly reach the subject.

One of the most important things we observe in the course of an analysis is the region of love, since everything that has happened to the subject is related to that emotion. We came into this world in order to succeed in reaching this place and remaining there. Human energy strives to reach this place of love, i.e., balance; each person pursues this goal in his or her own way.

Our subjects are not in a state of balance; if they were, they would not have come to us. We try to see if love is present in their lives. Do they know of its existence? Their lines of parting (see figure 74) indicate watersheds in their lives and opportunities to grow beyond the point they have reached thus far. We look for a sign of parting, inquire about these separations, and show them that we have found an indicator of something significant that is unresolved in their lives. When a matter is truly "over and done with," an opportunity for a new beginning is created. This is a moment of choice. There are no vacuums in life; the moment something ends, something new begins.

From the moment we are created, we are constantly undergoing separations—from the previous moment, from people, from times in our lives. Consequently, this is a significant issue in everyone's life. We should show people how to separate, how to declare things over, for only then can there be an encounter with freedom—freedom from the things they have finished. Through this training, people learn to let the pain and the power emanate whenever they must, for a great force will arise from this process. The stronger the pain, the greater the force that will emerge. The foot analysis process should address this point by asking questions such as, "What did you gain from your partings?" or, "What did you allow yourselves to lose from your partings?"

Separation makes some people younger and pushes others toward death. (An example of the latter would be cancer patients.) Most serious illnesses, such as cancer, begin as something general without clear symptoms. They are related in some way to love—love for some person or thing in our lives, be it an object, a place, a creation, a cat, or whatever. Such people gradually "fade away" and give up on life, like a flame that flickers before dying. There are people who, while not physically ill, live as if they were dead. They have parted with something, and the love within them has died. Not having recovered from the parting, they have not revived what has died inside. Love once filled them; when it perished they became empty and could not or would not replenish themselves.

It is extremely rare to find a foot with no signs of parting. Separations are inevitable when we love; anyone who has not experienced them does not know what love is. One cannot discern light without knowing the meaning of darkness. If we see adults without signs of parting, we know that they have never taken the risk, never loved, for it is impossible to have loved and never parted from anything. A groove signifying parting appears in the region where the point of balance lies. The groove tells us that our subjects loved and later suffered pain. The parting can be from an object, an animal, an ideology, a place, a person, or anything else to which they felt close. It must be something with which they formed a connection through their love. A sign of parting indicates to us that something they loved has gone away. The subject may deny it; he or she may even have forgotten about it. But we will find indications of it in the region of the heart and confirm our findings elsewhere on the foot.

We can observe such signs even in very young children, for children are constantly undergoing separations. There are many things in their lives that, at times, surpass even mommy and daddy in importance: a turtle, a cat that disappeared, a flower that was picked, grandpa, or grandma. The sign can emerge quite quickly in children since they don't repress themselves. They have the strength to love and to suffer pain. Later the losses accumulate and people become "immune."

Even so, there is no one who cannot love again. People are afraid to allow the power of love to surface and hold them in its grasp for a long, uninterrupted time; they generally forget that such a possibility even exists. Underlying many attributes such as creativity, sexuality, and intelligence is the matter of love or its absence. A loss of the power to love plays a large role in the process of maturation and senescence. Over the years, people lose the ability to give love from within themselves, lest this cause them pain. This is the ultimate tragedy. Indeed, most people who come to us experience little love, pleasure, or pain. In a love relationship, people pass between the various elements. The site of balance in a loving connection is the point of departure and the base that can always be returned to after we have selected different elements each time.

As long as we can leave confrontation behind and return to love, or call forth love when needed—even in the middle of a clash between spouses, for example—then love is still present. If we are unable to arouse this feeling, we know the tie has been severed, at least with regard to love. Some partings take place out of love, and the people involved continue to love each other despite their anger and bitterness. Each element has its own conditions that must be fulfilled if it is to play a role in love, be it sexuality (earth) emotions (water), or other aspects arising from the various elements.

Love is spoken of as a punishment. At times we may love people with whom we're "out of sync"; incompatibility on a sexual or other level is present, and our whole personality screams, "No!" But we love them anyway. The love that emanates from that place remains with us forever. If the heart loves, it allows the other elements to express themselves. Sadness and love are felt in the heart but pass through other elements.

Parting is like a sore, open wound. If there is no complementary process, i.e. resolution, the love is not restored and the energy is lost. When we complete a separation, the open, festering wound eventually heals and forms a scar. An indicator of parting and a scarred region appear when there is pain that has not been experienced. Through a process of treatment, people can be helped to get in touch with their pain and revive it, thus closing the circle and regaining the lost energy. People generally avoid doing this. They ask for a promise, impossible to give, that they will never again suffer pain. The unwillingness to experience strength as a "package deal" that includes pain, places them at even greater distance from possible encounters with moments of love.

At the point of balance, endless variations of the elements and their effect on love are possible. By using the reading to compare the potential of this point with its actual state, we learn about the subject's behavior and way of experiencing love. It is safe to say that every person has the potential to love. Those who have realized this potential exhibit signs of parting; if no such signs are present, we know they have never loved. Love is something of which people are generally unaware; or, more precisely, they are aware of it through different elements but not at the point of balance itself. When a relationship begins, we call this place "falling in love." Even here, however, the elements come into play, and pure unadulterated moments of love are rare and exceptional.

Love is true inner peace that also radiates outward. People who are capable of living at the point of love itself create a balance between their water and fire elements. The first step on the road to balance is to reach the point of balance, if only for a few moments. The apex of love is tranquility, with no planning or complications, with no effort to change things, no desire to make them different.

People with a mark of parting have experienced, at least once, what it means to be inside their own heart. Someone who experienced a parting three years ago, and has been feeling bad about it ever since, thinks that this feeling is due to the separation. In reality, however, such people feel bad because their heart is pleading for change and they are ignoring its wishes. When people experience a parting, they stop and look at their lives. At this point, all opportunities are open to them; it is a moment of choice, a new chance to change. When the break is not "clean" and the pain is not experienced, the chances for change/choice are diminished or blocked.

Parting indeed demands real change on various human levels. During the agony of parting, most people swear that they will never love again. They reject the possibility that they may be hurt in this way again, and they invest their energy in avoiding such an eventuality.

The first conclusions people should draw from a separation is that they have love, that love is possible, and that it places further demands on us. Influenced by other elements, we generally resolve never to let "it" happen to us again. Most of us succeed. This first conclusion is usually reached at an early age and is connected with our families—unless people are capable of accepting their parents' imperfections—with whom we often become angry, but still truly love.

People seek a way to "sew up" the parting in their first, their second, their third relationship, but unfortunately they never experience it properly. The attempt to avoid the painful feelings of separation obstructs the opportunity to choose and freezes it in its tracks. Life becomes restricted; we only pursue "sure things" and run from pain. The pain, however, remains there in any case, although it seems easier to live with.

We say people are "strong" if they don't show pain when someone dear to them has died. The truth is that they hurt inside no less than they would if they were to let themselves truly experience the pain; such people are headed for injury on the physical level. The Jewish practice known as *shiva* (the seven-day mourning period for a close loved one) exists for the purpose of allowing people to experience their pain. All saints, of whatever stripe, are people willing to suffer pain. They lost everything they had and were ready to confront the loss head on and, thus, to experience the pain. Partings and pain contain great latent power. People who are unwilling to experience the pain of leave-taking are incapable of loving, and vice versa.

During the foot analysis we try to uncover the separations that have accumulated over the years, examine them, show our subjects the opportunities for choice that existed at given times, and gauge the degree of change that took place in the aftermath of these partings. Most people in the middle of parting situations fail to recognize the chance being given them to love. Without love, the quality and power of life become something else entirely—unrequited potential.

In the physical examination with which we begin the reading, we should examine imbalances that exist at the point of balance. All states of imbalance are "windows" through which we may observe the outcome of the subject's love. If water appears there, we know that the person lost love due to an excess of emotion—more precisely, a great wave of anxiety. Even if subjects define this feeling as jealousy or anything else, it is nevertheless anxiety. People who break off ties before the other person can do so, are expressing their fear that the relationship will end.

Earth can appear only in the water or fire sections of the heart region. Earth in the fire area indicates that the subject's life is characterized not by giving but by stubbornness, stagnation, and impulsiveness. Instead of acting and creating with love, the subject's life is "stuck," stationary. Earth in the water area points to stagnation instead of the emotional strength and fear that are crucial to love. Fear always allows something new to happen. Since the new is always frightening, the connection is broken in the absence of fear and renewal. The new is exciting, but underlying that excitement is fear. Adults who have long blocked their feelings exhibit earth in their fire, fire in their earth, and grooves in their water. If fire is no longer in balance, then neither is water; the two processes are inseparably linked.

We trace the origins of the sign of parting by examining the potential of the fire element. (This is done by bending the foot backward to the highest possible line.) The location of the sign tells us whether this connection is more water-based or fire-based. We then know on which level love and the subject have met—that of masculine or feminine energy.

In addition to the signs of parting over the heart region, we may find such signs in other elements when a connection with someone or something was formed, sustained, and terminated, primarily on the basis of a specific element. For example, an interruption of studies represents a separation from creativity (fire) or from intellectual activity (air). Termination of a career is a departure from "doing" and creativity (fire). Frustration is a separation from something that the subject desired but hadn't the audacity to grasp (water).

Since basic needs have substitutes that are quite easy to find, we encounter relatively few lines of parting in the earth region. Every surgical operation we have undergone represents a separation from a part of ourselves. Failure to have consummated this process of separation will leave an indicator in the form of a line of parting over the region of the foot corresponding to the site of the surgery. Creativity is supposed to rise from the point of balance in the fire section; from this point downward, the subject must be capable of admitting the love directed at him or her from some outside source. When we do not accept love, we neither emanate nor admit it. When we do not love ourselves, we cannot love others. Such people are quick to criticize themselves; the good things—how much I love and accept myself—are seldom heard.

The foot analysts' role is complicated; they must approach their task from a position of love. If we're "in it for the money" (earth), or if we are doing it in search of self-importance (water), power-lust or desire to dominate (fire), or intellectual curiosity (air), we can give our subjects all kinds of information but will not succeed in reaching them and inspiring them to truly listen. Approaching a reading with love means that even if we err, we have touched our subjects and have facilitated an encounter with love—a commodity so rare in people's lives. The need to come from "a place of love" evokes immediate fear, insecurity, avoidance, challenge, and curiosity. The way to connect with this place is to connect with our own pain and be willing to truly suffer. The willingness to hurt opens up the possibility of loving as we strike a precarious balance on the tightrope between the active and the passive forces.

CREATIVITY—SOMETHING FROM NOTHING

Creation is the making of something that had not existed previously. In view of this definition, creative people must transcend their own limitations and touch something new. Creation is a divine act, originating in a person's contact with the fifth element. Between the air and the fifth element, something completely new is created. The emergence of this newness into the real world requires energy that ascends through all four elements, expanding the person's boundaries in the process.

The idea of creation originates in the heavens but is realized on the earth; we need our bodies in order to create. Any creative act on my part defines me, for creation is an expression of my energies. Creation signifies that we have succeeded in reaching the place from which we experienced our energies in a way that permitted us to create; that we have managed to form a connection with something beyond our own boundaries.

In any creative act (writing, conversation, body movement, painting), people create themselves and create by means of themselves. Creative people who learn to focus and motivate themselves spiritually (through meditation and similar techniques) succeed in connecting with the heavens, thus expanding their creativity. Artists in the throes of creation draw closer to the heavens. Most such people are dominated by bursts of creativity; they fluctuate between states where "the muse descends upon them" and periods when it is blocked. If they could succeed in deciding that they are ascending to air—that they control their ability to connect with air—their creation would be a flowing, continuous act rather than an intermittent eruption carrying them beyond their limitations. Some people attempt to make this connection by means of alcohol or drugs—substances that transport them to a place outside their usual bounds.

Creativity takes place, first and foremost, in a person's highest heavens, in the fifth element. Once the fifth element is engaged, all the elements collaborate. Earth is responsible for the creative framework, the discipline required in order to create, aesthetics, and the advent of the creation in the world of the here and now. Water endows the creation with depth and flow, and imprints it with qualities emanating from the inner world.

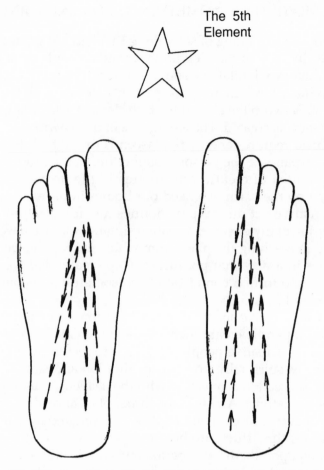

Figure 75. The flow of creativity. This is the flow from heaven into earth, and also, from the earth trying to reach its way to heaven.

Fire is responsible for the act itself, control of technique, drive and outward expression, and the creator's personal involvement in his or her work. Air permits the creation to communicate; this outward expression is grounded in choice and careful consideration (see figure 75). An imbalance in any of the elements will harm those qualities that the element contributes to the creation and may block its successful realization. A surplus in any element will tilt the creation in the direction of that type of energy; a deficiency in one of the elements will make creation impossible, since the energy of that element will not be harnessed for the creative act.

Earth may pull in the direction of stagnation, rigidity, preservation of the status quo, and a consequent inability to create something new. It if is in deficiency, it will cause a lack of vitality that makes creation impossible. Water evokes fear and other emotions that are threatened by the appearance of something new and, for this reason, may obstruct the creative process. Fire may induce the imposition of control, crowding out spontaneity and possibly introducing ego and prestige considerations that will harm the creation; alternatively, control may foster a lack of ambition that stymies the creative drive. Air can be critical and judgmental, blocking any creation that fails to meet the standards of pure logic; alternatively, it may cause a lack of concentration that will similarly impair the ability to create. A good two-way flow between earth and air is a prerequisite for any genuinely creative act.

During the foot analysis we examine the flow-line between the earth element and the fifth toe and gauge the quality of the flow in all the elements. We may expect to find a strong earth element, flowing water, and indicators of the many experiences undergone by the subject in his or her life. A large and powerful fire element in a foot with straight toes indicates that there is a drive underlying the creative force that permits its outward expression. If the air is free of all other elements, fire may ascend to it, meaning that the need to create is rising to air. We then examine the junction of fire and air to see if there is a flow between these elements.

All creative people possess their own means of expression. Those who are particularly creative have unique toes. For example, special qualities in toe 2, and a healthy flow from the fire element to the hands, indicate good hand-eye coordination. This, in turn, signifies special creative ability in areas entailing such a connection, e.g., the plastic arts. Unique fourth and fifth toes may suggest special musical aptitude and the like. In our examination, we seek answers to the following questions: Which toes permit a creative emanation? Which toes are strong and which are weak? Is something blocking the flow, and, if so, what is it? For example, earth that appears in the form of dry skin on the toes tells us that the artist has become "stuck" over earth-related issues such as money, the framework within which he or she creates, administrative matters, aesthetics, and the like. Signs of frustration in the water element indicate the presence of frustrated creativity, too; such a person will be judgmental and dissatisfied. The overall vitality of the foot shows us how likely it is that the subject's potential creativity has been realized.

Creativity is a power that exists within us. Creative people who have blocked their own creativity are sick individuals. The power with which they were born must be channeled toward some goal; if this force is unable to expand their limitations, it will lead to chronic physical patterns that will force these people to confront the creativity that lies within them. When people seal and obstruct their creativity, they generate an internal pressure that can drive them crazy. A plugged, i.e., nonflowing, creative force is damaging. The pressure that builds up inside will make such people so literally sick as to induce physical symptoms.

A foot in a severe state of overall surplus tells us that the subject's creativity is trapped and is accumulating as a destructive force. A foot with a general deficiency of vitality belongs to a subject who does not allow himself or herself to engage in creative acts; it often indicates a total collapse brought on by a creative force that, because it was never properly utilized, accrued in the subject and ultimately worked against him or her.

Our acculturation contains a bias for action. Although work is supposed to be a creative act, most people do not regard it as such. People dream of being involved in creative work, but when they achieve such a position, they do not know or remember how to function creatively and instead become accustomed to a set routine. Such people exhibit earth in their fire region. Earth in fire stymies creation by hampering and blocking the flow to the air element. Earth induces stagnation in a place where active, dynamic creativity should reign.

Study, too, should be considered a form of creativity. Learning represents internalized creativity; conversely, creativity is learning given outward expression. Learning that arises out of interest and motivation forces people to draw expanded boundaries for themselves. People who do not wish to learn have lost their creativity, since they no longer wish to transcend limitations. The characteristic indication of studies that have been halted is a groove on the big toe, signifying a break between air and fire—the very channel in which the two-way energy flow allows the new to enter and the creative force to emanate.

The following conditions must be met for the fulfillment of creativity: there must not be a severe imbalance in any of the elements; there must be an uninterrupted flow among the elements; and, even if a state of relative balance exists, there must be motivation and a persistent need to grow beyond one's boundaries, to experience the new.

RELATIONSHIPS WITH OTHERS

When we attempt to observe people's relationships and interpersonal contact through their feet, our basic assumption is that they relate to others just as they relate to themselves. In other words, if there is a particular element that dominates their feet, this same element will predominate in their relationships and mirror their attitudes toward others. If we understand the connection and the balance of power between the elements, as well as the way an individual operates internally, we may correlate these findings with his or her relationships with others. In men, the connection between active and passive energies reflects the nature of their relationships with women; in women, the connection between these energies shows us how they relate to men.

We note such connections during our foot analysis while observing other levels and issues in the subject's life. For example, if we see individuals who treat themselves repressively and exercise forcible control, it is reasonable to assume that they treat those close to them in the same fashion; their expectations of others reflect their expectations of themselves. Highly emotional people, whose feelings play a prominent role in their lives, relate to others, too, on an emotional level. Intellectuals forge connections based upon intellect. Creative people seek and form creative relationships, i.e., those in which sexuality is important. People with a surplus of earth as a dominant element will build secure, unchanging frameworks and reinforce them with all their might, and they will demand that those near them never change—just as they themselves never change.

If the equilibrium between the various elements is different in each foot, we realize that the subject expresses himself or herself one way with loved ones and another way with work acquaintances. Obviously, if individuals' chronic patterns are broken, the types of relationships that they forge change, too; they meet other people who come from a different emotional "place," who offer a fresh perspective. We observe people's relationships through the looking glass of their own individual dynamic; if this becomes altered, the nature and quality of all their relationships will change in quality or in substance.

15

RESOLVING
UNFINISHED BUSINESS

The art of being human demands all of one's energy and attention. In people who suffer from chronic patterns, some of this
attention becomes diminished; it turns in predetermined cycles,
leaving no room for anything new. The energy level of such
people falls, since freedom does not flow through them but is
obstructed and stuck in these same chronic patterns.

One type of chronic pattern is caused by a severe and sudden imbalance; in these cases balance is never restored and the
pattern becomes entrenched. One example would be people
who have undergone an episode of traumatic fear and have
become diabetic—a pattern that in fact permeates the entire
body and, under these circumstances, becomes a chronic state.
The same holds true for accidents and other sudden, intense
situations.

Another type of chronic pattern originates in numerous
repetitions of the same situation, or a situation that remains
constant over a long period of time. A chronic pattern may be
regarded as any habit or energy-related routine, irrespective of
origin.

Since we regard an imbalance as a state that impairs energy
flow, we may infer that a chronic pattern is a permanent state of
imbalance. The concept of an unresolved or "open" issue actually refers to a state of past imbalance that was never corrected,
i.e., one that remained open. In other words, the cycle of energy
flow did not close. This cycle resurfaces repeatedly over the
course of a person's life, reflecting each time an unsuccessful
attempt to close itself.

We generally perceive states such as this—which include
recurrent symptoms, entrenched forms of behavior, and constant feelings—as "not good"; we experience them as "bad" or

"sick." In actuality, we are experiencing our energy's futile attempt to seek balance. Because we understand the "open issues" concept, we may see that any chronic pattern causes us to expend a great deal of energy, which we are either unable to utilize in our lives or may use only in a way that is harmful to us. The vast inner space that these chronic patterns occupy within us robs us of the ability to change and renew ourselves.

By inference, people without chronic patterns are free and healthy. They are unpredictable, always "recharging" themselves, and possess a huge store of vitality. By contrast, people beset with many chronic patterns tend to say, "That's my personality," "That's how I am," or "That's how I've always been." In this fashion they defend these patterns and thwart the possibility of change in their lives. Such people are predictable; they see only one possible path in life for themselves. Suffering from the symptoms of various chronic states, they lack the strength to contend with themselves. People with a great many chronic patterns become "old" and set in their perceptions, behavior, opinions, self-experience, and experience of their surroundings. Consequently, they age both mentally and physically at a faster rate than people who are capable of change—those who are attracted to and curious about new things and who live their lives "full speed."

When we examine the feet of such people, what we see is essentially a whole series of open, unresolved states, or states of imbalance seeking balance. We must remember that, by nature, our energy needs to flow and to be balanced. The attempt to close these cycles exists in everyone, even if on an unconscious level only.

Before examining how these open (i.e., unresolved) issues can be closed, we must remember that each represents a past situation that was difficult for the subject. In other words, the subject experienced pain, fear, a threat to his or her existence, emotional difficulties, loss, physical trauma, and so forth—all those states that we do not wish to remember or reencounter in our lives. Our subjects actually resist the idea of returning to such an open state, even for the purpose of closing it.

Modern psychotherapy recognizes the stage known as denial, a point in the process at which many people become stuck. People deny the existence of a chronic, open state, and resist with all their might the notion of contemplating or confronting it. It should be noted that resistance, judgment, denial, forgetfulness, cynicism, guilt, and acquiescence are ways of placing distance between people and their own chronic states. They are actually defense mechanisms against the state and its completion (consummation), generating a state in which the chronic pattern is preserved and not allowed to close. These same defense mechanisms keep the pattern alive in its original form, and are often so sophisticated that people can neither comprehend nor perceive the existence of the chronic pattern. In other words, the extent of the gap between how people view themselves and objective reality is contingent upon this same understanding or its absence. Before we address ourselves to the chronic pattern, we must be able to accept the fact of its existence. Such acceptance does not take place on the intellectual level alone, nor is it limited to only one of the elements; rather, it must take place within all the elements, i.e., on all levels of our existence and experience.

One of the goals of foot analysis is to create a state in which such acceptance takes place, if only partially, during the analysis itself. We strive to show our subjects their chronic pattern in a way that allows them to accept its existence in the fashion in which we describe it to them—nonjudgmentally, without fostering revulsion or defensiveness, but with a readiness to examine it from all angles. The only prerequisite for acceptance is a willingness to listen without resistance or judgment.

What we call true listening has nothing to do with hearing; it is a special state of awareness. Many people, when engulfed in some type of crisis, invoke this listening capability out of a sincere desire to recover and become well again. When people ask themselves, "What next?" they are already considering the possibility of coping and changing; the process of restoring balance has already begun.

Our first goal is to create a state in which our subjects accept themselves—or at least some aspects of themselves—in a way that makes clear to them the need to complete the matter, issue, or state that remains open in their lives. If they ask, "So what do we do about this?" we know they have already taken the first step toward regaining balance.

If we complete the first stage successfully, we continue by considering how to close an open issue, i.e., how to expunge something old. In the courses that I teach, for example, I clutch a piece of chalk and ask how I can dispose of it. Very few people know that the first stage in the process of getting rid of the chalk is acknowledging the presence of the chalk in my hand. Once I accept this and focus on its presence, I can embark upon the next stage: that of doing.

Now the key question is what must be done, or what must take place, in order to close the circle. The answer is contained in the open circle itself. In principle, the stage of doing is the point at which we are willing to experience the unresolved matter in full. In other words, we experience the pattern without defense mechanisms, allowing the pent-up flow to surge forward at full force. The "doing" here is defined as the infusion of all our strength into this flow. Alternatively expressed, the entire person—with all of his or her energy—experiences the same trauma or "old" process in the fullest possible way, mounting no resistance; the entire self is invested in the struggle to close the circle and free the trapped energy.

In most cases, this state is achieved not immediately but gradually; the process is actually one of balancing. The more chronic and entrenched the pattern is, the longer the balancing process will take, and the greater the investment and "doing" needed to close it will be. We generally find that the stage of doing is where people encounter the greatest difficulties. Most people are somewhat aware of the existence of their patterns, but most of their actions with regard to the circle only reinforce it and do not contribute to closing it. These patterns exist on our practical/experiential level.

For example, people with a pattern of anxiety will act on the basis of this anxiety both consciously and subconsciously; thus, their "doing" will never close the circle. Once we see that this pattern has been modified, we know that the circle is complete. In other words, working on one pattern alone is impossible for all intents and purposes; since we would in any case be acting on the basis of additional patterns, we could not bring about a state wherein all our energy is available for the struggle. What this means is that dealing with the pattern through doing is tantamount to coping with *all* our chronic patterns, since all are involved in the process.

This is a process of genuine personal growth, in which new patterns are created and old patterns obliterated. It is a practical process and a therapeutic one; the moment we close one circle, we discover another that must be dealt with, so that the process of doing and coping continues ad infinitum. The principles that make the "doing stage" possible—and that make it an effective process, meaning that our energy is mobilized for the closing of open issues—are easy to understand but very difficult to implement. For example, I might be aware that instead of saying something I should have, I kept it inside. Acknowledging this is the first step, but actually going and saying what needs to be said triggers many other patterns, such as anxiety and insecurity. Even as I engage in my "doing," I must contend with these.

The first principle of doing is the courage to do what must be done, the audacity to tackle and experience hitherto incomplete cycles. The next principle is to make sure that the doing is complete. The struggle for completion must be coupled with an almost fanatical insistence that everything be closed as hermetically and completely as possible. For example, consider people who have experienced a difficult loss but who treat the attendant pain with such resistance as to have turned it into an internal, chronic agony never fully expressed or experienced. Such people carry permanent pain inside—pain they cannot expunge, even if they are aware of its presence.

The first stage would be to accept that the pain exists and must be resolved or expunged, i.e., "closed." The next stage is the "doing"—to experience the pain, to transform the loss into a state that exists in the present, to express the pain in the way in which it needs to be expressed, and to reexperience the loss in its entirety. When the energy thus far obstructed by this resistance is released (remember that the reason for the resistance, be it fear, social norms, or the like, is irrelevant), we regain the power that was lost and turn the chronic pain into life supporting strength.

The third stage looks easy. After all, the experience has taken place and we've crossed the abyss. It is at this point that people shed, or separate from, their chronic pattern; the possibility of complete liberation from the pattern now exists, because we may now utilize the released energy in a new and balanced way. However, if we are predisposed to neglect this new energy, we are at risk of automatically returning to the same old pattern—something which, in fact, often happens. It is at this stage, when we are ridding ourselves of something, that new issues arise in both our inner and outer worlds. Because of our fear or avoidance of the new, we may have coped with a problem or a chronic pattern without truly parting with it, since it has become a defense against the change that is starting to take place.

We return to the example of the chalk. When people have accepted the presence of the chalk in their hand, experienced its presence there, performed the requisite "doing," opened their hand, and turned it over, the chalk has fallen to the ground. Once the chalk began its descent, it began to be replaced, in this case by air, and something new was created on the spot. Human energy does not tolerate a vacuum, and the new is unknown. When we drop chronic longstanding patterns, what fills their place is unknown because it had not existed there in our perception, our consciousness, or our experience.

People are deterred by change, particularly when change means the integration of a new quality, strength, or perspective into their lives. Any change in experience threatens and intimidates, because our permanent "I" demands reassurance. Thus, most people, when parting with a chronic state, may hang onto it for dear life in order to avoid change. In many respects, this moment is a true test of that person's life force. To hope for any success in the third stage, one must follow these rules:

1) Acknowledge that there are many unrecognized possibilities within you, thereby changing yourself into a mysterious and intriguing place that harbors much potential.

2) Be willing to leave old things behind or to accept a type of inner detachment by which you are not dragged into events as they occur.

3) Be aware at all times of new possibilities, and be willing to explore them, so that the commencement of something new actually means the end of the old.

We can see that, from many perspectives, the process of accepting, experiencing, doing, and completing the new is a lifelong one. We are born; we accept that we are alive; we experience and "do" our lives; and then we part with them. This process is evident in every human experience, and is also the path that one must follow in order to close open issues.

The feet permit us to identify chronic patterns and open states. We can see how, and where, people have lost their strength. More often than not, we may pinpoint the time and situation in which a chronic pattern became fixed, and observe the objective context in which this event took place. Bear in mind that patterns relate to the region and the personal quality in which they are most pronounced. By inference, a particular pattern in a particular element will require the quality of the energy in question in order to become closed.

A pattern connected with the fire element will be closed when the quality of that element regains its balance, meaning that the energy of fire must be actively integrated into the process. Our subjects must play an active role through their own process of "doing." They must take certain actions, or cease doing certain things that they do in excess, in order to complete the pattern (in accordance with the states of surplus and deficiency within the element in question).

Many patterns include connections between elements and embrace several different elements. These are patterns in which all the forces of all the elements appear and engage in a struggle for balance. Allergic asthma, for example, is a pattern that mixes fire and water on the physical level. In the fire element we observe introversion, shyness, weak ego, low resistance, poor ambition, and a tendency to yield to others. In the water element we encounter extreme fear, strong anger and guilt, and a large surplus of water. We notice that the subject has two interrelated ways of coping, which actually add up to one coping mechanism—specifically, the bolstering of the fire element and the aggravation of its dominance with a concomitant mitigation of the influence of water. In terms of water, this means being able to cope with fear in a balanced fashion that refrains from transforming the fear into something that dominates everything else, fire in particular; and to give vent to anger and guilt in the way in which these need to be expressed. For the fire element, this means directing all one's energy toward the forces of control and ambition.

We attempt to carry out the first stage during the foot analysis, pointing things out and questioning our subjects about available "doing" options that may truly close the circle. It is often necessary to refer subjects to treatment or some form of support, such as hypnosis, psychotherapy, various body work techniques, conventional medicine, psychoanalysis, or homeopathy. These and other techniques may further the process of closure. To be of help in "completing" (i.e., closing) open patterns, a technique must play a supportive role in the closing process. Some subjects need no such assistance; they usually know what they must do, particularly if their patterns are not especially rigid or intense. For them, the stage of doing and experiencing is somewhat easier, although this may not be so when they advance to the stage of complete closure of the circle and separation from their pattern.

To make the reading a dynamic act that addresses itself to these patterns and their completion, we may reexamine the subject at least three months after the first session and compare the state of their feet in "before-and-after" fashion. This will serve as a measure of the subject's development and his or her true achievements.

16

THE BENEFITS
OF FOOT ANALYSIS

The process of developing and studying foot analysis has been, for me, a transforming experience that changed my world view and behavior, and, in fact, affected every aspect of my life. The partitioning of the human being by its elements, and the recognition that I myself embody an integration of forces of these types, has led me to observe, seek, comprehend, and accept these forces in myself. The very knowledge that I contain a certain energy has legitimized its presence and its emergence in my life in any form; this, in turn, has made me a richer person, my inner world blessed with a complexity and an abundance that had not been there before.

Much of the analysis is composed of observing the connections and relationships between inner forces that are outwardly manifested in one's life situations. If people knew, when faced with a decision, that they must scrutinize their entire self, and that the decision must emanate from the full self—not from one part that may dominate the others—their actions would be better balanced and would flow through the world more auspiciously.

The act of foot analysis is actually an attempt to reflect back to our subjects the place in which they find themselves now, and to reveal the open issues (i.e., chronic patterns) that have accompanied them throughout their lives and claimed much of their personal energy. It may be said that every person who approaches us for analysis reflects a particular aspect of ourselves; by means of the foot analysis process, the reader, too, contends with the very aspect being exhibited by the subject. By holding a mirror up to the subject, the analyst is given an opportunity to see and be seen with the clarity of an uninvolved party, offering the analyst insight into his or her own chronic patterns. Observing how others cope with these open issues is instructive, providing an opportunity to modify personal coping mechanisms. As a foot analyst, I have seen—in the process of developing the technique and in daily practice—how different people confront a similar problem (physical, social, or other), each devising or developing his or her own method of coping. Out of this vast storehouse, personal evolution and new learning cannot help but emerge.

For our subjects, the entire analyzing process is an attempt to achieve a breakthrough. They come to hear another person's observations—not to solicit advice but to try to gain a more complete picture of themselves. If they succeed, they undergo a change in attitude that, in turn, modifies their behavior and surroundings. The interplay of their inner forces reflects their external state—their life situation—since energy does not acknowledge any difference between inner and outer. People determine their life situation as a direct corollary of their personal inner state. In other words, the act of foot analysis is also an attempt to break through to a better life situation (in the subjects' own eyes). If they truly use the analysis to observe parts of themselves they had not addressed earlier—open issues that they now decide to close—there is a chance that they will modify their life situation by mere virtue of the new knowledge they have acquired. The ability to accept a situation for what it is—without trying to change it, fix it, wish it away, judge it, or wallow in it—is the first step in the process of transformation.

Our purpose in conducting the analysis is to call unclosed, i.e., unresolved issues, to our subjects' attention. If they see and accept the presence of these issues, acknowledge the need to take action to close them, and indeed follow through, we may assert that the analysis has opened up new possibilities in their lives.

The feet reveal our subjects' personal history, habits, and routines—all the issues that have never been closed. Insofar as these people drag around their histories with them, they not only drain themselves of personal strength but also forget that it even exists. They forget the principle that even when we close (i.e., complete or finish) something, we nevertheless retain its strength, which may be channeled toward the creation of some-thing new instead of moving along the fixed paths that we trav-eled before. The analyst would do well to provide subjects with a list of obvious issues that are "incomplete" in their lives, so that they may see where they are losing strength and where they should focus their efforts in order to complete and emerge from the chronic patterns that they carry with them.

As a foot analyst, I gain much more than the profound excitement and the strong relationships that are forged during the analysis. Each fresh pair of feet gives me the opportunity to reencounter myself and confront the unresolved issues in my own life. Each such encounter reminds me anew that it's time to wake up and do something about them. Foot analysis adds zest to my life and reminds me daily of my own humanity.

INDEX

A

abdomen, 23, 40, 42, 111
abdominal pain, 111
abdominal wall, 38, 39
abortions, 85, 156, 157
accidents, 16, 40
acetone, 50
Achilles' tendons, 60, 88, 89, 114
acupuncture points, 2
adhesions, 93, 128
adolescence, 173
age, 172
aggressiveness, 110
air, 3, 9, 12, 21, 23, 31, 32, 34, 35, 37, 44, 45, 52, 63, 64, 65, 67, 113, 161, 163, 167, 179, 180, 181, 182, 184, 187, 188, 189, 190, 192, 198, 200, 259
    dominated, 116, 117
    too much, 113
air in air, 192, 198
air in earth, 124
air in fire, 138
air in water, 130
air to fire, 163
air pollution, 61
alienation, 120

allergy, 41, 76, 79, 83, 111, 141, 213
ambition, 187
amoebic dysentery, 111
amputation, 49, 50
anal fissure, 89, 110
analyzing process, 49, 95, 102, 219
anemia, 130
anger, 23, 45, 136, 173, 184, 203, 204, 210, 211, 212, 215, 269
angina pectoris, 71, 75, 133
ankle, 11, 50, 52, 89, 156
ankle bone, 50, 60, 85, 89
ankle mobility, 114
ankle rotation, 54
anus, 24, 35, 88, 89, 124, 165
anxiety, 40, 93, 136, 139, 204
appendix, 24, 26, 38, 165
arches, 17, 51, 90, 91
arms, 26, 28, 69, 169
arthritis, 80, 84, 166, 213
artificial insemination, 50
ascetics, 125
assault, 40
asthma, 44, 61, 63, 73, 79, 83, 111, 135, 156, 163, 213, 269

athlete's foot, see mycosis
auditory nerves, 44
autoimmune disease, 93

B
back
 lower, 18, 38, 85, 87, 88,
  102, 111, 123, 124, 149,
  171
 muscles, 39, 60
 upper, 32, 53, 112
bad breath, 142
balance, 9, 70, 117
Band 1, 35
Band 2, 38
Band 3, 39
Band 4, 40
Band 5, 42
Band 6, 43
Band 7, 44
Band 8, 45
beauty marks, 67, 68, 70, 76,
  84, 153, 156, 175
behavior
 physical, 13
bile, 23
birth, 149, 152, 156, 157
birth trauma, 88
birthmarks, 70, 153
bladder, 23, 24, 35, 39, 82, 83,
  84, 85, 86, 165, 217
blame, 184
bleeding, 109
blemishes, 84, 175
blood, 23, 32, 216
blood pressure, 107
blood vessels, 42, 43, 45
 black-and-blue, 52
body fluids, 141
body work techniques, 269

bones, 5, 11, 17, 52, 53
bowel
 irritable bowel syndrome,
  208
brain, 32, 44, 45, 141
breath, 164
breathing, 71, 163
breathing problems, 76, 141
bronchial tubes, 42, 43, 135
bronchitis, 61, 63, 135
bunion, 192, 193

C
calcification, 128
calluses, 114, 115, 134, 135,
  175, 197
cancer, 93, 107, 123, 137
case history, 96
central nervous system, 32,
  113, 167
cerebral cortex, 45
cerebral hemorrhage, 107,
  143
cerebrospinal fluid, 23
cervix, 35, 110
cesarean section, 85, 86
chakra system, 2, 292
charisma, 182
cheeks, 44
chemotherapy, 50
chest, 32, 40, 42, 53, 112, 182
chest muscles, 32
childbirth
 difficult, 89
childhood process, 185
chin, 44
cholesterol, 217
chronic conditions, 10, 62, 63
circulatory problems, 49, 111
coccyx, 24, 35

colds, 111
colitis, 81, 84, 111
colon
    ascending, 26, 38, 39, 165
    descending, 26, 38, 39, 165
    sigmoid, 35
    spastic, 111
    transverse, 26, 39, 40, 165
colors
    blue, 33
    dark brown, 22
    gray, 133
    green, 32
    light, 115, 205, 214
    maroon, 22
    red, 52, 69, 74, 75, 76, 81,
        84, 85, 90, 112, 131,
        142, 175, 201, 211, 212
    white, 116, 138, 176
    yellow, 23, 130
common indicators, 61
communication, 44, 183
compulsive eaters, 217
compulsiveness, 32, 124
computers, 19
conception, 7
concentration, 45, 114
conception, 149, 153
    difficulty, 126
conflict, 119, 183
congenital markings, 11
conscience, 214
constipation, 76, 81, 84, 106,
        110, 130, 149, 159
conventional medicine, 269
corns, 52
cortisone, 50
courage, 43, 182, 215, 267
cowardice, 43
cranium, 167
creative drive, 43, 71, 113,
        179, 247, 258

crisis, 4
crisscross lines, 84
crystals, 176
cycle, 4
cysts, 112

D
death, 43, 75, 176
    of loved one, 74
deficiency, 10
denial, 264
depression, 113, 182, 215
destiny, 3
diabetes, 10, 40, 90, 126, 263
diaphragm, 26, 40, 41, 42, 76,
        77, 78, 131, 182
    flaccid, 15, 76
    ruptured, 111
diarrhea, 81, 84, 111
digestive system, 41, 45, 106,
        128, 131, 163, 164, 165,
        166, 193
disabilities
    physical, 9
dissociation
    fire and air, 139
    line, 159
    water and earth, 125
    water and fire, 130
dizziness, 107, 200
dominance, 120
dreams, 67, 70, 113
duodenum, 26, 40, 165
dyslexia, 67, 69

E
ear, 28, 30, 44, 64, 65, 69, 79,
        83, 189

middle, 68, 70
earaches, 171
earth, 3, 9, 11, 21, 22, 25, 34,
    35, 37, 38, 52, 63, 85, 86,
    87, 88, 89, 90, 110, 161,
    173, 176, 179, 182, 185,
    189, 190, 199, 218, 259
  dominated, 114, 116
  energy invasion, 136
  invasion by water, 206
  too much, 109, 111
earth in air, 140, 175, 192, 198
earth in fire, 133, 175
earth in water, 126, 127, 207
eczema, 137, 141
ego, 32, 44, 46, 137, 215
ejaculation
  premature, 110, 124
elbows/knees, 102
element
  fifth, 3, 192
  invasion, 122
  of mother, 152
  relationship, 119, 122
elements
  active, 36, 40, 43, 44, 45
  excessive, 109
  four, 8, 9, 21, 37, 63
  passive, 36, 38, 40
emotional potential, 203
emotional trauma, 132, 159
emotions, 23, 41, 76, 112, 141,
    184
empathy, 183
emphysema, 71, 73
endocrine centers, 2, 93
energy, 2, 7, 13, 143
  active, 35, 147
  father's, 150
  flow, 170
  passive, 35, 147

patterns, 159
energy zones, 21
epilepsy, 113, 141
equilibrium, 183
esophagus, 26, 28, 30, 42, 43,
    135, 165
ether
  quintessential, 3
examination, 52, 103
example session, 233
expectoration, 69
extrasensory perception, 183
eyes, 19, 28, 30, 41, 44, 64, 65,
    79, 83, 141, 188, 189
eyesight, 69
eyestrain, 19

F
fainting, 138
fallopian tubes, 24, 38, 110,
    126
fatigue, 90
fear, 10, 17, 23, 40, 42, 45, 76,
    112, 123, 136, 173, 179,
    184, 186, 189, 203, 204,
    205, 207, 215, 218, 263,
    269
fear of death, 203
fear of drowning, 217
fear of strangulation, 217
fear of tests, 198
feces, 38
feet/hands, 102
fertility, 22, 38, 131, 182
fetal development, 151
fetal experiences, 175
fever, 80, 84
fibroids, 109, 112
fight-or-flight, 140

fire, 3, 9, 11, 21, 23, 29, 32, 34,
    35, 37, 42, 43, 52, 63, 71,
    72, 73, 74, 75, 161, 163,
    173, 174, 179, 182, 183,
    186, 190, 193, 208, 215,
    216, 218, 259
  dominated, 115, 116
  too much, 112
fire in air, 142, 192, 195
fire in earth, 123
fire in water, 128, 129
flatulence, 111
fluids in body, 83
foot
  analysis, 1, 49, 219, 222,
      232, 233, 259, 271, 272
  ball, 11, 12
  cold, 217
  cold and trembling, 123
  cold and wet, 93
  color, 49, 115
  cracked, 114
  deficiency, 93
  division, 145, 194
  dominant, 51, 131, 144
  dominant element, 114
  dryness, 90, 114, 124
  flexibility, 52, 117
  narrow, 115
  old people/young feet, 176
  pale and cold, 90
  perspiration, 93
  rotation, 52
  size, 51
  slender, 117
  splayed, 117
  structure, 62
  tendons, 18
  texture, 49, 84
  webbed, 153
  wet, 115, 206

  wide, 112, 114
  young people/old foot, 176
fractures, 110
freckles, 156
frustration, 9, 10, 173, 203,
    204, 209

G
gall bladder, 26, 76, 78
gallstones, 76, 128
gastritis, 111
genetic disturbances, 16, 68,
    70, 153, 183
genitalia, 24, 35
general indicators, 90
grooves, 216
guilt, 173, 184, 198, 210, 212,
    213, 269
gums, 44, 45, 67, 69, 142

H
habits, 6, 17, 18, 19
  emotional, 19
hair, 44, 69
hands, 43, 45, 170
  dominant, 131, 144
hay fever, 83
headaches, 64, 113, 142, 171
health, 117
hearing, 184, 188
heart, 26, 28, 30, 32, 42, 43, 71,
    75, 107, 138, 182
heart attack, 32, 43, 74, 112
heartburn, 107, 112
Heberden's nodes, 109
heel, 11, 36, 50, 85, 87, 111,
    114, 123, 124, 171, 206

hemorrhoids, 36, 85, 87, 110, 133
hepatitis, 83, 130
hip joint, 24
hips, 35, 53
hips/shoulders, 102
hoarseness, 69, 102
homeopathy, 270
horizontal lines, 168
hormonal system, 93
hormones, 23
hypertension, 90, 112
hyperthyroidism, 139
hypertonia, 53, 112, 175, 176
hypnosis, 40, 153, 157, 269
hypotension, 90, 138, 217
hypothyroidism, 139
hysterectomy, 85
hysteria, 112, 123, 136, 159, 206, 218

I
ileocecal valve, 24, 26, 38, 165
illness, 14, 41
imbalance, 5, 13, 14, 16, 17, 19, 61, 62, 68, 83, 159, 263
immune system, 70, 92, 93, 107, 137
indentations
transverse, 166
inflamation, 52, 85
injury, 16, 51, 110
inner balance, 247
inner peace, 119
intelligence, 180, 194
interviews, 95
intestinal contents, 23
intestinal diseases, 111
intestine

large, 39
small, 24, 26, 38, 39, 165
intestines, 23, 82, 84
intuition, 39, 46, 179, 230
invasion
earth to fire, 63
IQ, 179
irritability, 204, 208

J
Jane Doe's feet, 100-101
jaw, 28, 30, 44, 45, 142
jealousy, 173, 213

K
kidney stones, 128
kidneys, 23, 26, 40, 82, 83, 84, 111, 165, 184, 204, 207, 217
Kirlian photography, 2
knee, 24
knuckles
bony, 113

L
lachrymal glands, 44
laryngitis, 16, 69, 102, 138, 139
larynx, 44
lateral division, 190
learning disability, 69, 195
legs, 22, 24
liberation, 267
limp, 50
liver, 26, 39, 40, 41, 42, 76, 79,

80, 83, 84, 111, 130, 165, 182, 184, 211
logic, 46
love, 247
low blood pressure, 217
lumbar spine, 24, 26
lungs, 26, 28, 30, 32, 40, 42, 43
lymph, 23
lymph glands, 40
lymphatic system, 35, 43

M
malformations, 153
malignancies, 107
manic-depressives, 182, 201
mapping imbalances, 98, 99
marks
   moist, 111
   new, 175
   star-shaped, 76
   striding, 162, 163
mastectomy, 74, 75
memory, 45
menopause, 64
menstrual cycle, 64
menstrual cramps, 88
menstruation
   painful, 109, 112
migraines, 64, 113, 141, 200
mirror, 218, 229
money, 182, 198
Months 1-9, 154, 155
mood swings, 115
mother, 126
mouth, 28, 30, 44, 141, 165
mouth/anus, 102, 163
moving fingers technique, 59, 60, 61
muscular system, 32, 42, 43

muscle tone, 71, 89
muscles
   hypotonic, 52
   stomach, 60
   trapezius, 43
mycosis, 49, 69, 141

N
nadis, 2
nail polish, 50
nausea, 107
navel, 39, 40, 217
neck, 18, 43, 66, 70, 71, 102, 149
neck/lower back, 102
nose, 30, 41, 44, 141
numbness, 69, 70, 107
nursing, 112
nymphomania, 124

O
odor, 23, 61, 111, 115
old age, 177
open-heart surgery, 75
operation, 86
organs
   internal, 167
   soft, 23
orgasm, 161
ovary, 24, 38, 110, 126, 217
ovulation, 110, 112

P
pain, 10, 69, 101, 112
palpation, 60, 105

pancreas, 26, 40, 90, 217
panic, 15, 16, 206
paralysis, 49, 50
paraplegia, 50
parasympathetic system, 23
pattern
  behavioral, 6
  chronic, 4, 10, 15, 18, 49, 62,
    71, 76, 120, 157, 171,
    175, 177, 203, 263, 269
  common, 17
  emotional, 6
pelvis, 22, 24, 39, 53, 123
perception, 182, 183, 200
perseverance, 193
perspiration, 112
pineal gland, 30, 35, 45
pituitary gland, 30, 44
pneumonia, 75, 135
postnatal events, 175
potential, 6, 7, 179
power, 128
pregnancy, 7, 110, 149, 151,
    152, 153, 157
  ectopic, 110
prolapse of heart valve, 75
prostate, 24, 35, 64, 88, 110,
    182
prostitutes, 42
psychotherapy, 269
psychotics, 36, 201
puberty, 173, 174
pulmonary problem, 75

Q
quadriplegia, 50

R
radiation therapy, 50
rape, 16, 40

rebirthing, 153, 157
receptivity, 224
rectum, 24, 26, 35, 163, 165
red spots, 84, 85, 175
relationship
  ending, 75, 261
reproductive organs, 38
resistance, 224
respiratory system, 63, 135
ribs, 28, 32, 42, 43
rites of passage, 173

S
sacrum, 24, 35
scalp, 45
scars, 6, 93
  on the head, 69
sciatic nerve, 24, 35, 85
sciatica, 85, 110
scoliosis, 90, 91, 112
screaming, 45
seed, 7
self-confidence, 43, 71, 185
self-expression, 44, 71, 139,
    187
self-pity, 215
senses, 19
sensitivity, 175, 183
sensuality, 22
separation, 75, 176, 250, 251
sexual disorders, 131
sexual energy, 124, 125, 161
sexuality, 22, 38, 42, 182, 198
shame, 123, 203
shock, 16, 176
shoulder
  blades, 32, 43
  joints, 26, 28, 30, 43, 63
shoulders, 18, 44, 53, 63, 71,
    72
sight, 183, 188, 189

sinuses, 28, 30, 44, 45, 79, 83, 141
sinusitis, 64, 197
skin, 5, 11, 12, 32, 111, 113
   changes, 175
   cold, 113
   dry, 52, 72, 87
   dry, rough, 52, 63, 66, 73
   dry strip, 71
   dry tough, 49, 69, 71, 85, 114, 126, 135
   grayish, 71, 73
   loose white, 116
   red, 74, 112, 212
   stiff, 71, 112
   taut, 115
   tough, 112
   wrinkled, 111
skull, 32, 45
sleeping problems, 113
smoking, 71
solar plexus, 40, 42
speech, 45
spinal column, 102, 149, 150, 153, 167, 168
spine
   cervical, 28, 30
   thoracic, 26, 28
   upper, 68
spiritual abilities, 46, 192
spitting, 45
spleen, 26, 40, 41, 76, 79, 80, 84, 182
   enlarged, 111
sports, 36, 110
sprains, 110
sterility, 110
sternum, 42
stomach, 26, 28, 40, 41, 76, 77, 86, 163, 165
   muscles, 60
   ulcer, 112

calcified, 176
striding line, 11
striding zone, 183, 193
stridor, 71, 73, 163
structure, 5
struggle, 9
   for completion, 267
suffering, 9, 10
suffocation, 44
surgery, 93, 132, 176
surplus, 9, 90
sweating, 107
swellings, 52, 66, 69, 86, 90, 211

T
Tantra yoga, 125
tears, 112
teeth, 28, 30, 44, 45, 69
television, 19
temperature, 5, 52
temples, 44
tendons, 57, 60
   calcification, 52
   muscular, 15
terror, 203, 204, 205
testicle, 24
thighs, 22, 24, 35
thinking, 182
throat, 28, 30, 43, 44, 45, 66, 69, 138, 141, 165
thymus gland, 28, 42
thyroid gland, 28, 30, 43, 102, 135, 139
time, 171, 172
tinnitus, 64
tissue, 11
   swollen, 12
toenails, 12, 50, 150, 190, 197, 199
   brittle, 199

crooked, 199
discolored, 67
horn-like, 198
ingrown, 64, 199
inverted cone-shape, 200
marks under, 69
marred, 201
mycotic, 199
none, 191
soft, 141
striding, 201
thick, 52, 199
thin pale, 113
transverse lines, 199
vertical lines, 199
watery, 200
toes, 11, 12, 50, 53, 56, 64, 70,
    171, 179, 182, 188, 196,
    200, 259
toe 1, 182
1 square-shaped, 183
space between 1 and 2, 183
square 1, longer 2, 183
long 1 and 2, 187, 188
1 and 5 elevated, 199
toe 2, 182, 183, 184, 191, 197
2 short, 183
2 and 3 callus, 134
2, 3, 4 longer than big, 113
2 and 3 same height, 201
toe 3, 182, 184, 198, 201
3 long or short, 68, 70, 184
3 and 4 peeling, 141
toe 4, 182, 184, 193, 197, 200
4 points to 5 or 3, 69
4 and 5 numb, 70
toe 5, 71, 182, 184, 191, 200
base of, 64
bent, 113
big, 34, 53, 55, 69, 70, 111,
    139, 149, 164, 190, 198
bloated, 142

conical, 182, 201
curled, 18, 64, 65, 67, 112,
    114, 186
division, 189
elevated, 71, 72
flexible, long, 113
length, 193
lines on, 69
little, 34, 64, 71, 162, 190,
    198
mycotic, 200, 201
overlapping, 185, 186, 187,
    201
pads, 34, 79, 83, 112, 113,
    182, 197
pale, 113
raised, 201
red, 142
short, 114
skin joining 2 and 3, 201
spots, 200
splayed, 180
spread out, 117
stride, 181
swollen red pads, 64, 197
tendons, 60, 71, 72, 112
walking, 114
tongue, 44
tonsillectomy, 69
tonsillitis, 102
tonsils, 43, 45
touch, 5
trachea, 28, 30, 42, 43, 71, 135
transverse lines, 71, 76, 84,
    85, 160, 167
transverse strip, 175
tumors, 93, 111

U
ulcers, 76, 77, 112, 164, 208
umbilical cord, 156

ureter, 26, 165
urinary tract, 35, 38, 39, 82,
    84, 110, 111, 217
urine, 38, 111
uterine infections, 110
uterus, 24, 38, 156, 182

V
vagus nerve, 40, 43
varicose veins, 109, 114
vascular inflammation, 110
vertebra, 43
vertebrae
    lower T, 39
    central thoracic, 40
    lumbar, 38, 70
    L4 and L5, 70
    S1 and S2, 70
    upper T, 42, 69
vertical lines, 84, 160, 168
vertigo, 64, 68, 113
violence, 42, 110, 204, 206
vision problems, 64
visions, 67
visual exam, 104
vocal chords, 69, 102, 139
vocal outbursts, 32
voices
    hearing, 113

W
walking thumb technique,
    58, 60, 61
water, 3, 9, 11, 21, 23, 27, 34,
    35, 37, 40, 41, 52, 60, 63,
    76, 77, 78, 79, 80, 81, 82,
    83, 84, 112, 163, 173, 179,
    182, 185, 186, 189, 190,
    193, 203, 204, 215, 216,
    218, 259
    dominated, 115
    invasion by earth, 206
    too much, 111
water in air, 141, 192
water in earth, 123, 195, 207
water in fire, 135
whiplash, 66, 69
will, 39, 113
womb, 88
workaholics, 129
writing, 46

Z
zones of the foot, 34

Avi Grinberg has worked with many body awareness and bodywork techniques—from reflexology, Chinese micro-massage, and biodynamic massage to hatha-yoga, visualization and various breathing techniques. His desire to work with the whole person—mind, body and soul—led him to combine Eastern philosophy with his bodywork techniques to develop the Grinberg Method. In 1986 he founded The Center for Alternative Studies in Haifa, Israel in order to make the Grinberg Method available to other people. Avi Grinberg is the author of *Holistic Reflexology* (Thorsons, 1989). He currently lives in France with his wife, and they travel internationally to bring these techniques to students around the world.